T0090460

Ronald Reagan &

The Evil Empire

~ a fictional autobiography of Ronald Reagan ~

an abridged edition of, *American Civilian Counter-terrorist Manual*
~ a fictional autobiography of Ronald Reagan ~

Order this book online at www.trafford.com
or email orders@trafford.com

Most Trafford titles are also available at major online book retailers.

Disclaimer

This contemporary historical novel is an allegory, a fable. For dramatization, all characters and
their alleged activities have been entirely fictionalized, based on their autobiographies, biographies,
journalism and history books, published intelligence sources, public radio broadcasts, and oral and
published investigative journalism. All apparent and/or alleged truths and/or falsehoods are to be
considered to be fictional statements and any resemblance between any characters in this book to any
living or dead people -- and/or to the truth of what may, or may not have happened in Reality -- is
merely coincidental and fictitious in Time.

Printed in Victoria, BC, Canada.

ISBN: 978-1-4269-2656-3 (sc)

*Our mission is to efficiently provide the world's finest, most comprehensive book publishing
service, enabling every author to experience success. To find out how to publish your book, your
way, and have it available worldwide, visit us online at www.trafford.com*

Trafford rev. 02/15/2010

 www.trafford.com

North America & international
toll-free: 1 888 232 4444 (USA & Canada)
phone: 250 383 6864 ♦ fax: 812 355 4082

Whatever You Did Unto One of the Least, You Did Unto Me

Mother Teresa of Calcutta
The National Prayer Breakfast — Washington, D.C.

On the last day, Jesus will say to those on His right hand, "Come, enter the Kingdom. For I was hungry and you gave me food, I was thirsty and you gave me drink, I was sick and you visited me." Then Jesus will turn to those on His left hand and say, "Depart from me because I was hungry and you did not feed me, I was thirsty and you did not give me to drink, I was sick and you did not visit me." These will ask Him, "When did we see You hungry, or thirsty or sick and did not come to Your help?" And Jesus will answer them, "Whatever you neglected to do unto one of these least of these, you neglected to do unto Me!"

Matthew 25:32-46 (New International Version)

[32]All the nations will be gathered before him, and he will separate the people one from another as a shepherd separates the sheep from the goats. [33]He will put the sheep on his right and the goats on his left.

[34]Then the King will say to those on his right, 'Come, you who are blessed by my Father; take your inheritance, the kingdom prepared for you since the creation of the world. [35]For I was hungry and you gave me something to eat, I was thirsty and you gave me something to drink, I was a stranger and you invited me in, [36]I needed clothes and you clothed me, I was sick and you looked after me, I was in prison and you came to visit me.'

[37]Then the righteous will answer him, 'Lord, when did we see you hungry and feed you, or thirsty and give you something to drink? [38]When did we see you a stranger and invite you in, or needing clothes and clothe you? [39]When did we see you sick or in prison and go to visit you?'

[40]The King will reply, 'I tell you the truth, whatever you did for one of the least of these brothers of mine, you did for me.'

⁴¹Then he will say to those on his left, 'Depart from me, you who are cursed, into the eternal fire prepared for the devil and his angels. ⁴²For I was hungry and you gave me nothing to eat, I was thirsty and you gave me nothing to drink, ⁴³I was a stranger and you did not invite me in, I needed clothes and you did not clothe me, I was sick and in prison and you did not look after me.'

⁴⁴They also will answer, 'Lord, when did we see you hungry or thirsty or a stranger or needing clothes or sick or in prison, and did not help you?'

⁴⁵He will reply, 'I tell you the truth, whatever you did not do for one of the least of these, you did not do for me.'

⁴⁶Then they will go away to eternal punishment, but the righteous to eternal life.

"If we ever forget that we are 'One Nation Under God', then we will be a nation gone under." – President Ronald Reagan

"Without History, Life is a Mystery"
– Dave Emory, radio &/or online broadcaster on
WFMU, KKUP, KFJC

ACKNOWLEDGMENTS

The author would like to acknowledge the work of the following authors, who document their research extensively for the common good without whose honesty, dedication, literary work and journalism, the understanding and oral tradition passed on from them, to you, would not be possible (also see unabridged edition): Mark Aarons, William Domhoff, Dave Emory, Sean Gervasi, Albert E. Kahn, Antony Kimery, Henrik Kruger, Martin A. Lee, John Loftus, Alfred McCoy, James Steward Martin, Eustace Mullins, Carl Olgesby, Kurt Riess, Michael Sayers, George Seldes, Peter Dale Scott, Christopher Simpson, Antony Sutton, T.H. Titans, Lou Wolf.

Special acknowledgment is given to Eustace Mullins – unique, brilliant and brave, with whom I corresponded the last few years of his life, and is one of the most significant researchers of American history and fiscal policy – all information about the American Revolution, the Federal Reserve system and precursors, associated national and international history, and financial depressions of 1907, 1920-1921 and 1929-1931 etc., is based on Mullins' scholarly and distinctive work, available online. Also, the scholarly work of intelligence community whistle blowers Antony Sutton; John Loftus and Mark Aarons; and online contemporary WFMU broadcaster Dave Emory for the last 40 years: "without history, life is a mystery". Dave, John, Mark, Eustace and the others mentioned above, are America's greatest treasures – because they alone have stood up for the American public whereas all our elected officials have failed, and continue to fail, to stand up for us and put our lives ahead of corporate.

Disclaimer

This contemporary historical novel is an allegory, a fable. For dramatization, all characters and their alleged activities have been entirely fictionalized, based on their autobiographies, biographies, journalism and history books, published intelligence sources, public radio broadcasts, and oral and published investigative journalism. All apparent and/or alleged truths and/or falsehoods are to be considered to be fictional statements and any resemblance between any characters in this book to any living or dead people -- and/or to the truth of what may, or may not have happened in Reality – is merely coincidental and fictitious in Time.

CHAPTER 1

How I Became Fiction

The daylight came in around Joan. Nancy had to squint. She flitted like a sparrow to another chair.

Joan lit a beeswax candle. It was carved with medieval priests. The priests were swinging lanterns of incense. Bayberry scented the air. Joan drew the curtain to block the sunshine.

She sat down beside Nancy. Joan stared into a crystal ball. Her eyes rolled back in her head.

Nancy was afraid Joan would be attacked by demons.

Joan shivered and shook. She grasped the wooden table. Her fingers turned white and she screamed, "I'll get that bastard out of my way!"

"Joan! Who are you?"

"I'm Neil."

"Neil? I won't let you hurt Ronnie!"

"I will!"

"Stop it!"

Joan screamed in tongues. She blinked her eyes, rose from the table. She swung the heavy velvet curtains aside. Presidio Heights lay smothered in fog. The pebble colored Victorian row houses faded away.

Joan watched as Nancy sank into her chair. "Nancy, What's wrong?"

"I don't know."

"What did I say?"

"Nonsense about a Denver developer, Silverado Savings & Loan, setting Neil Bush up in business." Nancy wondered why she bothered with Joan.

Other times, she was desperate without Joan's advice.

Joan was mid-aged, too. With a medium build, darting black eyes. She lit a cigarette, exhaling smoke like a devil, "Get this straight. You asked me, 'Who's pulling Ronnie's strings? Who wants to get rid of him?'"

Nancy ran her fingers through her hair. It felt stiff, hair spray barely fragrant on the dyed blonde like catch threads on her fingernails. "Joan, you're the seer. That developer's hooks would be in Vice President Bush, not Ronnie. I don't get it."

A cable car went by, steel wheels chattering on steel rails. Then, slowed. People start jumping off and on, reaching for handgrips or letting go of them, jostling for seats on the wooden benches like musical chairs. The bell clanged. As the cable car faded over the hill in fog, the bell grew fainter.

Joan exhaled smoke against the window. "I don't get bad vibes. Let's do your astrology chart, then Ronnie's, then Washington D.C.'s."

Nancy's eyes lit up. "Okay." She put five one-hundred dollars bills on the table, looked at her watch, "Joan, I don't know what I'd do without you."

Joan took the money then Nancy's hand. "I love you, Nancy. I'll keep you and Ronnie safe."

As fog whitened the neighborhood, night darkened the fog.

Nancy dropped me off beforehand at Jak's barbershop on Haight. I figured if Joan made Nancy happy it was worth five hundred bucks. Jak finished my haircut as Nancy's black limo pulled up. My guards whisked me in. We left the city behind us, heading down Bayshore to San Francisco International, a set of headlights on the freeway.

"Nancy, did Joan name anyone out to get us?"

"Neil Bush."

"Why?"

"I don't know."

"Do you get bad vibes?"

"No."

"Bush swore he'd never run as vice president under me, now he is."

"That was his father, Ronnie, *not* Neil."

"*I know* it was his father. I'm *not* senile, *yet.*"

"Thank goodness. I couldn't stand that."

"You won't have to. Y'know, the world would be better without Bushes, Thyssens, Browns, Harrimans, Rothschilds, Shroders and Rockefellers."

"Umm-hmmm."

I settled back into the limo seats. I got sleepy. I dreamed I had a standing ovation from the crowd and hurried onstage for my Oscar.

President's Oval Office,
First Cabinet Meeting

The day after my inauguration I walked royal blue carpeted halls to the Oval Office for my first Cabinet and Staff meeting, that CNN reporter from California shadowing me, stopped me at the door before I could get in. I tried walking past him towards the office. He was in my face, "Mr. President, will you issue an Executive Order on cost-cutting?"

How irritating. It was too early in the morning for reporters, not a good omen to start the day with. I shrugged. I didn't know the damn answer. How was I going to cover myself …Budget Director David Stockman, a short man about five-and-a-half-feet, with attractively styled brown hair combed back over his head like a rogue, suddenly appeared, nodding frantically at me. I got the message. I turned to the reporter, "Alan, that's your name, isn't it? This smiling man beside me, Budget Director David Stockman is dribbling his head up and down. That indicates to me, yes, we're going to issue an Executive Order on cost-cutting. Leave me alone." We left the reporter behind.

Stockman and I went into the crowded Oval Office of noisy Cabinet officers arguing loudly with White House Staffers I'd brought from California like comfortable clothes.

Assistant Chief of White House Staff Mike Deaver, thin in his navy blue three-piece Brooks Brothers suit, brushed his thin hand over his balding, brown hair. Mike was one of my best friends. He handled my public relations image my whole political career. He was Nancy's confidant and hit man.

"Ron, the other night, it wasn't my fault…"

"Mike, it never is…"

"You said I didn't believe in you. That's not true. I don't question your ability, just your judgment."

"My judgment?!"

"Well, your timing." Mike felt he knew me better than he knew himself, took me through two gubernatorial campaigns and reminded me at every opportunity.

"What about my timing?"

"If it wasn't for me you wouldn't be here. I believe in you, Ronnie. I always have. I always will. Don't doubt that."

"Then, don't doubt me. I'm not an actor for nothing." Mike spent more time with Nancy than I did … so I made him squirm. "I'm glad to hear that, but Christ! You're guilty! Were there gangsters at my inauguration …or not?"

"We're in D.C., not Sacramento."

"It feels like Hollywood. I never played a gangster. Don't get me impeached my first day."

"Okay."

I wondered why Mike sounded ashamed. "We didn't take campaign money from foreign nationals. Did we, Mike?"

Mike felt chills run through him. He wished he was in a bar. His hand ran over his breast pocket …yes, his vodka flask was there, hidden beneath his jacket. Relieved, he hedged the question, "Foreign financing of campaigns is illegal." He took the flask out.

As a trained actor, I noted denial all over Mike's face, heard it in his tone of voice. I wondered what his motivation was …I felt puzzled, so I played it.

"What's puzzling you?" Mike took a long swig.

"You knew, and you still…"

"No! I didn't know shit! Stop it! Are you nuts? You don't thank banana republic dictators in front of reporters …haven't you learned anything from me? I stopped you from doing it! You took it wrong, that's all. I was covering your ass."

"What the hell, Mike? Hello? …we pay Contra freedom-fighters to kill communists for us, I don't know what papers you're reading, the last time I checked, that's what it's about …you bet, I'll thank him in public."

"It's not politically correct."

"Oh. Why didn't you say so?"

"I guess I wanted to see you make a fool out of yourself."

"Hmm."

Mike laughed, took another swig, his face start sweating.

In a wall mirror, Director of Central Intelligence Bill Casey gave Vice President George Bush a high-sign, then mumbled something I couldn't understand. An actor with a successful movie career, I found myself in a riotous White House cast party reading people to figure out what was up, since listening to them didn't help me understand the masquerade. Watching the mirror, I saw Bill signal George to tone it down. We study stuff like this in acting workshops for years. If you're good enough at acting, you get an Oscar. I never did. Which is not to say I didn't deserve one, "Where's the rest of me?!" My best lines, ever.

"Bill, you irritate me more than Mike. I'm humiliated, you hide behind my back where I can't see you, you mumble to George like some kind of rebel. Look in my eyes. Talk to me … you think I'm not smart enough to understand? You think I don't see what's going on? You think I'm stupid? You're standing by the damn mirror, for Christ's sake." I was on a roll.

Bill was well under six feet tall, a little pudgy, mostly bald with wispy white hair on the sides almost too long, typical red face of a man who drank too much. Bug-eyed, he wore his half-frame, accountant-style glasses down on his nose, looking down on everyone, mumbling to himself inaudibly, condescending to speak with any nouveau rich newcomers not in the money-issuing class for generations, or more specifically, anyone not a private shareholder of Federal Reserve stock or original shareholder of Bank of England or Bundesbank ...or any blue-blood who's family fortune didn't come from slave trading, drug running, weapons trading, or counter-intelligence selling-out to the highest bidder. Bill was condescending to anyone who wasn't what patriots consider a traitor, who didn't put the central bank collective higher on the totem pole than any petty nation or petty national allegiance and petty national boundaries. He was a bona fide one-worlder, one of Brown's, Harriman's, and Rockefeller's new world order banksta gangstas believing in one world government and damn the torpedoes, full speed ahead. Bill considered me a pawn in his game. He'd been my campaign manager. Used to sit in on meetings with me since 1950, with Steve Bechtel of Bechtel Construction, Martin Andersen of Hoover Institute of War, Peace & Revolution at Stanford, and Henry Kissinger just six years out of U.S. CIC Army Intelligence in Germany helping get jobs in the U.S. for genocidal Nazi war criminals who appeared on Disneyland on TV then were hired into our space program and into CIA anti-communist programs and who helped finance U.S. presidential contenders behind-the-scenes. Kissinger and Nitze carried off the Crusade for Freedom in the early 1950s. That was the first domestic psychological warfare program in the U.S. and part of the Christian West program Dulles and Reinhard Gehlen and Martin Bormann, Count Sergei DeMohrenshieldt, Prince Max von Hohenlohe, Otto von Bolschwing, Klaus Barbie, and Otto Skorzeny the son-in-law of Hitler's banker Hjalmar Schacht, and Heinrich Himmler had set up the last 15 years with the Bushes and their coterie of goons. Bormann and Himmler represented different bankers and their competing oil companies in the central banking collective. They bickered about whose version of the Christian West plan was bigger. That has accounted for all the civil wars, coups and counter-revolutions, wars and covert operations since World War II between opposing economic destabilization fronts competing in global turf wars for natural resources, free labor, central bank ownership and drug monopolies.

In the early '50s, I'd finished my stint as the president of the Actor's Guild in Hollywood and me and Nancy got informant checks from the FBI for turning in communist and socialist actors to them. This was around the time I was hosting G.E. Theatre and Death Valley Days on TV after my acting career had faded, and Bechtel's interlocking directorate over at General Electric had hired me to speak around the country against the communists taking over America to promote the Christian West plan, which they called in Americanese, the Crusade For Freedom. Back then, at those meetings in the Fed's west coast summer camp redwood grove, Bohemian Grove, they thought they were smartening me up, so I let them think that. I went with the flow and here I was today, in the best acting role of my career, set in the Oval Office, where a small town boy struggled hopelessly against overwhelming odds to save America from the evil empire in a Cold War atmosphere of impending doom. I was fond of Bill, but wouldn't say he was a good friend, like Mike. Bill was in Washington to stay. Dulles had taught him the ropes, made him liaison between OSS and MI-6, took him off Wall Street right along with him. Bill, just like Dulles, worked for the Bush dynasty since 1920 along with Brown banking interests in the Fed and Bank of England and Bundesbank. He watched presidents come, and go ...probably helped Dulles get rid of Kennedy, since Dulles ran the CIA long before Bill did, conducting economic warfare and covert action precipitating war for their central bank collective that paid them and their intelligence org of hunch shouldered scholarly desk jockeys plotting annihilation and Arnold Schwarzenegger and Stallone Rambo-type covert operatives enacting it as mercenaries, rewarding them with heroin franchises, U.S. printing plates, gold bars, Kugerands and General Motors bearer bonds.

Vice President Bush had run CIA, too. He was dirty as they come. Secretly worked for CIA until J. Edgar Hoover blew his cover right after JFK's assassination, by not shredding two incriminating memos proving Bush was then an undercover CIA agent while working for Dresser Industries behind the Iron Curtain along with Sergei DeMohrenshieldt, and two, that Bush called the CIA and tipped them that fateful day about the Kennedy Assassination.

What the hell had I got myself into? I should've settled for 'B' movies. This hero 'save the U.S.A.' stuff had bubbled to my head and backed me against the wall. I wanted to get through the Presidency having stuntmen take the falls, not me. I wanted to make it out, alive. With luck, there'd be an Oscar on the other end rather than a smoking gun. It was quite a role. I needed someone at my back besides Jesus, and he was packing.

"Ronnie," Bill Casey said, "I simply remarked on the strange guests at your inaugural ball. I was surprised."

I was taken aback. Not far away from me and Bill, George seemed amused, managing to look chagrined at the same time ...his trademark look.

I was losing my patience, "What's going on, Bill? No one gets past you. You're old school politics, know where the bodies are buried, probably put most of them there. You ran Export-Import Bank a few years ago, when Bechtel was on the board, were involved when Bechtel bought Dillion-Read, probably sleep with informant secretaries you plant inside Halliburton and Kelly, Brown & Root, used to head OSS. Now you head CIA ...I'm surprised you're surprised. And, knock off that condescending tone in your voice when you speak to me. Cut it out. You can be fired."

"So can you."

"Yeah, yeah, tell me about it." I let it go to get the meeting over.

Casey mumbled something to himself, keeping score or at least counting cards. "Can not tell you everything, Mr. President ...it would implicate you in scandals ...like the theft of Carter's campaign notebooks. I was saying to George, it's a mystery how we got a hold of those notebooks. Remember Nixon's Watergate scandal?"

Bill's off-the-cuff remark amused George, who looked around to make sure no one noticed, then smiled sarcastically. George spoke right up. "Remember it? I'm still covering it up. It was illegal campaign donations from foreign nationalists, drug money and kickbacks from foreign aid we gave to dictators that came back into our own congressmen's campaign funds. It wasn't just covering up the Kennedy and King assassinations for the Fed, like everyone thinks, y'know." George always had to appear in the know.

Bill wished George would keep his mouth shut and interrupted, "Stealin' Carter's campaign notes'll be a mini-Debate-gate, unless we deny everything. That usually stops scandals."

George wasn't a happy camper, "Great, just what I need to start off as Vice President, a fucking scandal pissing on me."

Casey laughed. We all did.

That made George very serious, "Bill, it doesn't amuse me ...it's disgraceful for counter-agents to get caught stealing, it makes spies look bad."

White House Chief of Staff James Baker III had a genuine Texas accent. He was a slender, handsome man, with that peculiar Texas sense of humor. "Boy, I just couldn't decide to take advantage and keep those stolen notebooks, or not. We won the debate with them ...maybe the election. And, here we are. You can't argue with history ...we're making it up as we go, whaa-hu! Ride 'em, cowboy!"

Edwin Meese was now Presidential Counselor, he'd been with me almost as long as Deaver. Ed's was a new position never existing at the White house before my Administration invented it. Ed was a big, fat, rough and gruff, short tempered fascist farther right than me. He challenged Baker, "Jim, who handed the notes to you?"

Baker was surprised, "Are you kidding?"

Ed got pissed off, "Fuck you, who gave you the damn notes?!"

Baker laughed it off, playing it down in a sophisticated, gentlemanly way, "You did."

Ed was confused. "Me?"

"Yes."

"I didn't steal 'em."

I was starting to get the big picture. It wasn't pretty, "Bill, did you have an Agency mole in Carter's White House? ...did the mole steal Carter's campaign notebook?"

Bill Casey passed the ball, "Ask Jim Baker."

Baker wasn't amused, "Wait a minute Bill, you gave those to me."

Bill acted surprised, "I don't remember doing that."

Maybe this would be an Oscar role for me, "Jim, you said Ed gave you the notebooks."

"Not all of them."

I found myself following the conversation like a tennis match, watching the bouncing ball go back and forth over the truth which was a net and if you got caught in it, you lost the point or maybe your life. I needed to make it clear to everyone, "Gentlemen, this is an honest administration. That's what the history books will say."

The room was quiet. It seemed like the meeting was over, but I wasn't satisfied. I turned to George Bush. "I want it settled, I don't want it coming back to haunt me. Who knows about these foreign aid kickbacks into election campaign funds, George?"

George Bush wouldn't jump out of line, "I was out of the loop, I'll look into it."

"I'm not satisfied with that, just what loop are you in?"

"I'll get you a full report," George looked away.

"Bill, you're the senior intelligence officer here, what do you know about it?"

"I wasn't in the loop, I don't know."

"Who does know?! Bill, I'm asking you!" I lost patience, angrily threw my glasses and watched them skid across the table.

"I just get the reports off my desk," Bill was indifferent.

"Then, no one's in the loop! Great! When CIA has a coup installing puppet military regimes we give them foreign aid to run the regime ...does any foreign aid come back to the Presidency or Congress as illegal campaign donations? Did we, or did we not broker bribes to-and-from foreign nationals to get into office?! Deaver?!"

"I'll get back to you with a report." Mike took a nip.

"Give me a copy of that report, too," Bush calmly maintained his self-control, "...it's something I should look into."

"Only if you give me a copy of your report," Mike quipped.

George nodded.

"I want copies," Bill mumbled, smirking then looked at George, then shook his head at me. As Bill watched me, George saw Bill's look, that seemed to say, 'You sucker'.

Christ, as a trained actor I observed, studied and practiced 'looks'. I was a Zen master at 'looks' -- for every script in every movie I played in. I had no trouble spotting looks. Looks are what directors direct.

Bill saw George watching me and that George wore a look seeming to say, 'There's one born every day'.

"The public doesn't understand," Bill mumbled, "you can't stop covert-ops and Communism at the same time or there's no teeter-totter."

"He's right, Mr. President," Bush was emphatic, "covert ops stop Communism."

Bill grimaced a little like George's timing was off, or had agreed too soon, or jumped in too fast. I didn't think George's timing was off. After all, I was an eager-beaver Cold Warrior. I started feeling less frustrated. My mood brightened and I felt agreeable, "I'll do whatever it takes to save the world from Communism."

Bill must have noticed that knowing, 'insider' look on my face. It amused him, but noticed George was holding back a smirk. Bill couldn't hold off his condescending grin, "Ronnie, me and Deaver got you campaign financing from the Contras. What you gonna do about it, call Ghostbusters? ...resign? ...we got you financing from the World Anti-Communist League contingent. That's how we got you elected, with their money ...from the Bormann organization. Foreign nationals financed this production. We wrote your script. Wake up and smell the roses. I told you. Maybe you forgot."

I didn't know whether to be upset or not. Did he tell me? Did I forget? It felt like I was having an idea ...like something opening in my head. I caught my composure, "Well, I never heard you tell me. Those banana republic dictators aren't really puppets, they're our employees. They're actors, make things happen, make change. We produce and direct them ...long live the freedom fighters! If it's Armageddon, God's on our side."

"We leaked October Surprise, too," Casey said, "...that was a nice domestic intelligence operation ...planted disinformation stories in the corporate press. That's not treason, it's national security. To hell with Carter. He fired five hundred of our CIA covert action operatives. You know what? ...we got even. Us spooks take care of our own, one way or t'other."

The more Bill said, the more I wondered what he hid. He was born with a poker face plastered on his mug, "Bill, you rehiring five hundred CIA field operatives that Carter fired?"

"Yes, I'm rehiring them, and a lot more."

"Will that help the Contras get the weapons we promised them?"

Bush was startled, he shot a worried glance over to Casey.

Bill returned a fleeting 'not-to-worry' to Bush, before answering me, "It has to look like we're cutting back weapons sales to freedom-fighters in Taiwan."

George was visibly relieved, nodded knowingly at Bill like a hand puppet or a cheap little toy dog with a floating head Mexican vendors carry on trays between cars in parking lots and border crossings to sell. I was puzzled. I didn't understand what they were up to. I felt like a new kid at school, frustrated and new to the game, "You mean, you sell the weapons to Taiwan first? ...I don't want to know. Just get the job done. Spare me the details."

There was that feeling again, almost having an intuition, almost remembering ...I shook my head but nothing came into focus. I stared off, across the room for an eternity. Suddenly, like unexpected lightning I came back sharply. "Bill, I'm starting to resent the hell out of you. Don't treat me like I'm your puppet. That's George's job, not mine."

George was hurt and offended, "That's uncalled for, Ronnie."

"You're right. I'm sorry."

"Okay."

"It's because Bill treats me like my head's full of sawdust. I don't get by on looks and charm. I have a brain. I hired you. I know what's going on ...my good looks take heat off'a you, Casey! See what those words say on that flag on the wall, 'Don't tread on me'. Get the picture?"

"It's a two-way street," Bill wasn't in the least, intimidated.

"George, are you going to let Bill talk to me that way? Speak up! Say something!" I glanced at George, indicating I wanted some back-up and emotional support from him.

"My mind was wandering, Mr. President. What did you say?" George was caught off-guard, daydreaming.

"All right. Let's all be calm and let bygones be bygones." I felt upset, showing emotion was unforgivable, now I'd have to come to terms with myself for showing feeling.

Bill flashed that condescending smile I hated.

Chief of Staff James Baker laughed it all off, he'd seen it all before a million times.

I called the meeting and dismissed everyone but Bush. I had brought my Jimmy Stewart videotape in my jacket pocket to keep me company. I started it for George and me. Watching the movie helped me act sincere and concerned. Jimmy was good at that. I turned it off, "George, I was hurt by Watt's big mouth and disregard. But, this Savings & Loan shenanigans breaks my heart."

"I wish I could make it easy for you," George looked away.

"How can 3,200 Savings & Loans be worth 17 billion dollars in 1972, then be 17 billion dollars in the hole in 1980!" I felt my temper rising, "You tell me, 'fix them, deregulate them!' Now six hundred of 'em are failing, again! Twelve hundred more are going down! ...500 billion dollars in the hole at taxpayer expense! Where'd the money go?"

George scratched his head, "I don't know."

I didn't know whether to believe him, or shoot him. So, I said nothing, and just stared at him to shake him up, "This is the biggest bank robbery in the history of the world. I wrote the largest check in history drawn on the bank account of the American taxpayer and, it bounced. I didn't make a dime out of this! ...did you?"

George's Episcopal upbringing made him confessional, "No. Two of my sons did okay. James Baker III did okay. Lloyd Bentsen did okay. But, I'm not a banker, I'm an oil man."

"That's some consolation. 'Where's the beef?' ...is that where it's at?"

"It's bad for the middle class, working class, some upper class, a few ruling families ...but, corporate law prevents board member liability for board members, they'll survive."

"What do you want? ...a pat on the head."

"Sure, it's great for the money-issuing class. I did good."

"George, it breaks my heart."

"It's the price money-issuing families pay to own everyone. Our hearts are broken all the way to the bank."

"I'm not a money-issuing kind of guy! I'm a poor kid from Iowa. I made a million in Hollywood because of my looks. I'm a screen idol. I rode the American dream like a bronco. I got bucked off into the mud of the White House ... Do we have a cover? ...will the cover hold? ...will I get caught holding the bag?"

"I'll ask Bill Casey. I was out of the loop. I'm sorry for your broken heart ... the mud washes off." George left the room.

I turned Jimmy Stewart's movie, It's a Wonderful Life, back on. I talked to it. "Poor Jimmy, you have a failed Savings & Loan on your hands ... I got the whole failed S&L industry ... I outlived you, Jimmy, old boy." I felt frustrated, angry, and full of despair ...I turned off TV, sadly watching the blank screen.

<>

I heard my Cabinet and Staff raising hell in the hall, so I called them back into the situation room to fight it out behind closed doors. The White House Staff was mostly middle class or upper class people I brought with me from California. We were nouveau riche, going for instant gratification and the quick fix, immediate return on investment.

The Cabinet was old ruling family wealth, measuring percentage returns over several generations of their family dynasties. They were very conservative, since their wealth primarily originated with slave trading, opium running (and sugar, tea, cigarettes, booze), money-issuing, petroleum, war-making and war profiteering. California money liked to build bubbles around technology and the stock market by sinking venture capital into start-up companies for military or consumer electronics. But, established old money-issuing or ruling family money preferred making bubbles by sinking venture capital into banking, oil, gold, weapons, real estate, military-industrial concerns and war-making. Both old and new money liked real estate bubbles. Bubble-making and popping were their forms of economic warfare against each other.

Everyone plowed back into the Situation Room. I brought the meeting to order. Secretary of State Alexander Haig, a Cabinet member, professionally represented old wealth ruling families. He was the ultimate Cold Warrior. Haig start furiously yelling, "Nicaragua Contra support money's coming from the outside. I know who's financing Contras in Nicaragua!"

By now, Mike Deaver was sweating profusely and very drunk. He sounded worried and defensive, "You think you know who? Then, who?! Who, me? You're paranoid."

Haig glared at Deaver. "I have an informer!"

"Haig, you don't know shit!" Deaver nipped his flask.

I forced myself between them, "Gentlemen, calm down. We need an orderly meeting here, tonight. We're getting Congress to start financing the Contras, right Bill?"

"Yes," Casey said, "it's in the best interests of our G-7 finance ministers and central bank governors for NWO one world government ...I mean, it's in the best interests of the country."

"We can blow Central America off the map!" Haig stormed around the room.

"I get a kick out of your macho attitude, Haig," Defense Secretary Caspar Weinberger over-reacted, "When the Arabs almost blew Israel off the map ...where were you, then? Which side were you on, then, Haig?"

"I saved Israel. I sent the Israelis missiles, through unofficial channels. That earned me enemies. Weinberger, you're a Jew, but you're anti-Semitic. Is that from cutting your teeth at Bechtel?"

"Helping Israel the way you do, stinks!" Weinberger was uncontrollable, "The Arabs were right then. They're right, now! You blew it, that time!"

"He's right, Haig!" Deaver chimed in.

"Calm down! Shut up! Sit down!" I yelled, acting just as crazy. People took their seats.

Weinberger pulled out oversized cartoon drawings showing silhouettes of two soldiers. The Soviet silhouette was big. It had a red star on it. The American silhouette was small. It had Stars & Stripes on it, "As Secretary of Defense, I'm in charge of the military-industrial complex. We must keep the military supplied with more weapons, more vehicles, more food, more ammunition, more uniforms, and more communications. I need more money in a bigger budget to fight more communists. I won't back down on this!"

David Stockman, the youngest person there, was Director of the Office of Budget Management and was in a constant state of being pissed off by Weinberger. David wasn't old wealth, but he wasn't from California, either. "Boy the hogs are feeding tonight. Weinberger, you and your damn Laffer trickle-down economics fantasy will bankrupt America! Don't give in to Weinberger, Mr. President. Before the Reagan Administration, the U.S. was the biggest creditor nation in the history of the world. Your handlers will make us the biggest debtor national in world history ...with the biggest deficit in history! ...the U.S. will go bankrupt! Why? Casey's G-7 dynastic banking family financiers are collapsing our economy to take over the Soviet Union with debt financing ...like they've taken over the United States? I cook the budget every damn day! Fudge numbers so it doesn't stink and cost us all our jobs."

"Stockman," I tried bringing the meeting back under control, "Weinberger worked for Nixon. Weinberger worked for me, when I was Governor. You need to see the big picture."

Weinberger felt exonerated, "Stockman, I took this office convinced the U.S. was disarming itself for ten years while we were swamped with intelligence reports about massive arms build-up by Soviet Union communists. America's 1981 position, in relationship to the Soviet Union, is the same as Britain's was in the '30s to Nazi Germany. Churchill saved Great Britain by rearming her. Churchill said, 'In anything great or small, large or petty, never give in.' I need 10% defense more budget than Carter had. Over five years it's only 1.5 trillion-dollars. I'm not giving in."

I liked that, it played well.

"I made a mistake in my figures," Stockman spoke uncomfortably, "it's 300 billion dollars less ... even with my mistake it's over what Reagan said he wanted."

"It's your error," Weinberger smiled, "I won't trim it out! Any reduction in my budget increases the chance of war because of Soviet military might. We're way behind them. Anyone who cuts a nickel from my budget wants the Communists to win." Weinberger pointed to some large charts he'd put on the walls. "I superimposed Soviet defense plants on top of a map of Washington. Here's a chart superimposing Soviet nuclear and conventional forces on top of ours. See how the Soviets dwarf our defenses? They dwarf the defenses of the whole free world, combined! Mr. President our B-52 planes are older than their pilots."

"That's really something," I said, "that's embarrassing."

Stockman was in shock, his jaw dropped.

Caspar Weinberger went on. "Here, see this poster? See these three cartoon soldiers, Mr. President? The tiny pygmy-sized soldier with no rifle, he's Carter's defense budget. The tall, skinny pygmy soldier wearing glasses, the Woody Allen character carrying that tiny toy-looking rifle, he's Stockman's budget. But, look! ...this big giant GI Joe with muscles like the Hulk ...he has a brand new military helmet ...a brand-new flak jacket ...he's carrying a brand new M-60 top-of-the-line machine gun! This super-hero American warrior is my Defense budget."

Stockman watched me being happy then start yelling anew at Weinberger, "I can't believe a Harvard-trained Cabinet officer can bring Sesame Street cartoon pictures to the President as a legal argument! We'll be spending 300 billion dollars a year, not even counting CIA, Energy Department and National Security Agency defense figures! We'll go bankrupt. Why? To line the pockets of the Fed private shareholders? ...to bloat budgets of defense companies they direct? So Casey and his central bank cartel pimps can eulogize Dulles' Christian West plan reaping windfall interest payments off soaring national debt? This budget's a mess."

Stockman never impressed me, he lacked maturity and polish, "Stockman, you're not allowed to let the budget look bad!" I slammed my hand down on the conference table, "It has to look good ...Gentlemen, compromise. Calm down! Stockman, you were hired to make the budget look good, do it. Make Reaganomics look good. Trickle-down economics looks complicated, I know. So, simplify it so taxpayers can understand. Even George Bush understands it." I heard people in the room laugh, my timing had been pretty good on that one. "Why can't you? Take it from me, I made movies in Hollywood. K ... I ... S ... S ... keep it simple, stupid. Boil it down to a snapshot in your mind. We're supply-siders, small government with no services, lower taxes increases growth, makes savings, stimulates commerce. Lazy people must work harder to reduce inflation so the value of tax revenue rises. You're an economist! ...we pay you to say it better than me! I met with President Ford and Laffer the economist in a restaurant in California. Laffer drew a graph on the paper placemat ...a picture of what happens with cut taxes. It was a curve. Everyone called it, the 'Laffer curve' ...it means I.R.S. fails when taxes are 0% or 100%. At 0% percent, no money comes in ...no matter how much business sales revenues are. At 100% taxation, all business activity stops. Therefore, you have to set taxes low enough to encourage economic activity. Then, with more economic activity, the amount of total tax revenues increase. What's so hard to understand, Stockman?"

Stockman challenged me, "No one has figured out what best tax rate is, so the Laffer Curve is buried treasure with no treasure map."

"Well, Kemp of New York and Roth of Delaware are introducing legislation to reduce federal income tax 30% ...so we can have increased taxes when the economy responds to the Laffer Curve. How can you beat that story, we reduce taxes to get more tax revenue."

"Mr. President, you don't have the foggiest idea supply-side's a mirror image of trickle-down economics, a cheap way of saying cut taxes for business ...so the wealthy stimulate the economy like giving your kid less allowance each week. It's a Trojan horse that will bankrupt us. You promise increased military spending and a balanced budget but you must cut domestic spending. Cutting taxes can't grow the economy, it raises the deficit, Congress will say we're stimulating economic growth but cut social welfare spending, Social Security, Medicare, Veterans Hospitals, public housing grants, farm subsidies, public broadcasting, student loans, mental health. You'll create homeless people in America for the first time, let people starve, get sick, and die." Stockman shot his wad, felt defeated and sat down.

Mike nudged me awake.

"Do we have our new budget?" I said, yawning sleepily.

"Tell them about the stack of money going into space," Mike whispered.

"When I took office," I said, "Carter's runaway 80 billion dollar deficit and cumulative national debt of 908 billion dollars could make a stack of dollar bills 60 miles high into outer space."

Stockman was devastated, like I didn't hear a word he said ...he'd talked me to sleep, "Mr. President I'm trying to tell you, eliminate the deficit by curbing spending and raising taxes. You're wandering around in circles."

"Runaway spending is the fault of an iron triangle of Congress, special interest lobbyists and journalists," I said, "raiding the Treasury then blaming it."

Stockman took his last shot, "Red ink on the budget is revenue shortfall, caused by lowering tax rates and raising defense spending. It is not from new social welfare spending. The Pentagon spends 34 million dollars an hour."

My eyelids felt heavy and I yawned, "It's Jimmy Carter's fault. The national Treasury will recover when we cut taxes to stimulate the economy, then we can retire the national debt. When I promised to balance the budget, I was promising it was my goal to do that ...not that I could really do it. I remember when Cold Warriors Paul Nitze, Paul Weyrich, Dick Cheney, Robert Bowman, and Laffer came to see me. They tried selling me Starwars with a Darth Vader doll ...using it as a movie prop to show me the Soviet Union was an evil empire. Well, I picked up that Darth Vader doll. I told that doll to its face, exactly what I'm telling you, the Soviet Union is an evil empire! ...that's the true story how Starwars got priority in this Administration."

The Cabinet and Staffers fell quiet. The Situation Room was still. Everyone watched me ...as I stared off ... past the room ... into the distance. In my head, I was reliving my days on stage in front of Hollywood cameras, fighting Nazis. In the footage replaying in my head, I was saving America. I was preventing an orbiting death ray from falling back into Nazi hands.

Bill Casey wanted to steer, "Mr. President, the Solidarity Labor Movement in Poland looks like it might get swept away by a Soviet-supported Communist regime. Moscow clamped down on the Polish army. The Polish army declared martial law."

"How does this sound?" I said. "Moscow is unleashing the forces of tyranny against a peaceful neighbor. I'm asking Americans to light candles, in support of Poles."

Deaver pushed his palms alongside his temples and smiled, "That will fly on TV."

Bill Casey was thinking about a Christian West Full-Court Press to speed up destabilization of the Soviet Union and Eastern Europe, that he, Paul Nitze and Paul Weyrich kept preaching. Bill knew not to publicly talk about the Full-Court Press, certainly not to Cabinet and Staff members, Bush and me. Bill's mastermind played a three-dimensional chess game in his head at all times, keeping a tally on us, counting the cards we played, tracking the money-issuing class rivalries and economic turf wars, covert ops, captains of industry and petroleum who argued by deploying the unquestionable logic of paramilitary death squads. Bill needed to push the Full-Court Press along with invisible fingers, and mumbled, "I go along with Defense Secretary Weinberger. A stepped-up arms race will beggar Russia."

"It will beggar us, too," Stockman objected, but had run out of gas.

Bill didn't care who made the National Debt interest payments to the money-issuing, private owners of the Fed, as long as the debt climbed ... that was the whole point of private ownership of the money-issuing apparatus, a strategy too simple for people to get.

"What we seem to be doing," Haig joined in, "is substituting an arms budget with covert ops as a foreign policy stand-in."

Mike looked at me, seeing I was tired. He was a guardian angel for me and Nancy, always had been. I smiled and he smiled back.

"On the news front," Larry Speakes said, "an organization of Roman Catholic Bishops is taking an anti-nuclear stand, condemning nuclear weapons as immoral, saying the arms race robs the poor and sick and makes mankind choose between constant terror or constant surrender."

I yawned again, "Anti-nuclear groups are under Communist influence. Carter's SALT II treaty locks in the Soviet advantage, makes us vulnerable. Only way to close this window of vulnerability is us making more nuclear weapons." I saw Defense Secretary Weinberger raising his hand, nervously, "What now, Weinberger?"

"The Joint Chiefs of Staff disagree with you, Mr. President," Weinberger had finally spit it out, "they say, SALT II limits the Soviets from deploying more missiles. Let's resume arms control talks with Moscow. But, secretly deploy cruise missiles and Pershing II missiles in Western Europe. The Soviets say their intermediate range missiles are aimed at Europe ...to match French and British missiles and weapons on American submarines and planes around Europe. Let's take the advantage back. Me and Deputy Defense Secretary Richard Perle want our 'Zero Option' plan ... zero Soviet SS-20 missiles in Europe. In return, we'll promise no future deployment of cruise and Pershing missiles ...of course, after we already have them in there. Another aide, T.K. Jones, is starting to assure the public that most Americans will survive a nuclear war, that many Americans would prosper from nuclear war. In a nuclear attack, just dig a hole, cover it with a couple doors, throw three feet of dirt on top ...with enough shovels, everyone's gonna make it. There'd be rapid economic recovery. Fighting nuclear war is survivable when we have military superiority over Russia."

"It's my early religious upbringing," I said, "I see nuclear conflict as Armageddon, fulfillment of Biblical prophesy. The Bible says, angels have a civil war in Heaven. Satan leads a band of angels against God. God throws Satan down into the fiery pit. Armageddon will destroy evil people in the world. The good people, at least 30,000 anyway, will go live up in Heaven. The rest of good people are resurrected from their graves to live eternal life on Earth. We're good people. What do we have to worry about?"

The room was silent, again.

"I went with Martin Andersen from Hoover Institute to Strategic Air Command Center in the Cheyenne Mountains, in Colorado. The commander there told me, if the Soviets fire one missile, then all we could do was track it ...and fire back a missile at Russia. We've spent a fortune in equipment ...and there's no way to stop a nuclear missile from hitting us. American nuclear strategy is called, 'Mutually Assured Destruction'. Now, that's the same thing I was up against when I played Brass Bancroft in the film, Murder in the Air in 1940. I played a secret agent. I had to steal a secret inertia projector device. The device stopped enemy aircraft from flying. I remember my lines, 'The inertia projector will make America invincible in war ...and therefore, it is the greatest force for peace ever invented'. Does anyone remember, The Day the Earth Stood Still. A flying saucer makes all the machines on Earth stop running. That's how they warn mankind to seek peace. Well ...when Dr. Ed Teller and retired Air Force Lt. General Dan Graham founded the High Frontier lobbying group, they came to me. They told me about an anti-missile shield project. I called it, Starwars, after the movie. Can you imagine building an X-Ray laser powered by a nuclear bomb? Then, the U.S. can have laser beam death rays to shoot down Soviet missiles. Brass Bancroft likes the idea. We mount the death rays on a space station. We make an astrodome of electro-magnetic-spectrum light radio signals to protect America. It's based on a Nazi plan to orbit mirrors and focus sunlight and burn up targets. I like the idea of Starwars.

"This is how my speech would go, 'I have a vision of a peaceful future ...in which we have a Strategic Defense Initiative to make all nuclear weapons impotent ...and obsolete.' I'd let people know I still had it in me."

"That'll fly, Ronnie, it'll play," Deaver said, "I have no idea how it works ...but it's high concept movie storytelling. Why don't we test the idea on some focus groups. Get you a few photo-ops. Raise your approval rating a few points."

I stared off into the distance. I remembered my role as secret agent Brass Bancroft in, Murder In The Air ...I was dreaming. Cabinet members and White House Staffers were deathly still, you could hear a pin drop in the room. They watched me, as I stared off into the distance. I could see everyone in the room looking at me funny, with confused looks on their faces. But, they all knew I got that same confused look on my face whenever I was trying to get my mind working again, get my thoughts flowing, get my hand around an idea. I felt a wondrous feeling, felt wonder wash over my face, and refreshed. I got that 'winning feeling', "You know what I told Weyrich and Nitze. I said, You men have given me hope again. You've answered my prayers. This Starwars death ray's a good story idea. It'll sell at the box office. People'll love it. That's the ticket. America needs hope ...hope of a world with no mutually-assured nuclear destruction. Weinberger, you'll get your budget, you'll get your weapons. I promise that. We have to get rid of the communists."

Weinberger's smile could outshine the White House Christmas tree.

Stockman's disappointed face was the biggest frown in town. I told Stockman, "Stockman, your job's to promote my policy, not sink it!"

Ed Meese III seemed to be having a crises. Ed blurted it out, "Mr. President ...my staff wants better office locations, navy blue water coolers, not mauve that's for girls. God damn the communists, too!"

I felt something was off, "Ed, what's really bothering you?"

Ed was quiet for a moment, pensive, "I don't know."

I did. "It's because James Baker ended-up as White House Chief of Staff, not you. Isn't it?"

Ed shuffled his feet, "I don't know. It's hard to get used to these Washington types ...it's like shooting shadows. I never hit 'em. I know you chose Baker ...because, I hate details ...I provoke people who disagree with me. How could I move legislation through Congress like Jim Baker can? He's an old-time friend of George Bush, anyway."

White House Chief of Staff Jim Baker III bit his lip, but had a cunning 'devil-may-care' look on his face, "I'm sorry, if you feel bad Ed. It's just, I know my way around Congress. There's a new Republican majority in the Senate, just itchin' to lead legislation around. The President and each one of us has got to talk tax cuts and the defense build-up, then the rest of the agenda takes care of itself. Mr. President and the rest of us don't mind you keep calling for banning abortion, getting prayer back in schools, changing the U.S. Constitution to mandate a balanced budget. I just hope you don't actually expect Congress to act on things like that, they're controversial, Ed. You got to get a feel for Washington. Your best bet, is just go with more tax cuts and more defense spending."

More tax cuts, more defense spending ...I liked the sound of that, "If it's Armageddon, then God's on our side! ...I got the presentation down on those lines, huh, Mike?"

Mike was drunk, "Yes sir." Mike waved that the meeting was over.

I stood up and looked into a full-length mirror. I smiled at me, "How do I look, Mike?"

Mike was a quiet drunk, convinced no one could smell vodka on his breath, "You're handsome, Mr. President ...the American people like handsome."

It was at this point, when everything seemed most absurd to me, that Nancy entered the room carrying a lunch tray of finger sandwiches for her and me. She started to shoo everyone out of the room. Me and Nancy would enjoy lunch in peace. Nancy always soothed me, always calmed me down ...just by being there, "Why the long face, Honey?"

I didn't feel grumpy anymore. I smiled at her. "You know my management style. I pick good people. Then, I delegate to them all of my decision-making authority, so they can do their job, their way. Will my management style hang me? ...ask your astrologer for me. Ask her, if my Staff and Cabinet will always hate each other? ...and fight to the death. Ask her ...how can I can get approval from my Staff and Cabinet? ...when they're at each other's throats ...it's makin' me crazy, I don't know what to do. Go for Staff approval? ...or Cabinet approval?"

Nancy understood me, "Is it approval you want?"

"You know me, that's what it boils down to."

She led me to clear thinking, "Should you play to the director, the producer, or the audience?"

"That depends if I want the part, or if I already have it ...I've already got the part. I'm President. I don't have to play to my White House Staff ...or play to my Cabinet, do I? ...I'll play to the American people."

Nancy kissed me on the check, "It's the same audience you've always played to, that watched your movies, elected you governor, elected you President ...play to your biggest audience for approval. If that means you have to play along with jerks in your Staff, and with rough necks in your Cabinet ...then play along. Can you?"

I felt better, "Sure I can. Thanks. I love you."

Deaver walked back in and gave me a high-sign, it was time for my press conference.

I stood up, "How do I look, Mike?"

"Handsome, Mr. President. The American public likes handsome, don't we," Mike said drunkenly. Mike emptied his flask down the hatch. He'd stopped caring if anyone was watching, long ago.

White House Spokesman Larry Speakes walked back into the Situation Room impatiently tapping his watch crystal with one of his fingers, "Ronnie it's time for your press conference ...get happy, the American people's waitin'. Press conference time, Mr. President. Reporters waiting. You look great. Go get 'em, Give 'em hell."

I felt confident, I was a performer, a trooper ...just like Nancy, who always covered my back. I checked myself out one last time in the full-length mirror, like a stage actor going onstage, I washed all the upset off my face, put on a mask of effortless confidence that the audience always pays for at the box office. I winked at me, and smiled at my image in the mirror, it smiled back ...I still had it.

I walked down the hall into the adjoining White House Briefing Room to applause, to greet reporters, giving them a 'thumbs-up' sign, happy to be on stage again, vital, alive, accepted and at home. I was making a radio speech at the same time. I sat down. I tapped my finger on the radio microphone to see if it was live. It made that dull, thundering sound that always shocked everyone. I looked at the radio technician. The technician signaled to me. I smiled. I spoke into the microphone to test the sound levels, "My fellow Americans I'm pleased to tell you today that I've signed legislation that will outlaw the Soviet Union, forever. We begin bombing in five minutes."

The people in the room were shocked. They started to get frantic. I laughed off their reaction, "It's only a sound check."

The radio technician looked nervous, he signaled me, "No, Mr. President. We're live, you're on the air, use your script."

I looked at Mike Deaver, accusingly. He was laughing. Then, I laughed. I began reading my script, "The Soviet Union is the focus of evil in the modern world, led by men who reserve the right to lie, cheat and steal their way to world domination. A Soviet conspiracy underlies all the unrest in the world. If the Soviet Union wasn't playing this game of dominoes, there wouldn't be any hot spots in the whole world. Let's see what's next. Oh yes. As you know, former President Carter enacted the Refugee Act of 1980. This was designed to protect those fleeing their countries, afraid of persecution for religious, political, or racial reasons. Under my Administration, only refugees fleeing Cuba or Nicaragua will receive political asylum. Salvadorans, Haitians, and Guatemalans, whose regimes Washington considers as allies, are being labeled inadmissible ...because we consider them to be, 'economic' refugees. Today, I ordered the Coast Guard to tow out to sea any boats of Haitian refugees found approaching America."

<>

Patti, at home in the Hollywood hillside canyons, dragged a string back and forth in front of her cat, Jackson. Jackson pretended not to see it; then, suddenly Jackson jumped up high in the air. Jackson came down with all four paws on top of the string. He flicked his tail and walked slowly and proudly away. Patti heard her father on the radio, and turned the station to a news report, 'A small group of American activists have formed a Sanctuary Movement modeled on the Underground Railroad used in President Lincoln's era to smuggle slaves out of the South up into Northern States. Sanctuary Movement helps people fleeing oppression and death squads in Latin America and South America. It helps oppressed people fleeing dictators CIA installed after killing legitimate government leaders. Sanctuary Movement organized a network of churches and non-profit organizations to shelter, feed and hide refugees ...who would otherwise be sent home, handed over to death squads, then slaughtered.' Patti was glad she'd donated money to the Sanctuary Movement.

<>

As time passed, I enjoyed my radio broadcasts more and more. It was like the old days, when I was a young man, just starting out. I noted my broadcasts on my desk calendar with a check mark after I did them. Then, I flipped over to the next day's calendar page. As months went by, official Press Briefings came and went according to Deaver's schedule.

Bitsburg, Germany

Deaver and his advance team met with German Chancellor Helmut Kohl in Bitsburg Germany, at a cemetery. It was snowing on the graves. Secret Service people and German elite guards stood by at attention.

Chancellor Kohl smiled, "Here."

Deaver was surprised. "In a cemetery? You want President Reagan to kneel down here to honor the German war dead?"

"Yes. It's all right. Germans were victims of World War II, too. It's a gesture of reconciliation."

"I don't want to compromise President Reagan."

"You won't. There are no Nazis buried here."

"It's a real decision."

Kohl put his arm around Mike Deaver's shoulders. "If you agree, we'll go to the BMW factory. You and your staff can pick out new BMWs, at a discount."

In the BMW factory, Mike Deaver stood at the end of the assembly line. He turned to Chancellor Kohl. "I think navy blue is a better color than black or silver for a beemer." Deaver and his staff climbed inside new BMWs when the cars were unhooked from the assembly line. Deaver floored his car. He screeched out of the factory. Chancellor Kohl sadly shook his head.

White House Situation Room

Me and Nancy, Mike Deaver, and George Shultz met in the White House Situation Room. Mike felt sad, uncomfortable. "I'm sorry, Ronnie. I didn't know we were being set up. I thought it was a good photo-op for you to say a few words commemorating the deaths of the Germans in World War II. I didn't know the god damn cemetery is full of SS officers."

"Mike, you messed up this time!" Nancy was furious. She couldn't stand anyone making me look bad. "Half of Congress is having a shit-fit! They don't want their voters to think Ronnie's honoring the murderers of their boys who fought World War II. White House Staff, the Cabinet, Congress, everyone's split ... the majority's against us."

Mike was silent. Nancy turned to me, "Ronnie, our personal friends and the entire Jewish community of the United States are against you on this one. Put it in reverse. Back yourself out. Don't pray at the graves of mass murderers. It's wrong."

"I gave my word, I won't cancel the visit." I was stubborn when I made a decision.

Nancy turned to George Shultz. "George, can you help him out?"

State Secretary George Shultz bit his lip, then chuckled. "I've talked with German ex-Chancellor Schmit. I told him, Look,

Helmut, I have to get the President's rear-end out of the wringer on Bitsburg. He said, there are no Nazis and SS buried there."

Nancy was bitter about it, "He lied to you."

George Shultz nodded. "I know. Ronnie won't back down because Schmidt said, Kohl won't be re-elected if Ronnie changes his mind ... the German government will fall to communists in the coming German elections."

Nancy's eyes widened. "Oh, please spare me."

"I argued with Kohl. He guaranteed me there was no problem with the grave site. Now, all Kohl can say is he'll lose re-election if he loses face, and communists will get more power in Germany." Shultz bit his lip.

I was getting upset. "If Kohl and Schmidt save face, then me and America lose face."

Nancy frowned, "It's not right."

George Shultz shrugged, "We've got to protect America's banking and trade relations with Germany."

"You were president of Bechtel, of course you'd say that," I said. "What I'm complaining about, is none of you, not one told me this job was like this. George, you're a pal, but I'm holding fast. There's no way out. I gave my word. I'm going to that Nazi SS graveyard to pray!"

George Shultz snapped a pencil in his hands. "The Nazis screwed us again."

Mike Deaver hung up his phone. "Approval ratings are in, you're going down."

Nancy was besides herself. "It's too soon after Iran-Contra."

"My 'hero' rating's falling," I felt sad. "America doesn't like me, anymore."

"Germany loves it. It makes us look like Nazi-lovers!" Shultz spat out his words.

"What am I going to do? ...I can't offend Germany. I gave my word."

"I'm sorry, Mr. President. I can't get your ass out of the fire on this one."

"The show must go on. I learned that in show business. Never cancel a show, even if it kills you. It'll be hard. But, I gave my word."

"Well, if you're going to the SS cemetery you have to make the Jews and liberals happy," Mike said. "So, you're going to concentration camp ruins, too. You go pray at the concentration camp ruins for Jews who died in the camps. I've been telling you for years, that's a good photo-op for your campaign chest, and will save your popularity rating."

"I don't ever want to go to a concentration camp. It's too painful. It reminds me of the truth. I know what went on there. It's too upsetting for me."

Nancy felt bad for me, saw me fighting back tears. I wouldn't let myself feel the sadness overtaking me ...I forced a phony smile. I tried to joke, "I'd rather remember it, Hollywood style."

Nancy sadly watched my face. I stared at the ceiling watching an imaginary film of my Hollywood days, back in 1941. I was drafted into a World War II war propaganda film unit. I served my country as a war propaganda film producer, in Hollywood, starring in, 'This Is The Army', a musical comedy about World War II. In the Situation Room I start singing a few lines from, This Is The Army. I saw the Hollywood soldiers singing happily, marching off to war on a stage set. The cameras rolled. I kept singing. I got up. I marched around the Situation Room.

George Shultz got an upset look on his face.

Nancy had seen it before, she tried to cover for me. "Don't get upset, George. Ronnie's just giving you a private performance of, 'This Is The Army'. It's a musical film he starred in about World War II."

I was back in 1941 in the screening room watching the film. It stuck in the projector. The screen images melted, browned, smoked and burst into a white image. It hurt my eyes. When the film started again, it had been switched. 'Top Secret ... German Concentration Camps' appeared in a subtitle on the screen. I watched documentary footage of concentration camp horrors. I felt trapped in the movie. I closed my eyes. I couldn't bear to see the truth. I vomited in the screening room.

Nancy saw the look of horror on my face. "Ronnie! Ronnie!"

My eyes cleared. I smiled at her.
Nancy felt relieved, "He's back."
George Shultz sighed heavily.

SS Graveyard Photo-Op, Bitsburg Germany

I was in Bitsburg, Germany at the SS Nazi graveyard for the World War II commemoration ceremony, flanked by a goose-stepping Germany honor guard accompanying me to the grave sites. I knelt down, layed a commemorative wreath on a grave, and prayed at the graves of German SS death squad leaders to honor German and American war dead. I prayed to commemorate the end of World War II.

In the movie in my head I was back in 1941, sitting in the screening room in Hollywood watching Top Secret Army documentary footage of concentration camp torture and mutilation scenes. I blinked my eyes. I was back at Bitsburg. I stared at the SS Nazi graves. I was in both places, horrified watching the camp torture and here, maintaining my dignity as the U.S. head of state. I watched ghosts materializing around me, pointing fingers at me.

Nancy was shocked, wondered where my head was at and helplessly watched a tormented, frightened look on my face, while trying to decide if I'd gone over the edge or if it was it my Alzheimer's acting up. Nancy leaned down beside me, whispering, "Ronnie, are you okay? Is your mind playing tricks on you?"

I looked up at Nancy, "Something inside me's dying. I see spirits begging me for help. I'm living a nightmare." Trees, fences and buildings morphed into ghosts then back again into what they really were. I looked at Nancy, "Don't you see them?"

Nancy, in her long winter coat standing in the freshly falling snow was a small figure in a large graveyard. She straightened up and smiled pleasantly to our German hosts, then leaned over again, moving her head close to mine, "Who?"

To steady myself, I put my hand against a gravestone. "Victims of the Nazis all around us, lost souls begging us to save them."

Nancy was shaken up, but kept her presence of mind to act

normal. "I feel they're here, too. Be brave, Darling, I love you. It will be over soon."

"No. It won't, it never ends, it has a life of its own." I rested my head against a tombstone. We were going next to a concentration camp.

Bergen-Belsen concentration camp, photo-op

Me and Nancy went to Bergen-Belsen concentration camp on an overcast, foggy day with Bergen-Belsen frosted in falling snow. I was tense, cautious, didn't know what was next. Bergen-Belsen felt haunted. The first chance I'd get, I'll tell Deaver where to shove this photo-op. Right now I didn't care if it would raise my falling public opinion ratings at home. I just wanted to get the hell out of here and stop feeling watched and scared. I walked off from Nancy and left the photographers to spend a few minutes by myself. I stood still, staring into one of the concentration camp ovens I recognized from the Top Secret Army film from a long time ago ...an oven where children were shoved in, screaming. There, our humanity was burnt alive. I heard Hollywood theme music, looked at my reflection in a glass window in the oven door. I start talking to my reflection in the oven, "All my life I've run away from feelings because of places like this that hurt too much. I avoid emotional pain, I just deny it because it hurts too much." I watched a little girl's ghost, rise up like smoke out of the ashes on the oven floor. It spoke to me, "Don't forget me. I was innocent. I was good. I committed no crime. Why was I starved and burnt alive? Don't ever forget me. Redeem my eternal soul."

Nancy bravely walked over to me, feeling eerie, "Ronnie, Darling, who are you talking to?"

I ignored Nancy. I felt vulnerable and fragile. It was private. I started to cry. Nancy didn't know what to do. I spoke out, "I feel helpless. I want to stop denying the pain. But, I can't. I want to push it away, pretend everything's fine and I feel good, to accept my feelings, to feel the pain I've pushed away. I've got to ...but, I can't. It hurts too much. I promise, I'll never, never push feelings away, again. Never."

Nancy was helpless, and not being in control was tearing her apart, "I know, Darling, I know."

"I have to suffer, now and feel their feelings, I can't pretend, anymore, it didn't happen. I can't deny it, I owe it to them, those innocent people, I owe it to Jesus. It's my responsibility. My mother would agree." I started to grieve, to sob, to let myself feel again. So much of my life I hadn't let myself feel. I'd wasted Time. What would life have been like, if I felt myself living ... if I felt life living all around me? I felt tears falling from my eyes, steaming in the cold air. It was so long since I cried. It occurred to me, then. I realized life was feeling. It was feeling tears. It was feeling love. Why was I crying like this, tears were useless things for weak men. But, my heart argued with me, as if life was an act of love. Could it be that simple? My tears thought so.

Nancy walked away so I could have private time, over to Mike Deaver, the German press corps and White House photographers. Nancy acted matter-of-fact, "The President was always afraid to come here. It's too painful for him to relive the horror that happened here. He'd rather avoid those feelings, because it hurts too much. It reminds him of the truth. It's too painful. Ronnie avoids emotional pain. He just denies it because it hurts too much. The President of the United States doesn't want to talk right now. He's crying for the lost souls that haunt this place. He's praying to redeem their eternal souls." Nancy walked back over to me, she took my arm, helping me to stand. Arm-in-arm, we walked away in falling white snowflakes, some brushing my eyelashes in the falling darkness.

Mike Deaver was amused, he turned to an aide, "They ought to get Oscars for that! His rating's gonna soar!"

As we walked in the night, photographers' searchlights projected our shadows across the graves and tombstones and up over corners of surrounding buildings across rows of office and apartment windows. Nancy looked at me, the lights reflecting in her eyes. Nancy saw the look of confusion and devastation on my face, the lost look in my eyes. She felt sorry. She felt sad. Nancy was afraid I was having an attack of Alzheimer's. Nancy was afraid this was a look ahead at what was coming. Nancy was frightened this was a look at what the rest of her life would be like, with me.

CHAPTER 2

White House Chief of Protocol Ambassador Lucky Roosevelt's office

Lucky was a thin, attractive Lebanese woman, with dark eyes like a doe, married to a ruling family spook, who apparently never told her the truth ...or, did. Sitting in her White House office U.S. Ambassador of Protocol Selwa Lucky Roosevelt's problems began her first day on the job.

As White House Chief of Protocol and Decorum, Ambassador Lucky came on the job the first day, only to find her staff wearing blue jeans! And, chewing gum!

Then, totally embarrassing Lucky, George Bush's wife, Barbara, unexpectedly stopped by, walking in on her unannounced, catching Lucky off-guard. Lucky struggled to cope with her embarrassment about her staff's appearance.

"The last thing I do is stand on ceremony," Barbara smiled most of the time. "I've seen my own kids in blue jeans often enough. But, your job ...is to stand on ceremony. That's why you were hired."

Lucky was glad she no longer felt embarrassed. "Your husband, the Vice President, is a very lucky man to have you on his side."

Lucky appreciated how Barbara put her at ease, in a pleasant, social way.

"It'll be okay, Lucky, we CIA wives must stick together. We're always moving around the world with our husbands," Barbara said, "...or, wondering where they are today, if they're safe or not."

"Oh God yes." After that, Lucky felt at ease whenever Barbara was present. Lucky felt she'd found a friend in Barbara. "I don't even know where Archie is now ...maybe Africa with David Rockefeller. South Africa managing diamonds and gold, or Angola, overseeing oil operations, or overseeing hundreds of railroads for World Bank." Lucky remembered back in the '50s when her boyfriend, Archie Roosevelt, took her to a luncheon and told her, "Darling, wait a moment before you say yes or no to marrying me. There's something you have to know about me."

"What, Darling?"

"I work for Central Intelligence Agency."

"What's that?"

"Well, that's a government intelligence unit, a little private army thrown together after World War II to protect the Fed shareholders, when Office of Strategic Services OSS was revamped to protect American overseas business investments and fight Communism here, and overseas."

"How thrilling!"

"I sit behind a desk, I'm a pencil pusher, a desk jockey, a bean counter ...I'm an intelligence researcher. I get called on the road sometimes, but never into field operations ...so there's no danger for me. Most of all, Darling, we have to keep it a secret, just tell everyone my job's at the university."

Lucky was excited, "Wow. Marrying a spy!"

<>

Back in Lucky's White House office sipping ice tea with Barbara Bush, Barbara noticed Lucky seemed lost in thought. Barbara knew, from the look on Lucky's face, what Lucky was thinking ...because Barbara was remembering the first time George told Barbara he worked for CIA.

It was in 1976. George was appointed to Director of CIA. George hung up the phone, sat down at the table for dinner. The family butler served George a drink. The family cook delayed dinner five minutes, while George was on the phone. Now, the family waiter served soup. George got up. He walked past W, and his other kids, to the other end of the table. He kissed Barbara sweetly on the cheek. "Well it looks like I know who the new director of the CIA is going to be."

Barbara looked at the questioning look on her husband's face, "Really?"

"Yes."

"But, George, really. I've suspected you since after college, when you went behind the Iron Curtain for that conservative Dresser Industries oil exploration company, you were on Company business. When your friend Shackley used to run JM/Wave Radio in Florida against Cuba. CIA runs JM/Wave, that's what the girls say. Congratulations. Will this help you finally get rid of Castro? ...and get our family's Cuban offshore oil leases back, up-and-running, again?"

George adopted that look of feigned machismo, "I'm going to give it a hell of a try."

Barbara and Lucky stopped reminiscing. Lucky sipped ice tea. "Barbara, you know Mike Deaver's 'little shits' that work for him? I call them, 'munchkins'. One marched in yesterday demanding I hire one of their staffers as my chief assistant, can you imagine?"

"I'm afraid I can. A lot of the White House Staff came from California. What can you expect? When push comes to shove, they've been shoving, already."

"I told the munchkin, no. Then, Deaver called me, himself, to pressure me to hire his staffer. I said no. I had to decide if I'd let people bully me or not ...or tell him take this job, and shove it. I realized either way, I had to stand up for myself or munchkins would ride me out of town. I followed my intuition and did what's right, I stood up for myself. Now, I keep an eye out for munchkins."

"Good, Lucky. You did right." Barbara sipped some tea.

CIA Director's office,
Washington D.C., 1976

George Bush walked beneath a charcoal, stormy sky looming over the huge office complex in Langley, Virginia, noticing the brass sign on front of the building that read, 'CIA Headquarters', was getting tarnished more each day. He'd have to have the janitors polish it up to look more presentable because people believed what they perceived. He held up an identification card to a rent-a-cop inside the door, who verified it in a computer, then waved him past. George walked down the hall into an elevator, rode up a few floors, got out and walked down the hall to his office door, that read, 'George Bush, Director of Central Intelligence Agency (DCI)'. He looked suspiciously up and down the hall, then unlocked the office door and entered his office. He was startled, and nearly jumped out of his skin when someone swung around in his office chair to face him. In shadow, the figure appeared to be drawing a gun on him. George reached inside his coat, he drew his shoulder pistol out, pointed it. His desk lamp switched on.

"Happy Birthday," his wife said, holding out a bouquet to him for a gift.

"Barbara! Thank God it's you."

Barbara felt it go, she'd wet her pants a little bit, "You weren't going to shoot me, were you George?"

"Of course not," George was relieved, he holstered his pistol, "I'm sorry I scared you, Barbie."

"I'm sorry I scared you, too, George."

"Thanks for the flowers. How 'bout letting me have my chair back?"

"Of course, Darling. Soon as I put these flowers in the vase. They're white roses, your favorite."

"They're beautiful ...why were you sitting in the dark?"

"One of your friends recognized me, picked the lock to let me in to surprise you. Wasn't that nice?"

George shrugged and gave Barbara his look of feigned machismo. George loved Barbara and confided in her, whenever it didn't override her security clearance. And, off the record, sometimes when it did. It was his way of asking her for advice, it was one of those times, right now, "Barbara, when I took this job, I found out things the hard way I didn't want to know. CIA directors are front men, like presidents, cut-outs to blame, puppets to take heat or claim plausible denial, smoke and mirrors. We don't really do anything, just what we're told, like marionettes, except the strings that are pulled are our tendons, and we bleed."

"George," Barbara assured him, "it's the only way to protect our family and investment portfolio ... someone has to do it. We've six kids, and with grand kids, it makes twenty-seven in our immediate family. You're family patriarch, you have to financially protect everyone, build-up trust funds for the kids, grandkids, and great grandkids, so they never have to work like the subject population. Like we never had to work. We did it as a matter of choice and principle ...because, it was our duty. This world can be cold and uncaring. We want our family to go withdraw $5,000-to-$10,000 for out-of-pocket expenses whenever they feel like it, without cutting our family trust endowment. Your father and mine gave us that privilege, that's what ruling family values are, our family tradition. It's a great tradition. It's what we stand for. Just make sure the tendons that get cut aren't yours. As long as the blood on the ground is someone else's ...then, you're protecting our family. I know it sounds harsh ...but, you've heard it before. In a way, George, you're family patriarch for all the Blue Book American families, for Society. You're DCI, you protect the investment portfolios for all the ruling families in America, all 5,000 of us, puppets, cut-outs, sanctions, smoke, mirrors ...whatever." Barbara powdered her nose as she spoke.

George let loose a big sigh, "I feel so exasperated. There's so much dirty laundry in this job, it's a set-up waiting to happen ... like I'm a patsy finding out the hard way ...I can't trust anyone, here. Me covering up Nixon. Nixon covering up Dulles. Dulles smuggling Nazi and fascist financiers into the country to finance the Republican and Democratic parties since World War II. Covering up the Kennedy thing, both the brothers, Martin Luther King, Paul Robeson ... it changes a man, Barbara. There are more Nazis in our government all the time, in the National Republican Heritage Committee, those people were financiers and death squad leaders in Hitler's Eastern

Europe ...now, they're on the election committee as part of the official Republican party to get out and swing the ethnic vote. They're on CIA payroll, we give them foreign aid to keep modern death squads going in their regimes all through eastern Europe, South America, South Africa. It's Satanic ...how do you sweep Lucifer under the rug? How do you sweep Satan out of your heart? Keep him from looking out your eyes? Calling your shots? What do you tell the press, it's just one lie after another. It's demonic. You wouldn't believe how much business my father and yours did with Hitler before, during, and after World War II ... how much money we lost when the U.S. Government shut down our parents' business investing and laundering Nazi money and shipping them oil, working with Dulles to smuggle Nazi loot and gold from Dulles' House of Morgan financial interests through the Angletons, the Bank of England, the Baring brothers, Seligman, Speyers, Mirabaud, Mallet, Gould, J. Henry Shroder, Erlanger, Warburg, Grenfell, Hambros, Brown, Lazard brothers, Moses Seif, Rothschilds, and Vatican Bank. Then, how much money we made after the war on our Nazi partners that still check in with me through intelligence walk-ins and cut-outs. I never know when one's gonna contact me, every time the phone rings, I don't want to pick it up. It turns my blood black, makes my stomach feel sick. If there was only some way to make America clean again, to wash the blood off our family money ...or at least, get the damn money back."

"The Vatican Bank?" Barbara couldn't believe it. Yet, over time, nothing surprised her any more, "...even, the Pope was in on it?"

"Is the Pope Catholic? We've infiltrated the Knights of Malta, they're the walking Dark Ages, we've taken their Crusades from the Middle Ages right into today's headlines against the Muslims and the Jews ...the P-2 Lodge are the real Italian Mafioso controlling the Vatican Bank. The Pope is head of the Vatican National Government. It's like the Pope is a DCI in his own right, running a mind control experiment on a billion human beings. All this intelligence stuff gets to me, the double British-Soviet agents, the triple U.S.-British-Soviet agents, add German BND intelligence, KGB, Mossad ...it all goes around like a twister in a Scooby Do movie. Until there isn't national allegiance anymore, anyplace ...because, everyone's working for someone else, and they're subcontracted to the same central banks anyway, and international investment banks ...then, all the banking families start turf wars, and there's brothers fighting brothers, sisters fighting sisters ... add in Agency protection for drug-runners who run us gun-running intelligence, add in provocations to start wars to run up national debt for arms, or provisions ...and back and forth we go ...on a merry-go-round on an escalator on a roller coaster in elevator on a parachute drop. Everyone fills barf bags, Barbara ...we never get our feet back on the ground til we're planted six feet under. All of us just trying to grow our portfolios, shelter our family trusts, protect our fortune, that's our family values."

Barbara felt moved, she walked over to George, touched his shoulder, "George, I'm worried about you and your whining. Can you take a vacation?"

"I need a permanent vacation."

"That's a bad joke, George."

"There's too much stress on this job. I'm supposed to be protecting national security, but everywhere I look, it's the new World Order one world government crap ...that's not national, it's global. That's not the American flag, Barbara. It's dark angels against God and Christ, is what it is."

"I haven't seen you so wound up for awhile, George. We can't play God. You need this job to maintain and grow our family endowment. It's the way the ball bounces for you, your father, his father, my father and grandfather, for Abraham, Issac and Ishmael and the Gospel Apostles at the last supper, George ... no one has a choice, really. You put the family fortune first ...or, there's no family gonna be left, just anarchy."

"Think it boils down like that?"

Barbara nodded. She watched George's pet look of feigned machismo take over his face, again. George remembered being at his dad's, Prescott's, estate and mansion in Florida that time they had Selwa and Archie Roosevelt and Archie's parents over for dinner with Allen Dulles and several Rockefeller brothers.

Prescott was his usual circumspect self, "You can't beat Florida weather. You Roosevelts are the best neighbors I could have. Archie, I'm glad you brought your boss along."

David Rockefeller smiled, "Archie and me are off on business to Africa. We're interviewing ruling family reps for World Bank, IMF, and Export-Import Bank subservience ...from a host of countries that want credit ...have to weigh-in their collateral ...see what the House of Windsor and Bank of England will let me have ...where to send the Marines in. Half the time, Dulles' CIA and Queen Elizabeth's MI-6 are on the same side ...half, they're not and make a fiasco for everyone. Prescott, nice to see your son George, here. Hi George."

Barbara Bush noticed although Prescott didn't seem to, her husband George seemed aloof in Prescott's presence. Soon dinner was in full swing.

Prescott had nostalgia in his eyes, "These meals in our Florida estate are like the old days. George and the other kids were little then, 60 years ago, George was six. That's when I explained ruling family values to him. 'George, you're six, its time for our annual man-to-man. Serving family wealth is first.'" Six-year-old George looked blank, his face turned red. His mother had something to add, 'Ruling families of this world are one big family. It doesn't matter what country we're from, wealth makes us one big family, the 'World Order'. Our countries may fight ...but, not us, we stay allies ...because our country is personal wealth, all personal wealth of all ruling families ... the One World Order. 'Family values' means do not mix socially with the upper class, the managerial class, or working class ...only with the money-issuing class, or with the ruling class.' Little George spoke for himself, 'Yes mother. Yes father. Family fortune comes first ...or, we'll end up wage slaves like the upper class, middle class, and lower class. We're the money-issuing class, the New One World Order.'"

Yes, Prescott had a head full of memories about his son George ...when George learned money-issuing class and ruling family manners, etiquette, correct silver usage ...George complaining, he was tired going to debutante balls and prep schools ...George embarrassed about Prescott's Nazi partners that first year of college, when George pledged Skull & Crossbones German Society of the Order of Death in his Yale freshman year, where the inner circle was money-issuing class and ruling family college students who would be friends for life, the ones to follow in their fathers' footsteps ...carve up natural resources of the world in local and international turf wars ...decide which countries would war or, be at peace. His first year at Yale, George found out about his father's and grandfather's bust by the U.S. under the Trading with the Enemy Act ...the family banks and shipping lines were seized. When George confronted his father's pro-Nazi stance, at the time Prescott was a Yale board member in charge of racial quotas at the university ...and, George spoke publicly in opposition to Prescott's racial quota policies ...and, argued for Prescott to let more Jews and Blacks into Yale.

"Dad," George asked, "did you finance Hitler during wartime. The U.S. government shut down our bank and shipping lines. Did you and Grandfather Walker attack Nicaragua in your own private war in the 1920s, trying to take Nicaragua over for yourselves?"

"Those are tough questions, son."

"Dad, I'm going to enlist to change people's minds about us, and redeem our family's honor. If I fight against Hitler, people will forget you were in business with him."

Yes, Prescott remembered it well ... George went off to fight Nazis, later was described as a war hero. Prescott could feel proud of George ...and, still count his Nazi profits through the war years into the early 1950s ...and, make sure after the war when George finished college, to get George a good job with a reputable CIA-connected company ... to learn the ropes on his own ...learn how to make his own private armies ...to grow and defend their family portfolio ...and, keep it safe ...and defend and keep safe family wealth of all the money issuing class, and the ruling class families ... the World Order ...who fought unending war to keep their money from filtering down to upper, middle, or lower classes.

<>

"George, are you daydreaming?" Barbara said as she finished arranging the flowers she brought to George's CIA office for his birthday present.

"Yes. I was remembering what Dad taught me about family honor, keeping our wealth safe and some things he did I didn't agree with, like his Nazi fiasco."

Barbara finished arranging the flowers, "George, if you need to cover-up this or that to protect family honor and family fortune, don't come home until you do. Your father did the best he could, so should you. Being DCI is paying your dues, we have to earn twelve-to-fifteen percent each year ...or, inflation will ruin us, that's the facts of life."

"It's not that simple, Barbie, as fighting wars to grow capital and quarterly returns. John the Apostle told us before Messianic Millennial peace comes, which is the peace the Reich also promises, the human race will have a ruthless, new world order government to enslave mankind ...and, no man or country can buy or sell without bearing the mark of the new world order and world trade organization, it's fulfillment of Bible prophecy." George took a bible off a bookshelf, opened the book, read the inscription, "'God bless you ... from Ronald Reagan'". He flipped through the book. "Here it is, Revelations 13:15. God said it would compel all men, 'Both small and great, rich and poor, free and bond' to be identified with it, and 'no other man might buy or sell'. The beast ...Apocalypse ...God destroys Lucifer and his Satanic legions on Earth in nuclear battle. It's what Governor Reagan's talking about."

Barbara comforted George, "It'll be okay, George. One day, you'll run for president. I know, you'll fix the new World Order so nothing happens to our investments." She watched George shrug bravely with that look of feigned machismo on his face she got a kick out of, kissed him on the cheek, then left the room.

Bill Casey walked into the room.

George was startled, "Forget how to knock, Bill?"

Bill Casey wore a gruff look on his face that went away when he smiled as he knocked his knuckles on George's wooden desk, "Knock knock, who's there?" He'd brought with him a British MI-6 merchant banker and an Arab sheik from the new World Order petroleum community. Bill introduced them, "Our British friend here sits on The Bank of England, he's high up in MI-6. The Sheik is putting up the capital to start us a new bank, BCCI, Bank of Credit & Commerce International. When 'ex-CIA' assets Wilson and Terpil got busted selling U.S. arms to Kaddaffi, training his mercenaries, trading arms-for-drugs, it got traced to the Agency's Nyugen-Hand Bank in Australia, so BCCI is now where the New

One World Order intelligence agencies will launder payoffs, foreign aid kickbacks into campaign funds, bribes, drug money, illegal arms sales ...and, this time ... an all-around tighter operation handling black budget covert operations against communists and terrorists. Today, we're here to sign paperwork and found ICIC, International Credit & Investment Company, with its own ruling family investment portfolio to target which natural resources go to whom. ICIC will direct covert operations and wars to re-divide ownership of natural resources by wiping out ruling families whose wealth we want to takeover, clear out subject populations with genocide, decolonize then recolonize countries with bombs, install puppet governments, legislate new infrastructures, then award redevelopment contracts to our own developers and make 'em buy American. ICIC has BCCI launder and disperse money to our mercenary armies. ICIC's a holding company, its board directors are heads of different western intelligence agencies who sit on Central Bank boards. ICIC manages BCCI ...and, CIA and MI-6 are represented on the board ...but, we put up no money, the sheik here handles that. Quite a financial coup, don't you think?"

"Dulles and Sir Gordon Richardson would be proud of you," Bush said, "You're my intelligence mentor, he was yours. Okay, I read the briefs yesterday. Handy. Good 'vision' kind-of-thing, great paperwork, can't wait to see how this ICIC-BCCI thing works, where do I sign for CIA's financial part in founding ICIC and BCCI?"

Bill Casey handed George the paperwork, nodded his head towards the MI-6 banker.

The MI-6 agent took the cue, "MI-6's my personal collection agency for the Crown."

George wore a blank look on his face, "Thanks, I just came onboard as DCI. Congress outlawed more CIA involvement in Angola. I don't want to start my tenure here by losing the war there ...there's oil and minerals we need in our investment portfolio. Rumors say, we're using biological warfare in Angola, not like we did in Cuba to make sheep blind and crops fail. Prince Philip's house of Windsor says, it's too crowded in Angola, starve them off, let them go back to cannibalism ...then get down developing African oil and gold reserves."

Bill wondered, "George, let's end this and make Wednesday's lunch special at the Seasons. We've traditionally use Margaret Thatcher's MI-6 to run mercenaries and covert operations for us before, that's how I met our friends Leslie Aspin and Bill Buckley, running covert-ops for us when MI-6 introduced them to me for under-the-carpet cleaning. Congress told me, as long as CIA is not over there in Angola fighting, and not officially pulling the triggers, we're breaking no U.S. laws."

The MI-6 operative watched as he spoke for any reaction George might have, "You see, we've been fighting in Angola for you before and we know how to do it, again. But, what you have to do in return, is beef up your American wiretap operations in Britain for us. As you know, British law prohibits us wiretapping ourselves, but it says nothing about covert foreign nationals setting up shop, doing our wiretapping, and leaking it to us."

DCI Bush understood but looked to Casey for confirmation. When Casey nodded, George felt relieved then nodded at the Brit, even though the Brit irritated him, somehow. George couldn't put his finger on it, "We got the same kettle of fish, you to beef up your wiretapping program of U.S. civilians here for us ... my people will tell you what we want. Let me sign off on this thing, I'm hungry." After George signed off, the Brit signed off, the sheik started to, but George pulled the paperwork back, "What else is he in for, Bill?"

"Along with financing the deal," Casey mumbled, "he wants his hand on the Angolan oil tap for OAPEC ...OPEC then controls all African oil."

"Okay," Bush said, "as long as we win in Angola ...and, the Sheik doesn't get Cuban oil, that's mine, when Castro's gone my family can get our offshore oil out of Cuba and out of Central and South America. I swear, Bush's and Castro are like Hatfields and McCoys feuding, when communists are gone, I can drill. Get ahold of our BCCI people, tell MI-6 Congress tied my hands on Angola ...but, we approve backdoor MI-6 mercenaries and I'll owe 'em one, we'll do the wiretapping for them they do it for us ...and, we'll kick the Soviets out of Angola and Cuba."

The Brit nodded in agreement.

Bohemian Grove,
Northern California, 1979

At Bohemian Grove, Steve Bechtel greeted me, and Shultz, Deaver, Meese and Bill Casey, my presidential campaign manager, then after the pleasantries, Steve turned to Casey, "What's the matter, Bill?"

"I've got to figure out how to make Ronald Reagan understand the difference between Fed new one world order money-issuing economics, taxes, and foreign policy ... and United States subject population economics, taxes, and foreign policy. Or, just leave him out in the cold and handle him, which you wanted me to do in the first place. I got to give him savior faire."

"Look Bill," I was upset, "you're a know-it-all. I've been a political spokesperson for you guys, twenty years. We're both millionaires. I started from poverty. I earned mine, without a drop of blood. I wasn't born with a silver spoon in my mouth, like you were. I didn't kill people for my money, or stage coups and revolutions for it, like you did. My father was a shoe salesman. We didn't live on the wrong side of the tracks, but close enough to hear the train whistles. I've been a construction worker, a lifeguard, radio announcer and actor. I've hated communists all my life. When Hollywood put me out to pasture in the early fifties, General Electric hired me to go around the country promoting your Christian West Crusade For Freedom, then, I was Governor of California for eight years. I love this country as much as you do ... I'm not as stupid as you think I am or stupid as you'd like me to be. I don't need your help to smarten up, not as much as you need mine as a cover for what you're up to. You misjudge me ...I feel let down, sad when you cop an attitude like this."

Bechtel shot Casey a glancing smile.

Martin Andersen watched to see what Paul Nitze's reaction would be.

Paul Nitze shrugged. He looked at George Shultz for sympathy.

I felt let down by all of them, but I stood up for myself, "All of you know, when Carter was elected President in 1976 we start gearing up to run me for President in 1980. I want the Presidency. Just what is it you think I need to know about politics, that I don't know already."

"Giving away the Panama Canal is like giving away Grand Canyon," Martin Andersen of Hoover Institute, said, "or Statue of Liberty."

"I agree with you," Paul Nitze, former vice president of Dillion Read, who'd written NSC-68 in the late forties as a one-worlder anti-communist roadmap that authorized CIA domestic propaganda operations, said, "The bad news is, the dictator of Panama, General Omar Torrijos, the bastard convinced John Wayne and William Buckley Jr. to endorse a treaty the Senate ratified."

I was shocked, John Wayne was a Hollywood hero, and, a national hero ...my competition. I sat back in my chair, "John Wayne wants to give the canal away? He was a bigger star than I was. The canal is a non-issue, now."

Bechtel nodded silently to George Shultz. George Shultz lit his pipe.

"My friend," Martin Andersen continued, "75-year-old Howard Jarvis, got California voters to approve Proposition 13. That limits Municipal and State property taxes. The point, here, is campaign hard on the theme voters must take control of government or else, it's going to take control of you. The next national election should be a voter's revolution against Government."

I hesitated but didn't want to be condescending, or did I? I didn't want to come off that way ...too much, so I gathered my wits, "We all hate liberals. We hate the welfare state. And, the public's fed up being taxed. We'll campaign on slashing taxes, on blocking social welfare programs. That's nothing new. I did it in California for eight years. Was I supposed to learn that today, too? I've been nixing high taxes since 1950."

Mike Deaver let me swim without water wings, but felt he had to focus the picture, "Ronnie, we've been complaining about high taxes. Now, we want to emphasize reducing taxes. We need to make Jarvis look like a demi-God. We want people to bow down when they hear his name ...like he's Jesus.

"How's this?" I said, "... Jarvis triggered hope in the breasts of hard-working people to stop big government taxing people to death ...like dumping those cases of tea off the boat into Boston Harbor. We need a national movement to make giant cuts in Federal Income

Tax rates. When we look at America, we see Carter trying to pardon Vietnam draft dodgers, to cancel the West's water projects. Where does Carter stand on abortion? Nobody knows ...on Affirmative Action? ...he's morally confused ...on national energy policy? Carter told the American people, turn down your thermostats, wear sweaters. But I'm telling you, the energy crisis in America is not from a shortage of oil, it's from a surplus of Government." I looked at Mike for his reaction.

Mike smiled, "That's good, Ronnie. Hit him below the belt."

Bill Casey felt a renewed interest, "The revolution in Iran. Carter couldn't do squat about that. That made oil and gasoline prices high at home."

Henry Kissinger hadn't spoken and was observing everyone carefully, "Carter waffles between Secretary of State Cyrus Vance and National Security Adviser Zbigniew Brzezinski, like a volley ball knocked back and forth. Vance wants arms control ...GATT management of the world economy. Brzezinski plays hard ball. Brzezinski wants power politics. Brzezinski doesn't trust the Soviets. Vance put together SALT II as a arms control treaty with Moscow. It limits the U.S. and U.S.S.R. to 2,400 nuclear delivery systems, each. But, Soviet involvement in Africa proves the Kremlin is still expansionist."

"I suppose that means something to you," Deaver said, "but I deal with Ronnie's TV image ...shaping public opinion. Carter's approval rating's are low as Nixon's was. The country's sleeping. Let sleeping dogs lie."

Casey smiled, "My friend, Paul Volcker, told me he's going to be appointed Chairman of the Federal Reserve Board. He'll kick rising prices in the ass ...give slow production a shot in the arm ...stop inflation by going after rising unemployment, will drive up interest rates, over 15%. So, get ready for the next recession."

I thought for a moment, visualizing it, "That's good speech material, Bill."

Kissinger nodded, "What's Carter done? Handling foreign policy for him is a hot potato. He made Camp David Accords to make peace between Israel and Egypt."

"We need allies over there, to protect King ibn Saud," Steve

Bechtel said, "to protect the stability of his regime, to protect our, I mean 'American' interests, there."

Casey mumbled, "Carter came into office. He thought he could kick the Cold War in the ass. Now, the Soviet Union is in the Middle East, Africa, and South America and kicking us in the ass." Casey took a pocket tape recorder from his pocket and played a recording of Carter speaking, "We are now free of that inordinate fear of Communism, which once led us to embrace any dictator in that fear." Casey lit his pipe, "The bastard's reducing CIA by 500 field operatives. His God-damn brother's an agent for Libya. Muammar Qaddafi paid Mr. Billy Beer $200,000."

Bechtel saw the direction the conversation was taking, he needed to position the conversation fruitfully, "Qaddafi is militantly anti-Israel. King ibn Saud is militantly anti-Israel. My company works with Qaddafi and Kin ibn Saud. We have oil pipeline construction contracts in Libya and Saudi Arabia. I understand, in December, Soviet forces are going to invade Afghanistan. They're invading on the pretense of bolstering up the Communist regime, there. To keep it from an internal collapse."

Bill Casey clamped his teeth down on his pipe, and mumbled, "The Soviets want control of the Afghan opium trade. It's no big, fucking secret."

I didn't know what he meant by that. So, I ignored it.

Kissinger spoke up, "National Security Adviser Zbigniew Brzezinski will make Carter understand, this is the gravest threat to peace since World War II. Secretary of State Cyrus Vance will get more arms sales out of it, so, he'll go along."

Deaver had a flash of intuition, "That's going to look to the public like Soviets are driving to take over oil in the Persian Gulf.

Bill Casey nodded, "They are."

Bechtel didn't sound happy about that, "Carter will embargo grain sales to Russia, boycott the Moscow Olympics, revive draft registration, speed up production of new weapons like cruise missiles, withdraw SALT II from Senate consideration."

Kissinger was awestruck, "How do you know this?"

Bechtel felt flattered, "Here, at Bohemian Grove, we decide who will be President twenty years ahead of time, what wars will be fought and spin the spin doctors, dictate world events. It can be nasty. Bohemian Grove makes decisions for America. Or, Sir Gordon Richardson who runs the Bank of England, will make those decisions for us."

"Now, wait a minute," I said, trying not to be so frustrated, "can't we put this in Hollywood terms? I've got to understand, first. Then, I can explain it to the American people. Then, they'll vote for me ...Big Government should not regulate the private economy, risking prosperity and fundamental freedoms. Federal bureaucracy is a permanent monster so big, and powerful, its policy hurts ordinary citizens and people they elect. There's too much waste and fraud in Government, gross mismanagement by Federal regulators, no Government oversight, hostility towards ruling families that control private enterprise and money-issuing families that control the ruling family elite, smothering American business creativity, that destroys the American family and the American way of life. I'm against that! I'll make speeches about that! But, this foreign policy stuff, you've got to make up your minds, already ...tell me what I'm talking about! I wish I knew!"

Conversation in the large Bechtel lodge tent in the redwood forest came to a stop. Deaver was embarrassed. Bechtel looked at Casey. Bechtel dealt with the trans-Atlantic Axis central banking consortium, that Allen Dulles represented, for years. Bechtel knew, if world affairs Dulles or Casey managed misfired as our foreign policy, then exactly what Dulles and his protégé Bill Casey would do is point an accusing finger at the person standing next to them, and make that person or regime disappear.

Bill glared at Mike angrily, "I guess you didn't explain things to Ronnie the way I told you."

George Shultz felt offended, "Bill, you can't hold Mike responsible for events and speaking points you mismanaged."

Kissinger felt slighted and implored Bechtel with his eyes, "Gentlemen, I too was in the picture when the CIA coup in Iran installed Shah Reza Pahlevi, twenty-five years ago. Since, he's been an excellent American client, and customer for you. The Shah is a whore for the Seven Sisters. He's spent his petro-dollars buying billions of dollars worth of American weapons. That's a win-win, for everyone. As I'm sure you know, we supplied nuclear power generating capacity to Iraq and Iran in the early '50s. And he promises not to create an Iran Oil Bourse, a new oil exchange that won't be dominated by the four existing exchanges that we own. Times change. Oil interests shift. Oil monopolies evolve. There's too much world oil, already, it confuses polity. Untapped reserves in southern Ethiopia, alone, could run the world far into the next century. So, Central Intelligence had to get rid of the Shah. He's a sick man, anyway. Who should they replace him with. And, how? The Shah's always been a dictator, treated his subject population like shit. He's corrupt. When this information hits prime time then it's time for another coup, our next cover, a distraction limiting damage control as far as CIA and MI-6 grooming and financing is concerned, is the Ayatollah Khomeini. During exile in Iraq and France, Khomeini encouraged revolution in Iran. Feb. 1979, Ayatollah Khomeini drives the Shah from Iran ...Carter allows the fatally ill Shah to enter the U.S., for medical treatment. Khomeini denounces the United States as the Great Satan, and Great Whore of Babylon. Khomeini demands Carter turn over the overthrown shah ...and his foreign wealth to the new Islamic regime. Then, the press reports a mob sacked the U.S. embassy in Teheran, scizing its staff. But, you and I know that Ayatollah Khomeini's intelligence operatives captured the American embassy in Teheran and fifty embassy staff ... who were CIA counter-revolutionary operatives, agents provocateur."

< >

"Spare me details," I said, getting frustrated again, "what am I supposed to say?"

Shultz watched Bechtel nod to Casey. Andersen watched Casey nod to Deaver, who looked to me, "Ronnie, I see your TV new image like this. You say, America is held hostage. That makes Carter look impotent. Christ, Ronnie, our friend the Shah would still be in power if Carter didn't criticize him for torturing political prisoners."

Bill Casey felt vindicated that the meeting was back on track. George Shultz watched in amazement, as Deaver planted seeds of thought. I felt like I was going to have an idea at any moment ... I looked up ...into the distance and felt it coming, "It's Carter's fault there was a revolution in Iran in the first place."

George Shultz seized the moment, "You're right. Senator Ed Kennedy's complaining in Congress, all Carter does is lurch from crisis to crisis."

My thoughts sharpened, "Even Carter's own democrats are against him. Ed Kennedy said, Carter can't put one foot in front of the other. Look how Carter fumbled rescuing the hostages by crashing his helicopters in a desert dust storm ...it embarrasses the country, it makes me wonder if the Three Stooges are directing foreign policy."

Everyone laughed. That made me feel good. Bechtel nodded at George Shultz, who began talking, "Ronnie when you're President, give us some de-regulation of the nuclear power industry, will you? ... get big Government off our backs? ...and off the backs of the people."

I listened carefully, taking it all in.

"I'm close with Prescott Bush's trans-Atlantic banking group," Bill said, "I think his son, George, knows his way around the petroleum-intelligence community. He's a good running mate."

"I want Gerald Ford for my running mate ..can an ex-President be Vice President? ...I don't know foreign affairs, he could run it. George Bush gives me the creeps. He says I'm full of 'voodoo economics'. Bush is too liberal ...soft on abortion, women's rights, gun control."

Martin Andersen shifted gears, "Carter doesn't have a chance at re-election. Carter's dogged by hostages he can't free ...an economy he can't improve ...a brother on Libya's payroll he can't disown. Ronnie's an opponent Carter can't shake off ... once we get in office I'd like to run Office Of Management & Budget and for Commerce Department see Peter Grace and George Bush working together in a task force. With a task force like that, we'll cut hundreds of rules bad for 3rd Quarter profits, eliminate rules for disposal of hazardous waste, air pollution, nuclear safety, exposure to chemicals, get rid of financial waste policy protecting worker health and safety. It's too expensive to protect the environment, when big Government bureaucracy has to pay people wages to police big business, and tell us what we already know. This isn't Nazi Germany."

I was sleepy, "Well, what you've all said sounds good to me, but I'm too sleepy to make sense of it. Besides, I knew all it all, already. I'm going to sleep." I nodded off.

Later, back at our Santa Barbara ranch with Nancy, I told her what had happened, "Nancy, this is our chance to be in the spotlight and steal the show. Top billing everywhere, my damn campaign backers think I need words put in my mouth, that I'm stupid and can't think for myself!" I felt deflated and low-spirited.

Nancy was besides herself in anger, "Ronnie, treat them like script writers, directors, or producers. They don't know any better."

"It's the principle, they think I'm a pretty face to get votes they can hide behind."

"You are handsome. It will get votes. It's their fault. If they think you're dumb, if they think they can use you ...we'll outsmart them, at every step. Let's play along. Get elected, then do things our way. We'll show them what real acting is. With me by your side, we can do it!" We kissed.

"Nancy, you've always believed in me. I love you. I'm back."

"I believe in us, what we share. No one gets between us ...not Bechtel ...not Casey ...not our kids. This is our last chance to be bigger stars than ever. I won't let it slip away. Let them think, whatever! Who cares? It's on them. You accept political coaching, or lose Casey, Deaver and Meese on your campaign. You think you invented the circus?"

"Mommy, you're on the money. I don't like them doubting me. It's like losing the audience ...when it stops paying attention or caring ...then you're playing to an empty house, will no confidence. I need their approval. I want the damn Oscar. But, I want to help America, more. I need everyone to like me. That's the way I'm put together ...everything you said was right on."

"Beat them at their game like me."

"You're the best. I'll play along to get along."

Nancy gazed adoringly at me with big, brown eyes like a deer. That night, sex was good.

Israel combat exercises, 1979

George Bush went to Israel for a Mossad anti-terrorism conference, called, 'preventive counter-kidnapping'. The spin they put on it was renaming it, 'pre-emptive retaliation'. You go in there. You kidnap the kidnappers and their families ...before they kidnap you. It made sense to George, sort of an upside-down pyramiding kind of thing, would be how he'd later describe it.

< >

In 1980, I finally succeeded in getting the Republican nomination for president. At the convention, I wanted President Gerald Ford as my running mate, but, ultimately was told by Casey and Bechtel to go with George H. W. Bush, who I considered a creep. Bush had been my opponent, during the presidential primaries and thought so little of me, he said he'd never be my Vice President. Bush was many things I wasn't ...a lifelong Republican ...a combat veteran ...a one-world NWO internationalist with U.N., CIA and China experience, and a CIA director. Bush's economic and political philosophies were way more liberal and moderate than I cared for. Bush called my supply-side proposal for a 30% across-the-board tax cut, 'voodoo economics'. How would you like to have a guy like that at your back?

August 1980

"I want to accept the Republican Presidential nomination," I said, "and thank you all. America is an island of freedom. I want to ask all convention delegates here, join me in thanking Divine Providence for making this nation a haven for refugees fleeing oppression and disaster."

Mike smiled, knowing his WACL friends and clients would appreciate that touch, and knew where my speech was going as he settled back in his chair, shifting around till he felt comfortable.

"A lot of you know I come from humble beginnings," I continued, "I've been a lifeguard, a radio announcer, a soldier, an actor, an actors' union president, a Democrat ...who became a Republican, and a Republican Governor of California. My grandparents were farmers during the potato famine in Ireland. My parents suffered during the Great Depression. My father lost his job on Christmas Eve."

Mike waved excitedly, pointing to my toe-marks. I moved a little to my right, till my toes lined up on the marks for my best camera angles then looked into the TV cameras, wiping a tear from my eye, "I cannot and will not stand by, while inflation and joblessness destroy the dignity of the American people. Recently I made a speech to the Veterans of Foreign Wars. I told them this. I blame past administrations for not fighting to victory in Vietnam. Ours, in truth, was a noble cause. President Carter is wrong to establish diplomatic ties with China. When I am elected, I will restore recognition of Taiwan as the real government of China. I'll tell you about an American pilot in World War II, who sacrificed his life for his country. He posthumously won a Congressional Medal of Honor. The pilot's plane was strafed. It was going down. The pilot cradled a wounded comrade, rather than bail out from his crippled plane. 'Never mind, son,' the pilot of the doomed plane told his injured belly gunner, 'We'll ride this one down together.' That's the America I believe in. America doesn't want to be second rate. We need to have a bigger, stronger military and get rid of liberal spending programs. They've made big government more wasteful than the New Deal. I'll roll back social welfare programs, limit Federal courts for hearing civil rights and civil liberties cases, eliminate government regulation of business, banking, and the environment, remove the dead hand of Government regulation from private enterprise to unleash market forces, and create new wealth for us. I'll reduce Federal taxes, promote a Conservative social ethic against abortion, against drug use, and promote religion in daily life, and in schools. It's time to realize, we're too great a nation to limit ourselves to small dreams. Past policies of big Government, past tax-and-spend mortgaged our future, and our children's future. America must stop living beyond our means ...or, face disaster. I pledge when I am elected President, I'll cut taxes, end deficit spending. To paraphrase Winston Churchill ...I did not accept this nomination with the intention of presiding over the dissolution of the world's strongest economy. America will be back, it will be morning again."

Mike Deaver listened as nomination convention center exploded in applause, cheering and whistling. I'd brought many in the audience to tears. Mike felt things were going his way, under his control, and smiled proudly.

Ed Meese looked at Deaver, "I almost felt a little sad, myself. They love him. You did it again, Mike. I don't know how you do it. But, you do."

"I keep apple pie and the flag going the whole time," Mike said quietly.

Reporters swarmed around me. Alan, the CNN reporter, elbowed his way to the front of the pack, "Mr. Reagan, Mr. Reagan! When the two pilots went down in the doomed plane, and crashed, how could anyone know what the two dead men said to each other moments before the crash?"

I got a puzzled look on my face. That CNN kid was obnoxious. I'd tell Ted Turner to swap him out.

Apr. 24, 1980

Carter's handlers tried to rescue American hostages. Eight helicopters took off from an aircraft carrier in the Persian Gulf, flying into a desert sandstorm where one chopper had engine trouble then returned to ship. Seven helicopters got lost in a sandstorm, two had to land because flight crews forgot to put sand filters on carburetors. The commander of the covert action team said five helicopters weren't enough, aborting the mission. Then, a helicopter collided with a re-fueling plane killing eight servicemen, five more men were injured and seven aircraft were destroyed in the crash. Sad as road kill, Carter gloomily announced details of the failed mission on TV. To many Americans, the mission was a cartoon branding America as a has-been and branding Carter as a joke.

As Mike Deaver put the scrambled puzzle pieces together, an image emerged of how he wanted me to paint Carter, his handlers and their foreign policy apparat in my Presidential speeches campaigning against Carter, as a joke ... to get useful emotional responses from voters. My campaign, managed by Bill Casey, wallowed in the shallows and shadows of the Iran hostage crisis. Many people felt Carter's presidential failure to bring the hostages home foretold his political future ... he was doomed. Carter couldn't handle double-digit inflation, unemployment, shabby economic growth and instable petroleum markets making long gas lines ...his perceived weakness was national defense ...it influenced the electorate college against him.

Oct. 1980, meeting of Ronnie & handlers

Mike Deaver and my other handlers were afraid. If President Carter got the American hostages released before the election, Carter might win.

Deaver went to Casey, "If I was Carter I'd pull off a surprise in October get the hostages free just before the elections in November. The public would go wild and joy would roll over America like a tidal wave of people standing up then sitting down sweeping around a sports arena. Carter would be a hero. Everyone would forget he makes America second-rate and he'd win the election, for sure. Get us out of this one, Casey."

Casey mumbled almost to himself, "I'm directing Ronnie's campaign. I hear you. I hear things, if the hostages aren't released until after the election, as soon as we get into office we sell arms to Iran, again. Their military is all U.S. weapons ...that need replacement parts. Selling 'em arms takes pressure off Teheran. Israel and Iran will get more arms under Reagan than Carter ... Ronnie, it's time for your campaign to start attacking Carter for bungling this hostage mess."

I looked to Mike for confirmation, "That's right, Ronnie. I already have a speech for you ...get righteous ... say, 'Why have fifty-two Americans been held hostage for almost a year! I promise, if I'm elected, I'll make CIA stronger, make all intelligence agencies stronger ...so we can punish terrorists and communist regimes, everywhere. Like it?"

"No. I love it."

<>

President Carter's CIA Director, Admiral Stansfield Turner, read an intelligence briefing to learn Israel was secretly shipping critical U.S.-made military equipment to Iran ...Turner found out three of my aides, Lawrence H. Silberman, Richard V. Allen, and Robert C. McFarlane met at least once with Ayatollah Khomeini's representative in Washington. Meanwhile, Carter's aides made progress negotiating with Iran. Carter's aides expected to get the hostages released, any moment. That was their only chance to get Carter re-elected.

Suddenly, the Iranians broke off the talks.

Turner looked at Carter, "Silberman, Allen, and McFarlane say they made no bargains ...that was their only meeting with Ayatollah's people. Any allegation Reagan or his aides making a hostage deal is too callous for me to believe ...but if they didn't make any deals with Ayatollah, then why is Israel shipping U.S. arms to Iran and why did Iran break off hostage talks with us."

Carter smelled a rat, "I don't know if there was a secret deal."

"I've interviewed a dozen Iranian arms dealers and intelligence operatives who gave me enough details to confirm that Casey's handling a secret deal," Turner said. "Everyone was in Madrid when Casey was on vacation, someplace out of sight all October. Nobody knows where he is."

Meanwhile, in Washington, me and Bush played golf. Reporters dogged us on the fairway. Alan the CNN reporter called out a question to me, "Is Casey doing a secret deal in Madrid to free the hostages?"

George Bush grabbed it, "Absolute fiction."

"We've tried some things," I said, "...the other way, to get the hostages home."

"What do you mean?"

"No comment. This stuff's classified ... Fore!" I said and teed off the green. Soon after, televised debates boosted my campaign because I was graceful deflecting Carter's criticisms with comments such as, "There you go again". Perhaps my most influential remark was a closing question to the audience during a time of rocketing global oil prices and unpopular Federal Reserve interest rate hikes, "Are you better off today than you were four years ago?"

Nov. 4, 1980
Pacific Palisades voting booth

Nancy and I arrived at our neighborhood polling place in Pacific Palisades on Election Day and voted. When I came out, reporters swarmed around me. Smiling, I stood around looking for my toe marks and felt better when I saw the masking tape, walking in front of the video cameras to my toe marks. "I can't answer any questions till I get on my mark."

Alan was there, as usual, "Are you going to win?"

"I'm too superstitious to answer that."

Nancy nudged me, I turned my eyes towards her. Nancy spoke quietly, "Cautiously optimistic."

I winked at Nancy, then turned to the reporters, "I mean, yes ...I'm cautiously optimistic."

"Who did you vote for?"

"I voted for Nancy."

<>

On the other side of the country, President Carter finished making his televised concession speech then moved off-camera with his wife Rosalyn. The TV announcer spoke into the network camera, "Reagan won. The Democrats lost the Senate for the first time since 1954."

Carter's ouster carried a 12-seat change in the Senate from Democratic to Republican, giving Republicans a majority in the Senate the first time in 28 years. The camera cut back to President Carter as he spoke to reporters, "I'm not bitter. Rosalyn is, but I'm not."

First Lady Rosalyn Carter glanced at her husband, "I'm bitter enough for both of us."

The camera cut back to the announcer, "Among the losers, are liberals Frank Church, George McGovern and Birch Bayh, defeated by two-term congressman J. Danforth Quayle."

*Jan. 6, 1981, California
campaign headquarters*

Surrounded by reporters, I read from a 5"-by-8" note card, "I'd like to announce the appointment of James Brady as White House Press Secretary. C'mere, Jim."

A reporter was shocked by Brady's homely looks, "Have Brady's visuals been approved by Nancy?"

"I'm getting irate at the things I'm reading you reporters say about my wife. None of it's true!"

Los Angeles Airport, farewell ceremony

Freelancing, CNN's Alan flew back and forth between California and Washington D.C. on a regular basis. At LAX, Alan watched at a farewell ceremony as I was given a huge jar of jellybeans. I felt nostalgic and teary-eyed leaving Hollywood behind me, "I used to pass a jellybean jar at the conference table when I was Governor of California ..you can tell a lot about a fellow's character, if a fellow picks out one color or grabs a handful."

CNN waved me down, "What can you tell?" Alan said, sarcastically.

CHAPTER 3

Hinckley estate, Mar. 29, 1981

The Hinckley family gathered at their father's estate to party. Scott, John's brother, placed a phone call to Neil, George H. W. Bush's son. Scott confirmed a business meeting with Neil, for the next day. While Scott Hinckley talked to Neil Bush, at Neil's home his brother Jeb looked and felt like a kid who'd stolen cookies from the cookie jar and didn't get caught. This was one of Jeb's happiest moments of his life, he told his brother, "I got the Contras on Medicaid in Florida. Can you believe that shit? I'm fuckin' the taxpayers now, Mom and Dad would be proud of me making taxpayers pay for Contra casualties in our private war in Nicaragua." Jeb made an obscene 'up their butt' gesture.

While talking on the phone to Scott, Neil gave brother Jeb a thumbs-up.

On the other end of the phone line, Scott Hinckley adjusted his portable phone in his hand as he walked into brother John's room and was stunned ...Scott's mouth dropped open. John was wearing a torn Nazi uniform and lying spread-eagled on a Nazi Skull & Bones flag spread on the bed, his pants down, masturbating at Taxi Driver movie posters of Jodi Foster he'd pinned up on his wall. Hard as he tried, John's fantasy couldn't block memories of his American

Nazi Party meeting a few days ago, when out-of-control neo-Nazis screamed at his, 'You're an FBI spy!', then beat him and kicked him out.

White House press briefing room

In my White House Press Briefing Room, I prepared my speech so I had motivation for acting furious ... I remembered not getting an Oscar for my most dramatic performance, delivering the lines, "Where's the rest of me?" Now prepared, I introduced the press to my well-rehearsed 'get-tough-on-drugs' speech and my 'no-compromise-with-terrorists' policy, then continued, "Can we who man the ship of state deny it's out of control. Waste and fraud in federal government is national scandal. Our nation's debt is approaching a trillion dollars. Can we continue on the present course without coming to a day of reckoning? I want to cut the budget 41 billion dollars, cut back welfare, cut back government bureaucracy that regulates business, the environment, and public health, get rid of conditions that let Welfare Queens ride around in new Cadillacs. We must stop punishing people who make a lot of money by taxing them more, till it makes no sense to work anymore. What will happen to America if the rich will not work harder ...because we take 90% of their money ...and the poor will not work harder, because they get too much welfare?" I finished my speech and looked over to Larry Speakes.

Larry addressed the press, "The President will now determine the answering order of whose questions by drawing names out of his jellybean jar."

I drew out names of reporters. Then, reporters fired questions at me that I answered til I was answered-out, always telling the truth, "Just because no reporters from NBC, ABC and AP were chosen from my jellybean jar doesn't mean you boycott my next press conference! After all, I'm the first president who draws names of who gets to ask questions out of a jellybean jar." That shut them up for a while.

Larry led State Secretary Alexander Haig to the podium to address the press. Haig composed himself, "I'll have to caveat my response and use careful caution and not saddle myself definitizing my statement, 'cause this isn't an experience I haven't been through before. Perhaps the four American nuns shot to death in El Salvador were killed because they were trying to run a road block."

I took the microphone away from him, "Thank you, Secretary of State Haig. The news is, I'm putting George Bush in charge of my administration's Crisis Management Team."

Of course, Haig over-reacted, "That doesn't make me happy! I want that position!"

Vice President Bush laughed to himself.

At that point, Larry Speakes officially terminated the press conference. Walking back to my office, I took a few jelly beans out of my jar, and popped them in my mouth. Back in my office, I flipped the calendar page on my desk calendar to a new day, one day at a time.

Evergreen Colorado,
Hinckley Sr. Mansion

A young John W. Hinckley Jr., so the story goes, was depressed over John Lennon's murder. Alone, in his parents' house, John sat in a chair, quietly looked at a torn picture of John Lennon he kept in his wallet drunkenly singing Lennon's lyrics, 'Imagine all the people sitting in a world of peace. You can say that I'm a dreamer, but I'm not the dreaming kind.' John fit the 'Lucy in the Sky with Diamonds' LSD-type profile better, as he sang he drank peach brandy. Picking up a portable tape recorder, he recorded a special message for the woman of his dreams, Jodie Foster. "Dear Jodie. I don't know what's going to happen this year. It's just gonna be insanity. Jodie, you're the only thing that matters, now. Jodie. Jodie. Ever since I saw you starring in, Taxi Driver, with you playin' a 13-year-old hooker ...I fell in love with you. Anything that I might do in 1981 will be for Jodie Foster's sake. It's time for me to go to bed. I love you."

Mar. 6, 1981, Jodie Foster's college dorm, 1 A.M.

John Hinckley stood outside Jodie Foster's college dormitory at one in the morning, yelling ...then, pounding on the door of the college dormitory, "Telegram for Jodie Foster!"

The dormitory house-mother opened the door a crack, she looked through a chain lock, "Slide it through the door. Stop yelling. Go away."

Jodie Foster sat in her dormitory bedroom. She read the telegram the house-mother brought her aloud to her roommate, "'Jodie Foster Love, just wait. I'll rescue you very soon. Please cooperate. J.W.H.' ... ... I don't understand, Who's J.W.H.?"

"It's a practical joke," her roommate was still drowsy, "Go to sleep.

Later that night at 3 A.M., John Hinckley was back outside Jodie Foster's college dormitory, yelling and pounding on the door.

Jodie Foster got another telegram delivered by the house-mother. Jodie read it aloud, "'Jodie, Goodbye! I love you six trillion times. Don't you maybe like me just a little bit? It would make all this worthwhile. From John Hinckley, of course' ... ... Who's John Hinckley?!" Jodie was starting to feel threatened and scared. Her roommate start hugging her.

American Nazi Party & Ku Klux Klan meeting

John Hinckley looked sharp and felt wicked, almost demonic, in his black Nazi uniform, watching another Nazi burn a picture of the White House. The other Nazi pointed at him, "That one! John Hinckley! He's a Reagan liberal."

John sensed danger immediately, "I hate Reagan."

"Hinckley's father, Prescott Bush and Allen Dulles are friends. Their families do business together. Hinckley's brother's dating Bush's daughter. Hinckley's in bed with the establishment."

"Just because my father and Bush's father are friends doesn't make me a spy!" John tried defending himself, "Prescott financed Hitler, stupid! Dulles was Hitler's friend! You're dumb and dumber!"

"He's an FBI Cointelpro infiltrator!"

Suddenly, John felt the eyes of all the Nazis glaring at him like hounds catching a whiff of blood. It was already too late to talk his way out, the Nazis start beating him, punching him, kicking him. He tried to run away and stumbled. They kicked him some more. He struggled to his feet, grabbing a Nazi SS Skull & Bones flag to help pull himself up ...it ripped off in his hands as he ran off as fast as he could, yelling behind him, "You assholes, I'll show you I'm a Nazi! You'll see!"

Nov. 11, 1980 press conference

Me and Deaver were surrounded by reporters. I went first, "No personnel decisions have been made."

Deaver shrugged, then filled the reporters in, "James A. Baker III will be White House Chief of Staff. Edwin Meese III will be White House Counselor, with a Cabinet rank."

I'd been caught off guard and was surprised, no one had told me.

White House, Oval Office

As President-elect, I had met with President Carter in the White House Oval Office to get a job briefing from Carter. Carter briefed me about duties and responsibilities of being President as I looked out the window. Nancy waited for me in the hall. Carter watched me watching Nancy through the window in the door. Nancy was briefing reporters. I start preening in front of a mirror.

Carter rolled his eyes, "You're listening to my briefing, aren't you? Taking notes? Any questions?"

"Can I have a copy of your presentation?"

I could hear the reporters grilling Nancy, "What are you going to do when you move into the White House, Mrs. President-elect-Reagan?"

Nancy was no-nonsense when she answered, "Ronnie and I are going to set an example for America to return to a higher sense of morality ...it trickles down from the top."

My friend and Nancy's, and backer, stood nearby talking to a reporter, "Running the government's exactly like running General Motors. Cabinet secretaries will be like presidents of Chevrolet and Pontiac. Chevrolet competes with Pontiac. Competition is good. But, their competition stops, at what is good for General Motors. Know what I mean?"

I smiled and wondered at Alfred Bloomingdale's comments, who in hell did he think he was, Suzie cream cheese?

Patti's headline scrapbook

Patti had a collection of headlines she cut out from newspapers. She cut out today's headline from *New York Times*, 'El Salvador Troops Shoot U.S. Churchwomen To Death'.

Reagan home in Hollywood

Home in Hollywood, Nancy and I prepared for bed listening to Beatles music on the radio, 'Little Darling, it's been a cold dark lonely winter, little Darling it seems like years since you've been here. Here comes the sun, here comes sun, tomorrow may rain, but here comes the sun.' Radio talk show host Paul Harvey interrupted the song unexpectedly. Nancy was alarmed as she listed to Paul Harvey, "We interrupt this broadcast to bring you sad news. John Lennon has been shot in the back outside his New York apartment."

Nancy was in shock, "That's terrible."

"Shot in the back," I said, "by a coward."

Nancy questioned me with a strange look on her face as Harvey argued with a call-in listener, "We don't need gun control because John Lennon's been murdered. Death has claimed many rock musicians prematurely, none with guns. Keith Moon and Janis Joplin OD'd on drugs, along with Elvis Presley, Brian Jones and John Bonham. Plane crashes killed Jim Croce, Otis Redding, Buddy Holly, Ritchie

Valens, and Ronnie van Zant. In fact, Lennon at 40 lived much longer than most of those."

Mike Deaver was downstairs working over my living room bar, planning to crash on the couch for a few hours then fly to D.C. I came down the stairs. Unsurprisingly, he sounded tipsy, "I'm pouring myself a drink. Here's the press statement I wrote for you to look over."

"No, that's okay. I'm sure it's fine. It always is."

"Just one more, for the road."

I poured Mike another shot of vodka, he smiled as his Old Fashion glass filled up, "I'm here and Washington so much I think I'm a yo-yo." The next afternoon Mike was at Reagan Campaign Headquarters in D.C. presiding over a press conference, "We have major appointments to announce. Donald T. Regan will be Secretary of the Treasury ...David A. Stockman, Budget Director ...William French Smith, Attorney General ...William J. Casey, Director of CIA."

Still back in our home in Pacific Palisades, me and Nancy stayed late in bed, talking. Nancy was emphatic. "I don't see why the Carters can't move out of the White House early. Then, I can get in there and start a good cleaning. There's gossip your son is gay."

"Ron Jr?

"Because he's dances ballet. He got married yesterday to stop the gossip, he loves us that much."

"I don't recall any wedding invitation," I said. "I'm sold on having space-based lasers to protect the U.S. Do you remember my film? ...in the '40s, when I saved the orbiting death ray from falling into Nazi hands? Was Dick Cheney in that movie?"

<>

In Washington, Mike Deaver made more press releases, "Caspar W. Weinberger, Secretary of Defense ...Alexander Haig, Secretary Of State ...Raymond Donovan, Secretary Of Labor ...Jeanne Kirkpatrick, U.S. Ambassador to the United Nations ...James Watt, Secretary of the Interior."

Nancy was busy in Pacific Palisades, "Ronnie, I've thought about it. Whoever's gonna be your press secretary in front of the cameras should be reasonably good-looking, because he's representing you."

In Washington, Mike kept the press busy, "Ed Meese will be Special Counselor to the President, a newly created position. And I, Michael Deaver am named Deputy White House Chief-of-Staff. President-elect Reagan issued this statement, 'These appointments are the exact combination to create the new beginning the American people expect and deserve."

Alan, the AP reporter was on freelance assignment, paid by the piece and interviewed Ed Meese, "I understand, Mr. Meese, you like to relax by listening to the police band on your radio. And, collect pig figurines as a tribute to police. Is that a pig tie tack you're wearing?"

Ed puffed on his cigar, "It sure is."

"Do you think President-elect Reagan is a bit remote? He's not here, with his transition team. He's not here, for his transition to the Presidency."

"Let me assure you, Reagan is running things."

"But, he's not even in Washington. Is he in California?"

Out west, I dressed casually, felt in high spirits, was enjoying that winning feeling and flanked by Secret Service agents. We walked in a butcher shop where I picked some veal and beef from my California butcher, then went to Drucker's Barber Shop, my favorite barber shop in Beverly Hills. Reporters quizzed me while I got my hair cut.

Harry Drucker, my old barber, answered a reporter's question,

"I've been cutting his hair the same way for forty years," Harry Drucker, my old barber said. "It's a traditional haircut. It's a conservative haircut. It isn't a hippie-type haircut."

"No," I said, "I don't dye my hair."

"President-elect Reagan ...was it a good idea for Attorney General-designate William French Smith to go to Frank Sinatra's party? ...when Frank's close to hoodlums?" Me and Nancy were Sinatra fans. "I've heard those things about Frank for years. Me and Nancy just hope none of them are true." I liked being surrounded by reporters. That made me the center of attention. That's what acting's all about. A few days later, I was being interviewed by CBS, on TV at a football game at half-time in the announcer's booth. I felt nostalgic,

"I was a radio sportscaster. I'd just make things up, to make life more interesting."

< >

When Patti smiled, her beautiful eyes lit up, "What do you want for dessert, Alan?"

"A flambé of Phyllis Schlafly going up in flames," Alan turned to the waiter, "Do you have that?"

"No. Fortune koo-kie, ice-keam."

"I interviewed Phyllis Schlafly," Alan said, "after she organized the Eagle Forum. She said, 'the Bible ordains a woman be submissive to her husband, just as she'd submit to Christ her Lord.'"

Patti was surprised. She laughed a small laugh, "I bet it was hard to keep your mouth shut."

Alan plopped a small portable TV up on the table, turned it on, start turning the channel dial to change stations, "It sure was. ...I got to catch Jerry Falwell's act, I'm interviewing him Wednesday."

"What are you gonna say?"

Alan had it down, something like, "The '70s had twenty-five Christian TV ministries on TV, the '80s, three hundred. Conservative, religious righters selling family values to half the families in America who can't afford doctors, go hungry, and have no jobs. ...Herrrrrre's Satan." Jerry Falwell was on the tube. A minister in Virginia on TV, before his congregation, Falwell gave his benediction, "This country is fed up with radicals and the unisex movement, fed up with departure from basics, with indecent departure from the monogamous home, with permissiveness. The Book of Proverbs clearly outlines free enterprise. We religious evangelical fundamentalists are the Moral Majority. We must seek out Satan's victims and save them, baptize them, and register them to vote. You've seen other televangelists, Oral Roberts, Jim Bakker, Jimmy Swaggart, Pat Robertson, who evangelize on TV to 60-to-100 million people watching electronic ministries to get God, country music, sermons, and Ronald Reagan!"

Patti reached to turn off the TV. Out of nowhere, Jerry Falwell introduced Ronnie, "Oh my god, it's Daddy!"

"Surprise."

"I want to introduce a man who needs no introduction. Our last speaker declared, God does not hear the prayers of a Jew. Here is a man, God does hear."

I smiled at TV cameras like I loved 'em, "I had strict, religious upbringing when I was a child. My mother taught me what the Bible says is the Truth, I believe in literal interpretation of the Bible, in God's Truth. I went to religious college. I studied to be a minister. The unfaithful say, 'Reagan don't go to church, he don't count'. They say, 'Reagan was divorced, he don't count. I am born, again! The world's problems are answered in the Bible. I support teaching the Bible's story of creation in public school, I'm against feminism, against gay rights because I believe, in the Bible. This destructive permissiveness in our society is the Evil One destroying American family values. I am born again!'"

Jerry Falwell raised up his palms, "Hallelujah!"

Patti looked pained so turned off the TV set, "I'd rather watch TV commercials."

When Alan stepped onboard deck, the small yawl rocked in slow motion in the water. They went below, layed down and were gently rocked to sleep. Alan dreamed of house-sized wontons and margaritas in martini glasses, a bead a salt around the rim, tasting of lime.

Contra field office, Argentina, 1980

Contra leaders training at CIA School of the Americas in Georgia and in Texas on the property of one of the largest Texas landowners, who later became one of the largest landowners in Belize, later deployed at Belize, a major staging ground and cocaine trafficking hub for Contras. After CIA training, highest-ranking Contra leaders were stationed in a field office in Argentina. There, was a picture of me over a dart board on the wall alongside framed pictures of Mike Deaver, Henry Ford, Allen Dulles, Adolf Hitler, Benito Mussolini, Emperor Hiroshito and senior Nazi officers of the Wehrmacht ...Martin Bormann Odessa mastermind, and Reinhart Gehlen, head of Hitler's anti-Soviet intelligence forces, the Gehlen Organization.

Maps of El Salvador and Nicaragua were on the walls.

Contra soldiers threw darts or knives at them. Nazi Count Otto von Bolschwing and Mario Sandoval Alarcon bet on their throws ...then, went outside into a helicopter carrying Contra death squads. It raised into the air, soon landing in Nicaraguan jungles. There von Bolschwing and Alarcon evaluated Contra death squad ambush, capture, torture and butchering techniques. Their victims were peasant families. And, Catholic nuns ministering to the village. Von Bolschwing demonstrated to Contra Leader Mario Sandoval Alarcon how Contra terrorists should interrogate prisoners, torture them, rape women and children with rifles, castrate men, gouge-out nuns' eyes using crucifixes, skin them, dismember them, burn their bodies, scatter their ashes ...then, search the ashes for gold fillings ... your basic Nazi procedures, based on saving bullets and recapturing wealth. Sandoval ordered his Contras to pick up a few hundred kilos of cocaine at one of his underground cocaine factories nearby the village ...once inside the factory, Sandoval received a radio communication from Nazi Klaus Barbie, who had founded the Bolivian cocaine industry, and ran Odessa regional Bolivian headquarters. Nicknamed 'Butcher of Lyon', Klaus Barbie fled to Bolivia after World War II ...thirty years earlier, led a successful Odessa coup d'état under orders of Fuehrer Martin Bormann to take over Bolivia, grow the fledgling cocaine industry and establish Nazi control of the cocaine drug trade.

<>

Sandoval's Contras loaded cocaine into a jetliner. The jetliner had a giant Coors beer logo painted on the rudder ...as a thank you to the company that supplied money to buy the plane ...once in the air, Contras, naturally, drank Coors beer ...and looked out the plane's windows, towards the ground. Many hours later, they stared at 50' tall white letters spelling out the word, 'Hollywood'. They passed around pictures of hookers on Hollywood & Vine, made off-color gestures, and sucking sounds. The plane happened to fly over Patti Reagan's ramshackle hippie cottage in the Hollywood hills, back in a canyon, on a hillside facing the sea.

Patti's writing time, 1988

The sun refused to shine. Patti liked the drizzle, clean taste of the air, the heady feeling of clarity hinting how good life could be. She drew in deep breaths, sighed, yawned lazily. Salmon-pink underbellied clouds flattened slowly into dusk, ...then, darkness fell, and bright stars appeared. Patti stared down the street, into the shadows for her connection ...the buildings felt like gargoyles looking down, the people in the street felt like aliens ...she start singing a Ray Charles song, and waited. Then, she saw Alan coming towards her and smiled, "Hey."

Alan smiled back. "Yo," he whispered.

A sensual woman, when she smiled, it melted him.

Together, Patti and Alan were writing a fictional autobiographical novel about her dad, President Reagan. It was a winning team, since Patti liked writing and Alan was an investigative reporter for CNN, and knew his way around Washington. He'd gotten them an interview with the White House Historian, Bill Barnes. They found him in the White House library surrounded by books, "There's Bill," Alan said, resting the rising and falling palm of his hand on Patti's hips as they walked.

After cordial introductions, Patti flipped on her tape recorder, "What's your job like? ...know where any bodies are buried?"

They cabbed it to the White House, the guards knew them all and let them pass without I.D. checks. Patti saw President-elect George Bush, and Vice-President-elect Dan Quayle disappearing down a hall, and wanted to catch up and interview them.

Barnes shook his head, leading them over towards Larry Speakes, the White House presidential spokesman. Larry Speakes walked briskly over, "Welcome to the ministry of propaganda."

"Larry's leaving President Reagan's White House," Barnes said, "Not staying on."

Patti hardly had time to wonder why or get the first question out of her mouth, when Larry threw his hands up into the air, "I've had enough, I'm only human. Don Regan set me up with Merrill Lynch, where he worked before he came here ... y'know, we had a three-headed monster running the White House ...Baker, Deaver and Meese. They loved limos ...private parking behind White House gates ...the way people defer to you ... when you're a White House big shot. Libyan terrorists stalked us back in '81, when your dad got here ...they threatened to hurt us. Baker, Deaver and Meese ordered personal, Secret Service guard details ...Deaver's way to be somebody. Nothing can sink someone here faster than a nickname. I had turf-wars with that s.o.b. David Gergen, Director of Communications, I called him 'Tall Man'. White House staffers, then press, called him, 'Too-Tall', too big for his britches."

Patti was after the inside scoop, trying to find out who was pulling her Dad's strings.

Larry kinda sensed that.

"They started the Reagan Revolution," Patti said, "...cutting taxes, cutting spending, cutting social services when they start running the White House."

Larry laughed, "They didn't really run it. Reagan's first term, his inner circle was Chief of Staff James Baker III, Presidential Counselor Edwin Meese III and Deputy Chief of Staff Michael Deaver. Reagan delegated everything, gave everyone more power than they were worth, they were boys going at each other's throats."

<>

James Baker was walking by, overheard, and chimed in, "Larry, Meese is damn dogmatic, thinks he's Genghis Kahn, politically correct as a bull in a china shop."

Speakes agreed, "He's another prima donna from the planet of California."

When Meese appeared, quickly figuring out what was going on, Baker cringed. "Here comes poppin'-fresh doughboy."

Speakes smelled the stinking cigar in Meese's mouth, even when it wasn't there hanging out. Ed Meese III didn't talk, he bellowed, "I'm a God-damn conservative! ...I'm not negotiable! Baker's so damn pragmatic, he'll compromise me out of town if I let him."

"I know, Ed," Speakes said, "What do you expect from a Texas prima donna?"

Deaver was walking with Meese and argued with Baker, "You

shouldn't be slandering Ronald Reagan, he doesn't have a bone of prejudice in his body!"

I walked into them all and was immediately out of patience. I was the god-damn President, "Baker, I don't know what Blacks' problems are, I got no feel for a person living in a ghetto."

Baker pressed, "You can't appear insensitive to Blacks, women and Jews."

Yes, I could. "If Nixon could do it, I can do it."

Ed supported me, "It doesn't matter what Blacks think! They're not disadvantaged ...they're lucky to live in America! Show me evidence there are hungry children in this country! They have soup kitchens where food is free! I eat there!"

Baker felt discouraged, "You're wrong, Ed. I'm with Deaver on this ... minorities are a voting block, that's why Nixon brought in the damn Nazis from Eastern Europe to stomp out the Jew vote."

< >

Larry Speakes stopped reminiscing, "Patti, Baker's staff was capable. Meese's aides were ignorant. Baker had the White House along with Congress. Besides Deaver, Baker had Richard Darman who'd worked with him at Commerce. Darman and I fought. Baker and Darman created the Legislative Strategy Group, early in your dad's first term, limited to as many who could sit around Baker's conference table. They were elite White House decision makers, the engine running the White House car. Baker made policy decisions over lunch, in cocktail parties, in the men's room. He wasn't supposed to, but he did. Baker's conference table was the magic key He used it to take control of the White House from Meese."

Patti fumbled with her fanny pack, "Wait a second, have to change batteries." She got it together.

Larry thought Patti was cute, "Meese held his policy apparatus together with spit and chewing gum. I call Meese the prime minister of the United States. When they were in Sacramento, Meese had absolute authority advising your father. I saw what Meese was up to in Washington, weeks before the inauguration. I warned Baker. So, Meese and Baker decided between them, who would do what, which offices they'd have, which duties. Meese was more conservative than Baker, or Deaver. Baker didn't join Reagan until the 1980 campaign. I don't know who tossed his hat into the ring. Meese was old-line Reagan, tuned-in to California players, knew how to work Reagan, played to his conservative side. Meese screwed up, deciding not to wake your dad up, when Navy jets shot down Libyan fighter planes off Libya's coast. The press made your dad look lazy. Baker won arguments with Meese, because Deaver sided with him, Meese should have got him up. Deaver worked with Meese when Reagan was governor, knew Meese's shortcomings, watched Meese manipulate your father, with cheap dogma. Meese wasn't organized. I always said, when Meese put a document in his briefcase, it was gone forever. Now, I think he did it on purpose. It was a good move when U.S. Attorney General William Smith resigned in '84 ...Meese replaced him. After that, the President relied on Meese, sometimes. I remember Reagan asked Meese for advice when Iran-Contra broke, in Nov. 1986. Meese wasn't in the inner circle any more ...a member of the Cabinet may have rank, but, it's proximity that counts. Now, Deaver was also a personal aide to your father, and mother. Deaver controlled your dad's body ...scheduled everyplace he went ...was your mother's confidant ...spent hours on the phone listening to the First Lady, on the hour. Nancy, ranting and raving, rehearsed Deaver on everything over and over. Deaver became the conscience of the Reagan White House, suggesting things to both your parents, engineered Baker's spot as 'first, among equals'. Deaver got more credit for public relations than he should have ...he wasn't brilliant ...he knew what stories Reagan could play to, and look his best ...he had second sense, that way ...a genius at knowing. At the London economic summit in '84 ... Deaver smelled how dramatic it would for your dad to make a speech at Normandy, on D-day. At Point du Hoc field, Ronnie stood by old geezer Rangers who'd invaded France in '44, turned out to be one of your dad's best photo-ops and Deaver raised your dad's public opinion poll points that day. Deaver's idea to have the President visit dead Nazi's in Bitsburg, wasn't bright. We fought over it. Remember it, clear as day. Deaver walked up to me, 'I toured the cemetery, myself. It was covered with snow!' I told him, 'We'll be in trouble, if this is a German military graveyard ...we never went to a concentration camp ...the press will pick our bones.' Deaver protested, 'Leave it alone, the theme of this trip is reconciliation!'

"'Every time we go to Europe, reporters say, 'Will the President see a concentration camp?' This will be a feeding frenzy.

So Deaver says, "'The President doesn't want to visit a concentration camp for personal reasons. He doesn't like reminders about how horrible it was. I can't blame him. I've been sheltering him, I admit it.'"

<>

Speakes looked over Patti's body, "I was surprised Deaver got in trouble when he left the White House ...accused of lying to Congress ...accused of lying to a federal grand jury. People said, after he left the first time, he illegally lobbied Reagan aides in '85, when he had that public relations business in Washington. His office was full of pictures in solid silver frames, pictures of him with kings, queens, prime ministers and Contra cocaine runners. He talked them all into posing, he enjoyed trappings of power ...but at heart, was still a small-town kid from Bakersfield. I guess, he got carried away with his own importance, it's a fatal disease in this town, being full of yourself. He got convicted on three counts of perjury. All in all, Don Regan, George Shultz and Jim Baker were superb Cabinet appointees. Ed Meese, Caspar Weinberger, Jim Watt, stunk. Your dad liked to say, 'The Cabinet is a board of directors. I'm the CEO. But, I'm the only one who has a vote at the end.' But Ronnie knew better. Deaver was the one who argued for women's issues, and minority issues. He was sincere. But, he was from California ...tuned-in to how important women and minorities were, politically. Baker thought, Meese was Neanderthal. Meese thought Baker threw the baby away with the bath water. Baker played your father differently than Meese did. Baker taught your dad how to get half a loaf now and get the other half, later. Meese wanted to eat the whole loaf now. I liked watching Baker manipulate your father, around to his point of view. Baker wooed the press, spent half his time with reporters and editors, had real control how his policies appeared in the press ...there's your propaganda ministry. Meese only played to right-wing reporters and the California press. Considering, you had a three-headed monster running the White House ...Baker, Deaver and Meese worked out okay, until Spring of '85. Then, the troika dissolved. Deaver left to start a public relations firm. Meese moved over to Attorney General, to head the Justice Department. By second term, after being Chief of Staff, Jim Baker was hunting around. He came to me.

< >

Baker felt he was always right, disregarding Speakes, "Speakes, I told you we'd get everything done at the beginning of Reagan's first term. We got a camel through the eye of a needle. We accomplished everything. I always said, the second term would be sitting-out retirement. I don't feel like sitting, I don't want any Liberals scowling, breaking wind, pointing their fingers at me. I want the Attorney General position."

Speakes felt strange, "Deaver said, Meese locked that up."

"Shoot! ...then I want Secretary of State," Baker said. "That's the way it is."

Speakes knew better, "Shultz will keep it."

"Then, head of CIA!"

"Too far back in line."

Baker blew it off, "Bernie Kuhn's being forced out as baseball commissioner. I was offered that job, it looks good."

"Baseball commissioner?! You don't like baseball!"

"I like it good enough. I'm just not an avid fan."

< >

Patti continued her interview, "Baker liked baseball?"

"Yeah, sure," Speakes said. "So Baker swapped jobs with Treasury Secretary Don Regan, cause Regan took over as Chief Of Staff ...then, only one man ran the White House, Don Regan. There was no question who was running things. Before he got into politics, Don fought his way to the top of Merrill Lynch on his own, a self-made multi-millionaire, just like your dad was. Your dad always got a kick out of how their last names were close. You dad liked Don's locker room jokes. When Bud McFarlane ran the National Security Council, Bud made Don mad. Bud used to sneak things for your dad to approve, into the Daily Briefing book, a leather-bound collection of top-secret intelligence the National Security Council makes and gives the President every day. In the first Cabinet, when Don Regan was Secretary of the Treasury, he was one of two take-charge guys in the Cabinet, Secretary of State Alexander Haig was the other. Don's debonair and polished, self-assured. He got me my new job at Merrill Lynch. You happy now?"

Patti was happy, she listened carefully, trying to piece together the father she had never known. Patti nodded, a questioning expression came over her.

Night fell on Washington.

Jan. 1, 1981, White House, Nancy's office

Nancy was in her White House office, on the phone. She called me in my Oval Office, "Ronnie, National Security Adviser Richard Allen called. He got $1,000, and a pair of Seiko watches from Japanese journalists ...because he arranged an interview for them with you ...okay. I won't. The Oval Office furniture is worn threadbare. In my office we have mousetraps! Mousetraps! Why doesn't one of those investigative reporters write an article about that?!"

Jan. 27, 1981, airport

I welcomed the hostages home. Deaver had arranged a photo-op for me. I made a short statement to the press, "The policy of the Reagan Administration dealing with terrorists will be one of swift, effective retribution."

Deaver waved to the audience shills to clap. The Marine Band start playing, Hail To The Chief.

I put my hand over my heart.

Nancy reached up and took my hand, whispering to me, "Don't do that to, Hail To The Chief! Take your hand down!"

"Oh ...I thought it was the national anthem."

Feb. 6, 1981, briefing room,
press conference #1

I looked over the reporters in the room. This was my first official presidential press conference in the Press Briefing Room. I snapped into my rant automatically, "The goal of the Soviet Union is promoting world revolution ...a one-world, Socialist communist state! They reserve for themselves the right to commit any crime ...to lie ...to cheat, to get world revolution!"

Nancy interrupted the press conference carrying a 4-tiered birthday cake, singing, Happy Birthday To You. The White House Staff joined in. Some of the reporters, too. I smiled and was very happy. I bragged to everyone, "It's the 31st anniversary of my 39th birthday."

Feb. 18, 1981, my first
joint session of Congress

I addressed my first joint session meeting of Congress, "I'm warning Congress, the national debt is approaching 1 trillion dollars! A trillion dollars would be a stack of 1,000-dollar bills, 67 miles high!"

Both Houses of Congress were silent.

Mar. 3, 1981, interview
in press briefing room

One night, I was interviewed by Walter Cronkite in Press Briefing room. I was adamant, "In 1939, Franklin Delano Roosevelt called on the free world to quarantine Nazi Germany. That's what we have to do with the Soviet Union, quarantine it."

The interview ended, lights and cameras were cut, mikes taken off me and Cronkite. Walter Cronkite cleared his throat, "FDR never made a speech to quarantine Nazi Germany."

I was genuinely surprised, "He didn't?"

Walter sadly shook his head.

Jan. 13, 1981,
Senate confirmation hearing

In the Senate Confirmation Hearing room, Bill Casey waited to be confirmed as our new CIA Director. The Hearing Chairman questioned him, "Mr. Casey, are you willing to cooperate with this Senate Committee, today, at your confirmation hearing to be CIA Director?"

Bill publicly underestimated himself, "I can't conceive now of any circumstances which would result in my not being able to provide this committee with the information it requires."

A murmur went up among the reporters. CNN's Alan, looked around the other reporters and couldn't restrain himself, "Right on!"

7 A.M. Jan. 20, 1981,
Inauguration Day

Me and Nancy were sleeping in a bedroom at Blair House, the White House Guest House across the street from the White House. In the Oval Office, President Jimmy Carter looked at his watch at 7 a.m., wanting to keep me informed about progress on the hostage release. A plane to bring the hostages home was parked on the runway at Teheran Airport. Carter called me at Blair House.

In Blair House, Mike Deaver listened to the phone ring in a small office alcove adjoining the room where me and Nancy slept. Deaver picked up the phone, "Hello. I understand. But, President-Elect Reagan is sleeping and is not to be disturbed."

Carter was surprised, "But this is good news, about the release of the hostages."

Mike took a morning nip, "Look, I'll tell the President when he wakes up. If he's interested, he may call you." Mike hung up the phone and settled back in his chair, drinking vodka and stared out the window then went for a walk over to the White House Briefing Room, returned to Blair house, sat down and dozed off. When Mike woke up looked at his watch, it was 9 a.m. and figured he better wake me up. Slowly entering mine and Nancy's bedroom, he saw I was still sleeping, "Ronnie, get up! Get up! I can't believe you're still sleeping. You're going to be inaugurated in three hours, at noon!"

I woke up in a happy-go-lucky mood, "Does that mean I have to get out of bed?"

"You better get used to it, Ronnie. In three hours, you'll be President. Then, every day the courier from the National Security Council is going to be your alarm clock at 7:30 each morning, to brief you," Deaver took another nip.

"He's gonna have a hell of a long wait. You tell them not to come before 9:30 in the morning. Have you seen Carter this morning?"

"I took a walk to the White House Briefing Room a couple hours ago. Went over there and watched Carter pacing around like a cat in a cage at the zoo. When he wasn't pacing, he prayed. I was there with him at 5 A.M., he made a press announcement. He wasn't even shaved."

President Carter was up all night. Reporters surrounded him. He wanted the satisfaction of having the hostages released while he was still President, "I want to announce an agreement with Iran that will result, I believe, in freedom of our American hostages, held there."

Deaver had leaned towards the press, "The Reagan Administration will not negotiate with terrorists!"

I laughed, "You mean, Carter wasn't even shaved. I guess washed-up means you're not washed-up."

"No, Ronnie. He wasn't shaved and wasn't dressed for your inauguration, at noon, either. So, let's get with it. Ronnie, it's lights, camera, action time."

I was in one of the best moods of my life, "Okay Mike. I'm getting ready. Nancy and me will meet you at the limo, at 11:30."

Mike left the room. I woke Nancy up. Me and Nancy got dressed. A couple hours later our limo arrived at the White House in route to the Capital Hill ceremony where Mike was waiting when we arrived.

I leaned over towards Mike, "Get a load of Carter. Look how gaunt he looks."

It wasn't Mike disliked Carter, Carter was just the enemy, "The Iranians are taking another poke at him. They're not going to let the plane with the hostages take off until five minutes after you're sworn in as President. That way, the Reagan Administration will get the credit."

I laughed, "That's how it should be."

My inauguration ceremony was at high noon. I promised to usher in an era of national renewal. After the ceremony, I was at the White House, in House Speaker Tip O'Neil's office. House Speaker Tip O'Neil showed his desk to me, "This desk was used by Grover Cleveland."

Grover Cleveland, I knew that part, "I played Grover Cleveland in a movie."

"You played Grover Cleveland Alexander the baseball player," O'Neil corrected me, "not Grover Cleveland the president."

"Oh. I was half-right."

President's Inaugural Ball, 1981

My Presidential inaugural ball in 1981 was totally Hollywood, a high society extravaganza. Since I was an actor and, naturally, a narcissist ...as Nancy was, we loved appearing in front of people costumed-up to the hilt in the spotlight. In the evening, following the high noon inauguration, I wore a tuxedo. Nancy wore a designer gown. We had toured the town together, party-hopping for three days ...already, making appearances at one party after another. The inner party of the inaugural celebration was already three days old. This was the final day, climaxed by my inauguration. Now, it was going to be climaxed again by this official, inauguration ball. It was like being young all over again.

Senator Barry Goldwater was there talking to a reporter, "This is the most expensive inaugural celebration in American history."

"So, Mr. Goldwater," Alan the CNN reported asked, "you have mixed feelings about the how ostentatious the Reagan inaugural celebration is?"

Goldwater watched me and Nancy waltzing. I was wearing tails. Nancy was swirling her lavish gown. We waved to Senator Goldwater. Goldwater waved back, "This party cost eleven million dollars, has been going on four days. All these white ties, limos and mink is out of place on TV, when most of the country can't hack it financially! It's bad taste!"

Nancy watched Frank Sinatra on stage singing a song especially written for the celebration, "I'm so proud, that you're First Lady, Nancy ...and so pleased that I'm sort of a chum ...The next eight years will be fancy, Nancy ...as fancy as they come!" Nancy clapped enthusiastically. Nancy was sincerely flattered, "Oh, Frankie ...thank you for organizing, producing and directing this inauguration party for me and Ronnie!"

<>

Bill Casey's reward, as he made clear and we'd understood from the beginning, was me appointing him from being my campaign manager to being the new director of Central Intelligence Agency.

George Bush, who used to be DCI, was now my Vice President of the United States. Admiral Haig, the champion of the Vietnam war, we made him Secretary of State. Caspar Weinberger had been treasurer at Bechtel ... Bechtel wanted him to be Secretary of Defense.

Bill Casey navigated through the Inauguration Ball crowd, over to me. Bill introduced Lucio Gelli, an Italian businessman and a P-2 Lodge member to me, then to Vice President Bush. I figured P-2 was like Rotary Club, Lions Club, or Moose Lodge, not knowing at the time Gelli was a hub of Italian mafia drug trafficking, money laundering and international banking with the Vatican.

Mike Deaver, who used to be my campaign public affairs man, I made my new White House Assistant Chief of Staff ...basically, the same job. Mike said he wanted to introduce Mario Sandoval Alarcon and campaign supporters from Taiwan, Argentina, Guatemala, South America, and North Korea. Mike arranged that each of them was with the Miss World contestant from each of their countries, wearing sashes with their countries name on it. I was confused, "Mike, why are all these people from foreign countries here?"

Mike boasted, "Politics ...foreign aid, weapons sales, special interest groups. Kind of a nice touch to have their Miss World contestants with them, huh? They're all WACL." Mike sensed I didn't know what he was talking about.

"Mike, what's that?"

He whispered, "WACL ... World Anti-Communist League members, you know, 'freedom fighters' from Taiwan, Argentina, Guatemala, South Africa, North Korea."

"Great! ...Just keep prompting me." I shook everyone's hands nonstop, all the time smiling that winning, handsome Hollywood smile of mine.

Mike was at full stride at the top of his game, "Mario Alarcon and his outfit tossed ten million dollars into your gubernatorial and presidential campaigns, each, way under the table. Leave 'em laughing." Then, he stopped whispering, "Mr. President, Mario Sandoval Alarcon, businessman and Contra training commander in Argentina."

We shook hands. Sandoval looked at me, "Mr. Presidente, I hate the communists, taxes, trade unions. To hell with them, putas." He made a gesture indicating the slitting of throats and let go an evil laugh, elbowing my arm.

I had a double-take and was about to have an idea ...a thought about something or other ...but I felt myself forget it ...it never came up ...it disappeared as I stared off looked through the party into the distance.

Mike brought me back somehow, nodding towards Alarcon. That was my cue, I looked for toe-marks but couldn't find any so did the best I could, "Thank you for your help, Mr. Alarcon, and for being who you are. I really appreciate it."

That upset Mike. "No!"

Mike had embarrassed me, was upset, "I want my supporters to like me!"

"It doesn't matter if they like you or not."

"What do you mean?" I wondered what Mike meant. I felt the

familiar confusion settle over me ...I stared off again through the party ...almost had a thought ...I forgot it, but I made it back.

Mike watched me struggling.

He'd irritated me, "Mike, I appreciate what you've done for me, from the beginning of my political career. But, don't make me look bad ...don't make me look ungrateful ...I don't like that."

Mike shrugged. "Sorry, boss."

I knew what was botherin' him, "Mike, you're wonderin' if I can cut the mustard, aren't you? You got questions about me, don't you. After all these years, about what I know, and what I don't."

Bill Casey watched Count Otto von Bolschwing like a hawk and caught the Count's attention, "Von Bolschwing, c'mere." Bill watched von Bolschwing excuse himself from the WACL contingent, then walk over. Bill whispered, "I can't get Justice or Immigration fixed to help you ...you've gonna be deported. I don't know when. There's a way out, a new identity."

Von Bolschwing hit Bill Casey on the shoulder and in disgust, pushed Bill away, "Bormann won't like this." Von Bolschwing angrily left the party. Being an actor, I noted human motivation. You've got to know where the other characters are at, to keep the pace up. I made nothing of it, then forgot it. Nancy came up to me. We began the first dance of the inaugural ball. The orchestra played Nancy's favorite waltz, Blue Danube. Everyone in the audience clapped and cheered for me, the new President, and my First Lady. We stopped for a moment and I took a bow, then held my pose for the cameras.

< >

Mel's Jesus came up and wanted to cut in on my dance but it was out of the question. I refused, "I can't believe this is happening!"

Nancy was confused, "What?"

Mel's Jesus understood what was going on, "It has to be." He swept me away into the sky, over my Santa Barbara ranch.

I didn't see Patti anyplace, "Patti's not here!"

Mel's Jesus didn't care, "She can't be." He steered us through clouds.

Nancy looked at me, wondering if I was okay, how long I'd stay in my Alzheimer's senior moment. Nancy's eyes darted around the room frantically for an eternity. She didn't know if she'd see me, again. But, it only lasted a moment and we continued dancing like it never happened at all.

CHAPTER 4

Bahia Brazil, onboard gaily decorated fishing boat

Selwa Lucky Roosevelt was standing alone, her movements suggesting a samba as she listened to a dance combo on a nearby fishing boat bobbing in the waves alongside the boat she was on. She never thought, in her wildest dreams, being a journalist for *Town & Country Magazine*, would bring her to Brazil. But, here she was, out on the open sea to cover the Festival of Iamenje, Goddess of the Sea on a fish-stinking boat. She bravely threw bouquets of colorful flowers and gaily wrapped gifts, overboard to please Iamenje, inquiring of an aide to the Brazilian president, "I take it Iamenje likes gifts?"

"Si," the aide said, "if Iamenje is displeased with you she refuses them, the gifts float ...if she likes you, she accepts your gifts, and they sink to her."

Lucky watched pink and red roses she'd thrown onto the surface of the water slowly sinking in the grey-green sea, "How thrilling! They're sinking! It's good luck!"

Later that day at dusk, back in port on land, Selwa slowly walked beside green hedges surrounding the house of a priestess of animal sacrifice ...*Town & Country* asked her to interview Mother

Menininha, a 90-year-old Candomble priestess. All around the hedges scattered on the ground, were rotten, broken eggs with yolks leaking out crushed eggshells, stinking ...and the bones of small birds and mammals. Selwa smelled strange odors she associated with animal sacrifice, entered the house, went in the bedroom where Priestess Mother Menininha lay, bedridden. Lucky stared at the wrinkled-up old face and boney hands of the priestess ...and feared, one day, she herself would be old, and felt uneasy.

Priestess Mother enfolded Selwa's hands in hers, speaking slowly, "Be careful, you are strong ... you will be famous, soon."

When Lucky's cell phone rang in her purse, she felt instant relief, took back her hand, excused herself, took her phone and walked away to speak, "Hello."

"This is Mike Deaver. I'm White House Assistant Chief of Staff. You've received a White House appointment from Rockefeller to become Chief Protocol Officer for the United States. It's an ambassadorial appointment. We'd like you to accept it. Can you be in my office, Friday?"

"Yes, thank you Mr. Deaver. I can." Lucky hung up her cellphone.

Priestess Mother saw the surprised, dreamy look of awe on Selwa's face, when Selwa turned to smile at her, "You were right on the money, Priestess Menininha."

Deaver's White House office

Mike Deaver was seated in his White House office as Assistant Chief of Staff for the President of the United States and was blunt about it, "Selwa, got skeletons in your closet?"

Selwa stiffened in her chair, "I'm pro-choice, of Lebanese origin and if you're looking for right-wing ideological robotics from me, then I'm not the right person for you."

Deaver felt amused, "President Reagan's pro-life, our other protocol officer is from Lebanon, too, like you are. Your attitude on abortion, and being a good protocol officer are not related. Don't make any speeches about it."

Selwa was diplomatic, "If someone asks me, of course, I'll tell the truth."

Mike felt coldly and there was no enjoyment in his smile as he nodded at Selwa ... he had no choice in the matter, "Fair enough. Would you go see if Secretary of State Haig is onboard with your appointment. I have a meeting with the President." He stood up, then shook her hand, "Glad to have you on board, Selwa."

She smiled, "You may call me, Lucky."

Secretary of State Haig's office

Secretary of State Alexander Haig enjoyed his reputation as a ruthless Vietnam war hawk, who was fanatically anti-Communist. To Lucky, Haig seemed cordial on the outside but tense and rigid, inside. She said he could call her Lucky.

Haig studied Lucky's face, said she was to call him Secretary of State Haig, "Lucky, I didn't know how important the Chief of Protocol's job was until I became Secretary of State. Did you know Deaver's staff's idea of protocol at Cancun was to give everyone jars of jellybeans?"

Lucky smiled warmly.

Haig continued, "Lucky, the powers that be, Brown Brothers over in London and Brown Brothers Harriman over here, told us, you're the right person for the job...so, you have my blessing. I'm off to a meeting with the President."

Deaver said it was Rockefeller, Haig said it was Brown Brothers, Harriman. Lucky guessed it was Dillon-Read. Never in her wildest dreams did she think Ronnie had no handlers and wondered how her husband, Archie Roosevelt, was enjoying his intelligence foray with David Rockefeller over in Angola, hoping Archie and David wouldn't be accidentally exposed to Soviet, South African or domestic biological and chemical warfare agents blown about in the fierce winds. South Africa was that continent's Bormann headquarters. She wondered if she'd been chosen for her White House Ambassadorial position because she was Lebanese and familiar with Arab and middle-eastern protocols of civility, and could appease the Saudis.

Nov. 5, 1980, post-election lunch

At a post-election lunch the next day, Nancy greeted George and Barbara Bush. George Bush was Vice President Elect. Nancy enjoyed Barbara, the apparently harmless, matronly maven who acted like she had no idea of what her husband was really up to. Nancy was ecstatic, "I can't believe it! I can't believe it! Ronnie just got out of the shower, he was standing in his robe. I 'd just gotten out of the shower, I was standing in my robe, too. And, we had the television on, naturally. NBC projected Ronnie as winner. I turned to Ronnie. I said, Somehow, this doesn't seem like it's the way it's supposed to be."

George ignored Nancy's conversation with Barbara, and turned to me, "A few years ago, I swore I'd never be your vice president. Well, what do we do now?"

Sacramento Governor's Mansion
waiting room, 1970

Patti pressed the blue transistor radio up against her ear ...but, the Elvis Presley song still filled the waiting room of the Governor's mansion. Listening to Elvis', You ain't nothin' but a hound dog, took Patti back 10-to-15 years, like she was 8. She saw the replays in her head, "But Daddy, Mommy hits me even when I don't do anything!"

"I hate it when you lie, Patti."

"You're not there, when it happens! You never see it! It happens, it does!"

Nancy yelled, "Patti's lying, Ronnie. She'll do anything for attention."

I scolded her, "Patti, you should be ashamed."

Patti started crying, "I'm sorry, Daddy."

"Now, apologize to your mother."

Patti remembered, like it was yesterday, like it happened moments ago ...but, it'd been years. But then, I remember things from 80 years ago like they were now. Sometimes, I remember things that didn't happen, like rehearsals in Hollywood making World War II movies ...and, seeing real films of Nazi concentration camps mixing up in my head and I don't know what's real ... and what's a commercial. *Hello?*

Voices played in Patti's head, over and over as she stared at the steel door of the auditorium, wondering if I would find time to see her.

Patti remembered it like yesterday, it never stopped. If she was tired, or needed help, when she felt unsure ... voices played in her head like dueling radio stations. She stared at the steel door for what seemed like forever, wondering what was happening on the other side of the door that separated her from me.

On my side of the door, Mike Deaver was rehearsing me for a speech. Mike was my public affairs man from the beginning of my political career in California, always trying to make me come off looking smarter, more decisive, sexy ...like a movie star, a governor movie star. Like Schwarzenegger, a movie star and governor at the same time. Only I did it first, before Schwarzenegger, and after Clint Eastwood was mayor of Carmel. Clint, then me, then Arnold. Deaver rehearsed me over and over again, fine-tuned me to make sure that debonair and handsome movie star look twinkled in my eyes, that the movie had a happy ending and the good guys won.

Mike was thrilled, "Lights!"

The auditorium suddenly lit up. A wide spot spiraled open around me. I began my speech, "Trees are the major source of air pollution."

Mike Deaver took a shot from his pocket flask, "Cut! What are you talking about?"

"Mike, I'm 64 years old, this is my acceptance speech. A scientist told me, trees sweat carbon. If you don't want me to add lib, give me a script to work from! I don't want to lose the house. Give me someone holding up those big cue cards for room temperature I.Q.'s, with big letters on them."

"If you read from cue card teleprompters, you'll be stale."

"I have to look into the camera to read a cue card. Tape down toe marks for me, Mike, so I can square up, you get the good angles on me."

Mike looked through a camera viewer, "I need a 'harder' angle, this is the 'hard' part of the speech. Be convincing, emotional."

I start laughing, "I can't do emotion. If I could do emotion I'd have 'A' pictures under my belt, and Oscars around the house. I'd still be in pictures, not politics. Are those cards done yet?" I felt confused ...I was going to think something ...I forgot what. Then, it almost came to me ...then, it slipped away. I stared in the distance of the empty auditorium ... trying to remember what I was here for. "I got it!" I said, turning to Stewart Spenser, another public affairs man working with Mike, "Stewart, I don't want to say anything stupid ...so, you script everything for me to say in speeches, and to reporters ...so, I'm convincing looking. Then, I'll concentrate on projecting my looks."

Stewart was always something of a mystery to me, I knew he and Nofzinger were part of Mike's mystique and power. Stewart handed me 5"x8" cards with scripted answers already written on them. I was surprised, "How'd you do that?"

Stewart grinned, "I'm way ahead of you, boss. You're goof-proofed."

Deaver nodded to the camera, then to the lighting crew as I pointed to masking tape toe marks a grip just taped to the floor, "Ronnie, read your lines, feel confident like Nancy's smiling at you, hit your toe marks. Roll 'em!"

I kept rehearsing ..when cue cards said, 'rant', I ranted ... 'pause to think', I reflected ... 'laugh', I laughed ... 'smile', I smiled ... 'act upset', I ranted, "The mess at Berkeley and the student bums there make me sick! They have sex orgies so vile I can't, I won't describe it to you! I won't allow student radicals to threaten democracy!" As I rehearsed, Mike kept an eye on reactions of the focus group, a test audience of normal people he made sure were there when I rehearsed ... they gathered in the corner, listening to me.

"When I ran for Governor of California, I promised to reduce the size of State government, to limit the scope of government, to throw the rascals out who got us in this financial mess. I'm not a politician. I'm an ordinary citizen, opposed to high taxes, government regulation, big spending, waste, and fraud. I endorse winning the war in Vietnam. As Douglas MacArthur said during war in Korea,

'There's no substitute for victory!' We can start a prairie fire that'll sweep the nation, prove we're number one in more than crime and taxes. This is a dream as big and golden as California." I heard the audience clapping. I felt the moment and was explosive, "I'll personally wage war against welfare cheats, commies, anti-nuclear protestors that threaten the American way! They want a blood bath! ...I'll give it to them!"

The focus group clapped. It was good entertainment.

Deaver smiled, "Cut! You've got it. Take five. Those cards make all the difference in the world." Mike turned to the audience, "That's enough for today, same time tomorrow. Pick up your twenty bucks on the way out." Mike walked over to Stu Spensor, "I think the media will eat up that image. That speech is going to appeal to people's emotions when they see it on TV. It doesn't have intellectual appeal, but it's sexy and will sell."

Stu Spenser nodded, "Let's see what Richard Wirthlin has to say."

Deaver and Spenser looked at Richard Wirthlin. Deaver spoke first, "You're the pollster. What do you say?"

Wirthlin held a script of the speech in one hand. In his other hand he was comparing a computer print-out that listed a word-by-word analysis of the speech, paired up with the audience reaction to each word, "I've been studying the pulse. We've got power phrases, here. They got the best emotional responses. Make sure we use them in the next draft of the speech. These lines I marked through are dead fish ... no audience emotional response to those. Cut them out. You've done a good job with Ronnie."

Deaver boasted, "I do a good job with Ronnie because I am Ronnie. Every morning after I get up I look in my mirror. I make believe I'm him. I ask what he should do today, where he should go today. Every day, I come up with the, 'line of the day'. Everyone in State government is supposed to stress that line to the press, that day. I make sure the press is here each day, taking pictures of Ronnie doing something positive. I make sure Ronnie gets onto the evening news, every night. With a face like his, it's money in the bank. I make sure he gets a front-page picture in the major dailies every morning I can. Every time I think of Ronnie's public image, I think in terms of camera angle. And, from now on every day I'm gonna hand Ronnie a deck of index cards that have the day's schedule on them, have the text written on them for every casual word Ronnie says and every word Ronnie says formally. I'm even going to have a card that says, 'God Bless You', written on it 'cause that's what I want Ronnie to say when he finishes his speeches. For Ronnie, those cue cards are gonna be like Linus' blanket."

I preened in a hand mirror, smiling ... I was getting old ...but, not fat. I cut a fine line, retouched my make-up. A few days later, I put down that mirror, walked in the auditorium and delivered the real speech to supporters, reporters, and cops. They liked it. Two days later I delivered the same speech, again, to students at University of California, Berkeley.

University of California, Berkeley campus

At University of California Berkeley campus, students and citizens were waiting for me. Radicals remembered me saying, 'trees are the greatest source of air pollution', because they'd put signs on the trees, 'Cut me down before I kill again'.

I started my speech ranting about Black Panthers, who'd armed themselves against Oakland Police, alleging police brutality. I ranted about anti-police demonstrators, anti-nuclear activists, communists, the usual. They heckled me. One kid, especially. I looked at him. I pointed my finger at his face, "Shut up!" I said, "I always wanted to tell a heckler to shut up! Now I have! It feels great!"

Ed Meese laughed.

A few days later, back in Sacramento in the Governor's mansion auditorium I kept rehearsing that same rant. Mike watched the focus group reaction, "You're doing good with the 'hardliner' bit, Ronnie. Keep it going as long as you can."

'Hardlining' was an unforgiving, angry act. After rehearsal, I snapped back into my handsome movie star look, sat down at the make-up table, checked out my profile in my hand mirror, winked as usual, touched-up my eyeliner, powered my face, practiced smiling and winking in my mirror ...I got that winning feeling back and froze that look on my face, turning my head to show Ed Meese.

Ed took the cellophane off a cigar, "How do you make that look stay stuck your face and look sincere?" He watched me remove my make-up and gruffly waved-in an L.A. police sergeant in uniform, and a couple guys in pressed dark blue business suits, "I took care of those death-threats on you, Ron. These guys are from SWAT and FBI Cointelpro."

I turned from my mirror to face them, that 'winning feeling' still plastered on ... I got the feeling I could almost remember something, but what it was, I had no idea ... I stared off. When was it? ...the early '50s, twenty, twenty-five years ago when I was a star in Hollywood, ...but, no loner making pictures. I was emcee on General Electric Theatre, on TV once a week. Between shows, GE sent me around the country giving speeches, ranting against Communism ... like my childhood hero, Father Kauflin did on radio in the '30s and '40s. I raved about Crusade For Freedom, explained how people in communist-run countries were prisoners ...then, collected my check. Back then, I didn't even know what the 'Christian West' plan was. There was a little more to it, than that ...because, in the early '50s when I was president of Actor's Guild in Hollywood, I ranted against communists trying to take over Hollywood who were trying to brainwash people who went to the movies. One time after talking to the Guild, I met a couple undercover FBI agents ...and, got a check from them, naturally ...I was an FBI informer.

Ed interrupted my revelry, "Ron, I want you to meet these guys. Ron, stop daydreaming, get your head back here."

"Death threats?" I said, "You mean that phone threat from the Commies to throw acid on my face, wreck my looks, so I can't act anymore?"

"No, Ron ...that, was twenty years ago. I mean the phone threats we got after the Berkeley speech last week."

"Okay. I'll try to get back here in the present, and focus. I saw the FBI patches on their blazers, that reminded me of the Actor's Guild, gave me a flashback." I had that feeling again ... I was going to remember something ... I start staring off. Ed looked worried ...but, I was getting that 'almost-remembering' feeling, and that was important cause lots of times after that feeling I did remember. "When I was President of Actor's Guild and got death-threats, I went into a gun store and bought my first, real gun. Sure, I used guns in movies ...but, they were props." I was daydreaming again. In the movie in my head, I walked down a street, patting a holstered gun beneath my jacket ...then, somehow I was in the audience watching myself walk down the street in my film, G-Men, playing a government agent, I was the star. Someone put a hand on my shoulder, it was Ed. I looked into Ed's face, the faces of the policeman, and the FBI agents ...they were waiting for me to stop remembering. I smiled, "I saved America in G-Men."

The L.A. policeman and FBI Cointelpro officers looked uncomfortable.

Ed turned towards them, "G-Men was a Hollywood film the Governor starred in mid-'40s, when he was a big star."

I remembered walking by my mailbox with the American flag and eagle painted on it, a horseshoe too, for good luck, going into the hallway, taking off my coat, hanging it up. Nancy came to kiss me, she jumped back when she saw the shoulder holster I was wearing, and the pistol butt sticking out of it.

I tried calming her down, "Mommy, I keep getting death-threats, communists calling me at Actor's Guild, talking about fixing my face so I'll never work again ...so, I bought 'old Betsy' at a gun store, I'm gonna keep her until the communists are gone, so you and me and the kids don't have to worry about the Red Menace."

Nancy hugged me, she felt better.

I rubbed grease in my hair, looked at Mike, "Where's my comb?" I was back, "We need secret police units and FBI Cointelpro provocateurs infiltrating anti-nuke demonstrations at Santa Barbara."

Ed let out a sigh of relief, "We're not ready yet, Ron."

"Ed. We're getting radicals off the streets put in jail, where they belong. No one's threatening California, I'm governor!" I felt confused. I looked off, across the room.

Ed sat down, shook his head.

Then, it came to me, "It's not California, it's America. When will Operation Cable Splicer be ready? ...mass arrests with Federal Emergency Martial Law judicial authority? That'll make me president."

On the other side of the room, on the other side of the door in the waiting room, Patti felt impatient and shifted her body so it came unstuck from the couch, threw down the magazine she was reading, onto the coffee table. This shocked my social secretary, Helena von Damm, "You can't go in there! I don't know if his rehearsal's over yet!"

Patti ignored her, "I don't care! I've been here 100 years, I've sat in on Dad's rehearsals before. It's no big deal." Patti let herself into the auditorium just as the FBI and police were leaving.

They looked her over.

Patti stared at them, flirting, "Oh, really ... you can't afford it." She loved male attention.

I felt amused, "Grandstanding again?"

"Dad, please change your views, stop being pro-nuclear power, it's dangerous."

"Patti, we've been through this before."

"But, dad?"

"Bechtel and his friends got me here, he builds nuclear plants, his friends own electric utilities, got me G.E. Theater. It's off the table."

"Daddy, meet Helen Caldecott and her anti-nuclear activists, listen to them. It's not just radioactive waste particles coming out smokestacks, it's miners, down-winders, babies born deformed, people getting sick, kids playing in bad playgrounds. It's not right!"

"Why tell me?! I'm not God! Money talks! State of California needs money! I need money! You need money! If you weren't a millionaire's daughter, you'd have a job! ...you couldn't hang out with radicals and commies at Berkeley and sound like this!"

Helena von Damm came in, "Ronnie, I couldn't stop her."

"That's all right, Helena."

Patti was startled, "Helena? ...Ronnie? Maybe Mom's right about you two."

"That's the first time I heard you say mother was right ...but, she's not."

Helena von Damm was indignant, "I doubt your father wants Berkeley radicals in the Governor's Mansion."

"I don't. Patti, you and your radicals are a pain in my ass. You're for everything I hate."

"That's how it is for me, for you!"

"This conversation's over!"

Patti stormed out, slamming the door. I looked at Helena, "What was that all about?"

We laughed.

< >

In 1966, I'd been elected 33rd Governor of California, defeating two-term incumbent Pat Brown. I was re-elected in 1970, defeating Jesse Unruh. In my first term, I froze government hiring and approved tax hikes to balance the budget. During the People's Park protests in 1969, I sent 2,200 National Guard troops to Berkeley campus to shut radicals up. I was responsible for dismantling the public psychiatric hospital system, because community-based housing and treatment would be better, although after that, California had a homeless population for the first time and still does. My first attempt to get the Republican presidential nomination was 1968, but damn Richard Nixon got it. When I was Governor of California, I used conservative rhetoric, the eight years I served as Governor. I said public programs were inferior to private business. In the movie playing in my mind I saw a California built by large landowners and railroad magnates, who carved out empires, Hollywood style ... from hostile lands. Patti said I ignored reality, that California was built on public power projects, public highway projects, and public water projects ... all financed by the State's use of public tax money, with experts supplied by the State, with project administration supplied by the State ...but, I was campaigning, playing an audience, my specialty. I really did care about making people happy, I was a professional actor ... a Hollywood star.

The phone rang, Helena picked it up, "Hello."

"It's Otto von Bolschwing. I need you tonight, to translate oil investment documents Sergei DeMohrenshieldt got for me, Klaus Barbie and Martin Bormann."

Helena lowered her voice, "Okay, as soon as Governor Reagan leaves. I bought into your company, is my stock headed up yet?"

"No, something else is."

<>

After my Presidential retirement back at the ranch one night in our continuing quest to find out who had been pulling my strings in Washington, Nancy read me Foothill Jr. College KFJC talk show host Mae Brussell's, *Nazi Connections to JFK*, in *Rebel*, about Otto von Bolschwing, "Otto Albrecht von Bolschwing was a captain in Heinrich Himmler's dreaded SS, and was Adolph Eichmann's superior in Europe and Palestine. Von Bolschwing worked simultaneously for Dulles' OSS."

I interrupted, "That means he was a double- or triple agent."

"When he entered U.S. in Feb. 1954, he concealed his Nazi past. He was to take over Gehlen's network in this country, and in many corners of the globe. He became closely associated with the late Elmer Bobst of Warner-Lambert Pharmaceutical, a godfather of Richard Nixon's political career, which brought him inside Nixon's 1960 campaign for the Presidency. In 1969, he showed up in California with a high-tech firm, TCI, that held classified Defense Department contracts. Trifia was brought to U.S. by von Bolschwing. Malaxa had escaped from Europe with 200 million dollars, in U.S. dollars. On arrival in New York, he picked up another 200 million dollars from Chase Manhattan Bank. The legal path for his entry was smoothed by Sullivan & Cromwell law offices, Dulles brothers' firm. Undersecretary of State Adolph Berle personally testified on Malaxa's behalf before a congressional subcommittee. In 1951, Senator Nixon introduced a private bill to allow Malaxa permanent residence. Arrangements for relocation in Whittier were made by Nixon's law office. The dummy front cover for Malaxa in Whittier was Western Tube. In 1946, Nixon got a call from Herman L. Perry asking if he wanted to run for Congress against Rep. Jerry Voorhis. Perry later became president of Western Tube."

"Wait a minute," I said, "That implies Nixon was put into office by Fascist financiers."

"In 1952, Nicolae Malaxa moved from Whittier California to Argentina. Malaxa had belonged to Otto von Bolschwing's Gestapo network, as did his associate, Viorel Trifa, living in Detroit. They were members of the Nazi Iron Guard in Romania, and had fled prosecution. When Malaxa went to Argentina in 1952, he linked up with Juan Peron and Otto Skorzeny."

"Nancy, they were reporting to Bormann and his Odessa!"

"Hmmm. It looks that way, doesn't it."

Governor's Mansion master bedroom

Fall turned into winter, it was the shortest day of the year, Nancy and I were in bed, watching my old Hollywood films ...my second favorite pastime. Twenty years ago, I was still a young man, "Hey, these films stay great, don't they, Nancy?"

"Yes Darling, you're still a handsome rogue. That's why I married you."

"I'm a pretty good actor, not as good as Bogart or Welles ...but, good as Flynn, don't you think?"

"Flynn yes, maybe Fonda too." She kissed me on the cheek.

"Thanks, Honey, I needed that ... Mommy, Ed Meese let me down on Operation Cable Splicer and that mass arrest program, he's late. When it gets here, I'm gonna lock up Black Panthers, peace radicals, anti-nuclear- power people ...and, all Patti's communist friends ... put them in internment camps." I switched videotapes.

Nancy noticed, "What's this one?"

"FBI footage of demonstrations at San Onofre nuclear facility and at Berkeley. See who's on stage in front of the mob?"

"That messy-looking one. Is that Patti? They all look the same to me ... it is Patti!" Nancy shook her head, "Sometimes I think we should just fix Patti and get it over with. My girlfriends are fixing their daughters."

"Maybe that's the answer ...if, a lobotomy would get Patti to shut up ... look there in the back."

"Why, it's those undercover FBI Cointelpro agents we had for lunch last week," Nancy said, "...going through the crowd pushing people around. Some people are pushing back. Look! ...police are arresting demonstrators. Ronnie, you didn't tell me they were agents-provocateur."

"Thank God for them ... it keeps those hippie communists away from me! Look at your daughter yelling into the microphone, dancing around, flipping her hair at the crowd. Now, she's playing Congo drums and passing a joint!"

"Smoking a joint ... on TV? I can't watch, anymore."

"Just hold on, here's a cut to People's Park with Patti on stage again ... one of those free speech rallies."

Nancy peeked from behind a pillow, "She's gonna talk. God help us."

"My father's politics stink."

Nancy watched me turn pale, "Ronnie ..."

"I'm not upset, I'm calm."

We got out of bed. Nancy put on hairspray, "Ronnie, aren't those FBI Cointelpro agents-provocateur the same ones from Hollywood in the early '50s, the ones who used to pay us for informing on actors when you were president of Actor's Guild?"

"Now, that's a coincidence, I was thinking the same thing, yesterday. I hope Ed gets my mass arrest law passed, soon." I looked in the mirror, smoothed my hair ... no white hairs to speak of.

"Ed's reliable as death and taxes, find any white hairs?"

"Just a couple." I pulled them out, winked into the mirror and laughed. "There's a cute guy in there flirting with me again."

Nancy jumped up, "What's that noise!?"

Patti burst in the room, "Mom, Dad, I've got to talk to you."

Nancy was furious, "You take that tone out of your voice, right now! How'd you get in here?"

Patti pulled up her mini-skirt, showing her thighs, "I have special arrangements with the guards."

I winced.

Nancy restrained herself, "You can't get shock value. Come, watch this FBI surveillance videotape of you disgracing us, in public ...tossing your hair ...dancing like that. You're not upsetting me."

Well, she was upsetting me, "Patti, I have an Irish temper, it's about ready to explode. Look how you act behind my back! ..attacking me! Your mother and I are talking about getting you a lobotomy, to get our family back together."

"What!?" Patti yelled, "Mom was the one always hitting me! ...fix her!"

Here we go again, I thought, "It never happened."

"Yes, it did!" Patti said. "You know it did!"

I kept calm, "Then, it was the best kept secret in California. I didn't know about it."

"Yes, you did!" Patti said, "I know you did!"

Nancy touched my shoulder, "Ronnie, control yourself. This is getting us nowhere."

I wanted to settle this once and for all, "Patti, you're wrong. Sometimes, you're not too bright. Sometimes, you're hopeless, a nut case. You should be ashamed. The only thing you and me have in common is good looks, and Irish temper!" I picked up a vintage movie magazine with me on the cover and began to read it, holding it in front of my face, blocking Patti from seeing me. Patti watched me and slowly closed her eyes, then stormed out of the room, frustrated.

Nancy triumphantly watched Patti leave, she'd given Patti a good scolding.

< > < > < >

Lebanon–Syria border,
Bekka Valley poppy fields, 1970

In Syria, in his brother's house, Monzer Al-Kassar reclined on a Turkish pillow on the floor, thinking about his opium poppy fields in Bekka Valley, Lebanon. He co-owned them with King Assad of Syria. Their fields and illegal arms trade together grossed about two-to-three billion dollars each year. Successful narco-terrorism was an art form that hinged on weapons trafficking between rogue and covert action teams ...from opposing intelligence services. The art form developed in World War II, when U.S. intelligence needed to find relative strengths of opposing groups, so sent in weapons traders via mafia, normally the drug warlords and mafia played both sides against each other, while having allegiance to neither ...only to themselves.

Monzer greeted his three brothers, "You want to see my new jet? Come with me, see my poppy fields in Bekka Valley."

The brothers boarded Monzer's new jet ... in a few minutes the jet landed on his private airstrip in Bekka Valley. When the jet door opened, a party was in progress. Monzer's harem of belly dancers approached him, with Middle-Eastern stringed instruments, flutes, drums and finger cymbals. The women were loaded on opium or heroin, its derivative. Sometimes, he kept women or sold them, trading them for girls or boys, threw them in to sweeten deals. From one tent stepped uniformed Soviet Military GRU intelligencers.

Monzer's youngest brother pointed towards them, "Your Soviet intelligence handler is here."

"I see him. Give him this report, it tells what Afghanistan Muhajidin rebels and their CIA handlers are planning against the Soviets. Tell them, I have a shipment of 100,000 American hand-held Stinger missiles for them. Get me my price, collect it, bring it here. I told them half in gold, half in printing plates for dollars, Deutchmarks and Yen," Monzer Al-Kassar said.

His brother walked to the Soviets, spoke with them a few minutes, handed over an attaché case, was directed to an open shipping crate with gold bars and printing plates in it ...then, returned to Monzer, telling him the deal went down with no problems. The Soviets departed by helicopter.

Several hours later, uniformed British Intelligencer MI-6 officers flew in, paid Monzer and supplied soldiers to protect Monzer's people loading opium and heroin crates onto Monzer's jet. An MI-6 British intelligencer grabbed a British officer, "The Brit over there, he works for us in MI-6 ...but, we caught him giving heroin delivery route info to a CIA operative ...then, followed him ... and he met with Soviet GRU operatives. He's a triple agent. What shall we do with him?"

Monzer took a ceremonial sword from his ceremonial guard, he lopped off the informers arms, legs, and head, "Eat him."

Stanford University, mid-'70s

George Shultz was president of Bechtel Corp. and invited friends, including Martin Anderson from Stanford University's Hoover Institute, to meet with him and me for dinner. Shultz felt, he needed to set me straight. Shultz's process of setting me straight was a continuing education program Bechtel pioneered years ago.

Shultz smiled at me, "Ronnie, my boss asked me, give you some pointers on conservative policies for California and the United States."

"That's humiliating ... treating me like I can't think for myself. I can, you know."

"Ronnie, I know that. You're gonna be 65 years old. I know, you know the forest from the trees and you're counting on going for the Republican nomination for president at the convention in 1976. I'm afraid Nixon's handling of Watergate is making it hard for us to push you into the Presidency as soon as we wanted to. Nixon has to resign, or he'll be impeached. Vice President Spiro Agnew's next in line. I understand he'll resign for taking bribes. Gerald Ford will be appointed after Agnew resigns. He'll be next President."

"I'll be President someday."

"Right on. Know Paul Nitze, Ronnie? Paul, come here. Paul's the universal Cold Warrior, drafted NSC-68, calls himself, 'neoconservative'."

Martin Anderson watched Nitze shake my hand. Nitze was husband of Standard Oil heiress, Phyllis Pratt and a vice president of Dillion Read, in the 1930s, had entered government service during World War II on the staff of James Forrestal before Forrestal became administrative assistant to President Franklin Roosevelt. In 1942, Nitze was chief of Metals & Minerals Branch of Board of Economic Warfare, then director of Foreign Procurement & Development Branch of Foreign Economic Administration in 1943. During 1944-1946, Nitze served as director, then vice chairman of U.S. Strategic Bombing Survey, for which President Truman awarded him the Legion of Merit. In the early post-WWII era, Nitze served in Truman Administration ...later, as Director of Policy Planning for State Department, 1950-1953. He was principal author of a highly influential secret National Security Council document ...NSC-68, which provided the strategic outline for increased U.S. expenditures to counter the perceived threat of Soviet armament.

From 1953 to 1961, Nitze served as president of Foreign Service Educational Foundation, concurrently serving as associate of Washington Center of Foreign Policy Research and School of Advanced International Studies SAIS, of Johns Hopkins University. Nitze had co-founded SAIS. His publications during this period included, U.S. Foreign Policy: 1945-1955. In 1961, President Kennedy appointed Nitze assistant secretary of Defense for International Security Affairs and in 1963, Nitze became Navy Secretary, serving until 1967. After Navy Secretary, Nitze was Deputy Secretary of Defense, 1967-1969 ...a member of the U.S. delegation to Strategic Arms Limitation Talks (SALT), 1969-1973 and Assistant Secretary of Defense for International Affairs, 1973-1976. Later, fearing Soviet rearmament, Nitze opposed ratification of SALT II 1979. Paul Nitze was co-founder of the 1970s 'Team B', created by conservative cold warriors, determined to stop détente and the SALT process. Panel members were all hard-liners. Team B reports became the intellectual foundation for, 'the window of vulnerability', of massive arms build-ups that began in Carter's Administration ...then, accelerated under my presidency. Team B came to the conclusion, Soviets developed terrifying new weapons of mass destruction, featuring a nuclear-armed submarine fleet that used a sonar system that didn't use sound ...and, was undetectable with U.S. technology. This info was later proven bogus. According to Dr. Anne Cahn of Arms Control and Disarmament Agency, 1977-1980, "If you go through Team B's allegations about weapons systems one by one, they were all wrong." Nitze became my chief negotiator of the Intermediate-Range Nuclear Forces Treaty, 1981-1984. In 1984, Nitze was named, Special Advisor to the President and Secretary of State on Arms Control. For forty years, Nitze was a chief architect of U.S. policy toward Soviet Union. I later awarded Nitze the Presidential Medal of Freedom, in 1985 ...for his contributions to freedom and security of the United States. The Arleigh Burke-class destroyer, USS Nitze, is named in his honor.

Nitze greeted me coldly, "I was invited here today, to shed a little light on the Committee On The Present Danger I formed."Paul Nitze remembered ... President Ford's Director of Central Intelligence, George Bush, had called him in. Paul wasn't too surprised. So, Paul visited CIA Director George Bush at his office in Langley Virginia at CIA headquarters.

At that time, CIA Director George Bush had set up serious shop in Angola and Jamaica and expanded CIA's domestic print media asset base of journalists moonlighting on Agency payroll during regular journalist jobs at domestic corporate media newspapers. They could argue any CIA perspective or disinformation story in the national media overnight, creating favorable public opinion in biased news stories and op-eds, and letters to the editor.

At the time, Bush's CIA was courting General Noriega, arming him, giving him payoffs, using Noriega as a mole inside South American drug cartels. Panama was cocaine central port of call. In return for letting Noriega traffic in cocaine, the Agency expected Noriega to provide the Agency intelligence Contra death squads could use eliminate people in South America and Latin America who wanted democracy, civil rights, fair pay or unions ... or otherwise got in the way of the drug trade. Those wanting democracy people were labeled 'communists' and murdered.

DCI George Bush looked into Paul Nitze's eyes, "I'm concerned about this Communist world take-over thing ... we should be able to milk it to get a bigger budget for the Agency from Congress. I'm not happy with annual intelligence estimates we're getting from Gehlen's Org out of Germany. Christ, the Agency's been dependent on him and Bormann for thirty years. I've decided, make up my own intelligence estimate team. I'm calling it, 'Team-B'. Team B will second-guess the annual intelligence estimates. I want you Paul, Richard Pipes, and Lt. Gen. Dan Graham to be, Team B. Be yourself. I want facts and figures from you and white papers to prove Moscow can get strategic superiority over the United States. I know there's smoke and mirrors involved. But, the Agency board of directors told me, you're the man for the job. How 'bout it? Help us beat the Communists?"

<>

Paul Nitze stopped remembering ...then, looked at me, "The Committee On The Present Danger is run by me and Richard Pipes, we're Cold Warriors, like you. We're real Reagan Republicans. Frankly, we didn't like losing in Vietnam, we didn't like losing to OPEC. We, in the Committee, are worried what would happen to the free world if Soviet military gains superiority over U.S. military. We're against détente with Soviet Union, at any cost. Détente means total American disarmament. It's American surrender. If the Soviets keep getting stronger militarily, they'll push us out of the Third World, push us all over the map, eventually take over here, at home. We have to convince the public and Congress to finance the largest build-up of military power the world has ever seen."

I watched Paul Nitze's eyes, "Of course. I know that. I've been saying it, 40 years. If that's what I was supposed to learn today, I'm sorry to disappoint you. I'm no dummy."

Martin Anderson smiled, "Let's say, you go after the Republican presidential nomination in '76. What do you think of this? ...you could save 90 billion dollars if you transferred cost of funding social programs from the Federal Government to State Governments."

I perked up, "Hmmm. That's a good idea, very interesting."

George Shultz smiled.

Paul Nitze spoke up, "I'd attack President Ford and, Secretary of State Kissinger for wanting arms control. Attack them every step of the way for any cooperation at all, with Soviet Union. It's a bad idea to placate your enemy. We need more American military power. These negotiations to give away Panama Canal are suicidal. If Ford has his way, he'll make United States No. 2, in a world where it's dangerous, if not fatal, to be second best."

I listened well. My training as an actor taught me, observe people closely. In my head, the ideas presented to me became my own. I visualized myself saying the same words I heard, at the same moment I heard them coming out my mouth to see if they would play, as if I was repeating them to captive audiences on radio and TV, in lecture halls and on the Presidential nomination convention floor. These guys were great.

When my second term as Governor of California ended, Jan. 1975, I continued on the speaker's circuit, went on radio with commentaries, and wrote newspaper op-ed columns. Bechtel and Shultz, my political handlers, decided I'd challenge Ford for Presidential nomination, in 1976. I campaigned hard, won the primary in California and many Southern states, fought all the way to the nominating convention floor, where I made a speech about dangers of nuclear war and the moral threat of the Soviet Union, winning many people's votes. My second attempt to get the Republican presidential nomination failed when Gerald Ford got enough delegates to win Republican nomination for President, on the first ballot. Ford chose Republican Nelson Rockefeller as a Vice Presidential running mate ...but, went on to lose the Presidential race to Jimmy Carter, a Democrat.

Bechtel Boardroom, San Francisco

At Bechtel company in his boardroom, Mr. Bechtel introduced his new company president, George Shultz. Two directors were also directors of California Chevron, and Pacific Gas & Electric. Outside the boardroom, Bechtel's treasurer, Caspar Weinberger felt he wasn't allowed to fit in at Bechtel ...because, he was Jewish ...and, Bechtel's biggest customers were anti-Semitic, the King of Saudi Arabia and King's family and friends throughout the Middle East. They hated Jews, they hated Israel. Caspar was the only Jew at Bechtel in upper management. He sulked outside until his temper got the better of him ...then, barged in the boardroom, where he saw George Shultz, "Shultz, I'm as good as you, I should be president of this company, not you."

< >

Nancy read Antony Sutton to me at the ranch, the last years of my life, he claimed the trans-Atlantic Axis, a Skull & Bones Society of the German Order of Death transcended national boundaries. But, Skull & Bones was just a recruiting stage and playground for the kids of the money-issuing class and ruling elite that served them. In 1965, Sutton put it this way, "Chevron Oil is Rockefeller owned.

Chase Manhattan, a Rockefeller-owned bank plays both sides of the political fence. The extent of Chase collaboration with Nazis is staggering, and this was at a time when Nelson Rockefeller had an intelligence job in Washington aimed against Nazi operations in Latin America. Chase Bank in Paris was a Nazi collaborator. Chase Bank, later Chase Manhattan Bank, has been a prime promoter of exporting U.S. technology to the Soviet Union, far back as early 1920s ... the first war crafted and managed by the Order was the Spanish-American War. The second war crafted and created by the Group was the Anglo-Boer war of 1899. The rise of Hitler and Nazism in Germany, and the rise of the Marxist State in the Soviet Union, and the clash between these two powers and the political systems they represented was a major cause of World War II. The Order financed revolutionary Marxism and its enemy, Nazism, to manage the nature and degree of the conflict to shape the evolution of the new World Order. The creation of the Soviet Union stems from the Order ... the early survivalof Soviet Union stems from the Order ... development of the Soviet Union stems from the Order. The Order created the Left and Right ... Soviet Russia, and Hitler, to be the two global arms needed for managed conflict to synthesize the new World Order. The arms were Guaranty Trust Co. of New York, and Brown Brothers, Harriman, private bankers of New York. In 1984 Averell Harriman (The Order 1913) was elder statesman of Democratic party while George Bush (The Order 1949) was heading CIA, then running for vice president then president to be head of the moderate-extremist wing of Republican Party. Order created and financed Soviet Union. Order created and financed Nazi Germany. Guaranty Trust Co., Brown Brothers, Harriman and Ruskombank developed Soviet Union's oil and manganese. In 1901 the Caucasus oil fields ... Baku fields ... produced half the total world crude oil output. After the revolution, which was a coup d'état orchestrated against the Czar, Soviet Union needed raw materials, technical skills and working capital to restore Russian factories. American firm International Barnsdall Corp. provided equipment to the Communists. They started drilling in the oil fields. International Barnsdall and Lucey Manufacturing Co. sent machinery and equipment from United States and sent American oil field workers to Communist Soviet Union. Chairman of International Barnsdall Corp. was Matthew C. Brush. Guaranty Trust, Lee Higginson & Co., and W. A. Harriman owned Barnsdall Corp. Barnsdall Corp. owned International Barnsdall Corp.

In 1913 Czarist Russia supplied fifty-three percent of world manganese, coming mostly from the Chiaturi deposits in the Caucasus. Production in 1920 was zero. The Soviets received modern mining and transportation facilities for their manganese deposits, acquired foreign exchange, and finally shattered American foreign policy concerning loans to the U.S.S.R. in a series of business agreements with W.A. Harriman Co. and Guaranty Trust. Chairman of Georgian Manganese Co., the Harriman operating company on the site in Russia, was Matthew Crush (the Order 1913). While the Order carried out its plans to develop Russia, State Department was helpless, could do nothing. In 1920s loans to Soviet Union were strictly against U.S. law. There were no diplomatic relations between United States and Soviet Union. There was no government support or government sanction for commercial activity between United States and Soviet Union. Government policy and public sentiment in the U.S. was against Soviet Union. But, Harriman-Guaranty cartel didn't tell State Department of its plans. Averell Harriman sneaked an illegal project past the U.S. Government. He later became U.S. Ambassador to Russia. Guaranty Trust, Union Banking Corp. were Harriman & Nazi interests that funded Hitler and helped construct and finance Nazism, National Socialism. Meanwhile, the Order kept a hold on professional associations relating to Soviet Union. Anglo-Russian Chamber of Commerce was created in 1920 to promote trade with Russia. It was needed by Soviet Union to get the Czar's industries working again. Chairman of the Executive Committee of Anglo-Russian Chamber Of Commerce was helped by Samuel R. Berton, a vice president of Guaranty Trust. The Order was aware that 'issuing credits' to U.S.S.R. was illegal. It wasn't made legal until 1933 when President Roosevelt got elected. Even though it was illegal and treason against the United States Government, Guaranty Trust did more than trade in Russian credits. Guaranty Trust made a joint banking agreement with the Soviets and installed a Guaranty Trust Vice President, Max May, as Director in Charge of the foreign division of a Soviet bank, the Ruskombank. Meanwhile the U.S. Government told U.S. citizens Soviet Communists were murderers. Meanwhile the Department Of Justice was deporting 'Reds' back to Soviet Union. Meanwhile every American politician-lawyer was telling the American public the United States would have no relations with the Soviets. But behind the scenes, Guaranty Trust Co. was actually running a division of a Soviet bank. American troops were being cheered by Soviet revolutionaries for helping protect the 'Revolution'. The Order's law firm Simpson, Thatcher & Bartlett represented the Soviet State Bank in the U.S. In 1927 Simpson, Thatcher & Bartlett told U.S. Government, Soviets were starting to increase U.S. bank deposits. This increase was priming the pump for huge payments to be directed to a few favored U.S. ruling family firms to build the Soviet First Five Year Plan. At the same time, in 1928, Secretary Kellogg said the government of the U.S. maintained the position it would be futile and unwise to enter into relations with Soviet Government. At this time the U.S., with implicit government approval, was involved in planning the First Five Year Plan in Russia. The planning work was done by American firms. Order construction of the Soviet dialectic arm continued through the 1930s up to World War II. In 1941 W.A. Harriman was appointed Lend Lease Administrator to assure flow of U.S. technology and products to Soviet Union. Harriman violated Lend Lease law that required only military goods could be shipped to Soviet Union. He shipped vast amounts of industrial equipment.

< >

"Harriman shipped U.S. Treasury Department currency plates. Now the Soviet Communists could freely print U.S. dollars.

< >

"During McCarthy era, while Communists were persecuted in U.S., money-issuing and ruling family banking interests had well-established interlocking board members on Soviet Communist banks, and had been financing and issuing credit to the Communists, 40 years."

< >

For his troubles, not to mention his accurate and well-documented research, Antony was blackballed by the establishment in America, and feared for his life each day. He died in 2002, two years before I did. A star, a brilliant investigative journalist, and true American hero.

White House Briefing Room,
Mar. 30, 1981

White House Spokesman Larry Speakes was having lunch with his boss, White House Press Chief Jim Brady. Brady smiled, "May the best man win."

"Right."

Brady flipped a coin up in the air ... heads. Larry laughed, "You lose, Brady. You go with Reagan today."

"Shit, I wanted time off." Jim picked up his hat, left the room.

Larry's staffers swarmed around him as pontificated, "What do you do if the president's assassinated? I was with President Ford when Squeaky Fromm went after him, it's confusing." The phone rang, Larry watched a staffer pick it up, "Stop! The trouble light's flashing ... I'll get it." Speakes went over, got the phone, he held it to his ear. His face changed in a frightened, unbelieving light.

Air Force One

Air Force One flew smoothly through the sky. Onboard, Vice President Bush read the name tag of the decorated soldier sitting next to him, 'Oliver North', "Ollie, is our FEMA Federal Emergency Martial Law Contingency plan for the presidential-assassination drill on time?"

"Yes, in a few hours we'll rehearse federal, state, national guard, military, and police responses to the scenario of a presidential assassination."

Bush was distracted by a phone ringing, watched a staffer go to answer ...then, stopped her, "Trouble button's flashing ... I'll pick up." Holding the phone to his ear, George's face turned ashen.

Washington, First Ladies'
Just Say No' Luncheon

In a fancy restaurant in downtown Washington D.C., First Lady Nancy Reagan stood at a podium giving her anti-drug, 'Just Say No', speech. Nancy picked up a glass of water, quickly opened a pill bottle of diet methamphetamine uppers and Miltown anti-depressant downers prescribed to her by the White House physician, emptied several into her hand, paused in her speech, raised her hand to her mouth, acted like she was clearing her throat, drank the water, swallowed the pills and continued her speech. "Excuse me ... what's important is we get street kids and their parents in American off street drugs ... and prescription drugs ...by, just saying, 'no'. Just say, 'no to drugs'." Nancy was distracted by a phone ringing offstage ...from the corner of her eye she watched a staffer pick it up, then frantically signal her. Nancy finished her speech to applause. She knew the call was important ...but, she hesitated stepping out of the limelight because the attention was a tonic for her, as always. When Nancy got to the phone, the staffer was upset.

The staffer was lost, "Trouble callin'".

Nancy was scared by the tone in the staffer's voice. Nancy put the phone up to her ear ...the triumphant look on her face from the applause she'd gotten drained away ...Nancy's worst fears had come true. She started to sob.

Patti's Hollywood Hills canyon home

In her hippie pad in Hollywood hills, back in the canyons overlooking the sea, Patti Reagan sang along with a bootlegged concert tape of the Rolling Stones playing, Honky Tonk Woman, "Honky tonk, honky tonk woman." Patti danced wildly while partying with her rich, infamous counter-culture friends, all tripping on LSD. Feeling delighted, she continued shaking her hair around, popping pills, snorting illegal narcotic powders, drinking shots of Jack Daniel from the bottle in her hand, then falling onto her waterbed. A couple of Patti's girlfriends were in the room rapping. Patti heard their words as if they were a foreign language she didn't understand. Patti watched her friends' auras as little pieces of God's illumination spilled out around them. Even with her eyes closed as she was trippin' and passing out, Patti felt the presence of her friends in the room, it made her feel warm and fuzzy the way she felt hugging her dog or her cat ...so contented. Patti was sure everyone was one big piece of God, one party spirit. Patti listened to her friends laughing. Her girlfriends, Laura and Joie, rapped back and forth like dueling typewriters.

Laura laughed, "Cancel the national debt. It's just words. Money's just an idea, y'know. It's a thieves' agreement for hardcore idolatry."

Joie could care less, "Money's the nature of the beast."

Patti laughed.

Laura kept rapping, "Patti's father stopped Medicare-paid abortions and made funding birth control illegal but he lets Congress fund religious people staffing chastity clinics."

Joey's jaw dropped, "Chastity clinics!? What the hell is that? What horny kid with two cents for brains would go to a chastity clinic to have a priest or a nun punch her ticket and say, 'just say no', cross your legs, bounce your feet on the floor to get rid of the feeling, take a cold shower ... I don't think so."

While Patti listened to Laura and Joie laugh, the warm sounds reminded Patti of taking her clothes off in the sunshine on mescaline in the cold rapids of Yosemite River by the falls. Patti felt the explosive cold water ejaculating in big creamy white splashes on her naked breasts and thighs, felt her skin in a rebellion of prickly goose bumps ...raised her hands to the sun god ...felt heat of the sun on her palms.

"Nancy doesn't just say no," Joie laughed, "Why should Patti?"

Laura nodded, "Maybe I can get Patti's father to fix everything if I do a Divine intercession."

"You're shittin' me. Those far-right religious assholes think Aids is divine punishment for sinners. Patrick Buchanan said, 'Oh the poor homosexuals have declared war on nature and nature is exacting an awful retribution.' unquote! Maybe he's right ...I don't know, it's a free country."

In Patti's head, she watched the movie reruns over and over that sucked life out of her. She covered her ears, but could still heard the sound track, closed her eyes, but saw the movie frames flickering. Nothing or no one could stop the voices in her head, her flashbacks. *Nancy jerked the brush through Patti's hair, snapping her ends with a loud crackle, then Nancy slapped. Patti cried, "Daddy! Daddy help me! Stop mommy hitting me." "Patti, I'm ashamed of you, you're lying about what mother did ...now, apologize to mother and hurry up, I have to go rehearse." "I'm sorry, I'm sorry, I'm sorry, I'm sorry, I'm sorry!"*

Patti felt her acid flashbacks fading out, watched her friends on her waterbed with her holding her hand and trying to soothe her, while managing their own acid flashbacks with crazy looks on their faces.

Other friends tried to talk Patty down. Patti had motor-mouth, "You and Mom are ice statues. I wish you were dead! I wish you were dead! Keep your shit to yourself, get out of my head! I can't take it anymore! I won't carry your shit anymore, carry it yourself, Dad! ...even if it kills you!"

Her friends just looked at one another and smiled, after all, many volunteered in the makeshift hospital tents at rock concerts, where they had to bring people down safely at every major rock concert.

On the floor, Patti's phone was ringing and ringing. A friend picked it up, then shook Patti to get her eyes to focus, but Patti's pupils stayed dilated like an owl's. Her friend bravely looked her right in the eyes, "Secret Service on the phone."

Patti raised the phone to her ear ...her face changed. Horrified, she threw the phone down and cried out, "It's my fault, I said I wanted him dead. My parents were right, I'm a witch." Patti struggled to come down the rest of the way ...someone stopped the music ...the party was over.

Washington D.C., hospital

In a Washington D.C. hospital, I lay terrified on a gurney watching Death pushing my gurney, its wheels chattering, out of emergency down the darkening corridor towards the morgue. Paul Robeson's ghost walked alongside me. I was panicking as my fear turned into terror, I prayed. In a movie jumbling in my head I watched had happened.

I finished my speech, everyone was clapping, accepting and approving. Walking out of the lecture hall to my limo I was surrounded by reporters, photographers, Secret Service men. Most of all, I loved being surrounded by fans. When the shots went off, my whole body jerked in fear, something punched my side, Secret Service agents surrounding me got shot, Jim Brady fell to the sidewalk, a widening pool of blood syrup beneath his head. I glimpsed my bodyguards wrestling a young man with a gun to the ground, handcuff and ankle-cuff the shooter, then shove him into a Secret Service car as he yelled out the window the reporters engulfing the car, "Tell Jodie I love her! Jodie you and I will occupy the White House, the peasants will drool with envy. Until then, please do your best to stay a virgin. You are a virgin, aren't you? I love you forever."

<>

I was roughly thrown into the limo, down on the floor, my ribs hit the drive-axle hump in the middle of the car, knocking the wind out of me, pinching my chest, I sunk down on the floor, a Secret Service agent on top of me. I felt sharp pain, "Ow! You broke my god-damn ribs!"

He didn't hear me and yelled to the chauffer, "Drive to the White House!" He ran his hands over my body, looking for blood ...but, his hands came up clean, bubbles of blood-colored saliva mixed foamed out my mouth. I stared at the agent, frantic.

"Negative on the White House," the agent said, "Head to the hospital!"

The Cadillac limo jumped out of traffic onto the sidewalk,

speeding a few blocks to the hospital, where hospital emergency room staff ran out of the hospital to meet us. I got out the limousine by myself, start walking to the emergency room, waving to everyone ...then, collapsed to my knees ...I woke up on a gurney. Secret Service agents cleared the press out, Mel's Jesus pushed the gurney along, then Jesus, Satan and me were sitting on a room-sized scale model of Earth. Death and Jesus wheeled me down the corridor. I was scared to death, I looked at Death. I looked at Paul Robeson's ghost, "Have you come for me?"

"Death, walking beside Paul Robeson, wore the uniform of a hospital orderly, "Yes ... it's your time."

Death and Paul Robeson bumped the gurney roughly into the walls down the hospital corridor. Nancy entered the hospital emergency room, was shocked and immediately grabbed the gurney as Death and Robeson's ghost whisked it past her, struggling and jerking the gurney to stop it. I saw Death leave, a spirit no longer occupying the body and dispossessing itself from the face the orderly, now calmly but quickly wheeling me along. Paul Robeson's ghost disappeared, too. Only Mel's Jesus stood there, over me.

Nancy yelled, "What are you doing with my husband?!"

The orderly was dazed, "Sorry ma'am. I don't know how it got away from me, I've got to get your husband into surgery, now."

Nancy took my hand, "I'm here, Darling, it's okay now Honey."

I tried reassuring Nancy, gave her a thumbs-up sign.

Nancy felt abandoned as the gurney left her. I lifted my head from the gurney, watched Nancy grow smaller and smaller, listened to the sound of one of the gurney wheels, it was lopsided, off center, like a horse cantering the linoleum floor. I looked up at the bright lights over the emergency room operating table. Doctors saw fear on my face, their machines beeping, I heard my heartbeat get weaker as breathing machines wheezed, far away a member of the hospital emergency room operating team talked to me above the controlled murmur of a crowd of orderlies and doctors hurrying through life-and-death routines. My doctor start fading away as the light got dimmer and dimmer, "We're losing him!"

A feeling of calmness and reassurance came over me, I liked the attention I was getting from the operating team, yet didn't know why their voices were so far away, growing so faint.

My doctor looked in my eyes. "We're starting surgery."

I smiled, "I hope you're a Republican."

"Right now, Mr. President, we're all Republicans."

< >

The surgeon removed a bullet from my left lung close to my heart. It was an illegal bullet. The kind that explode. But this one hadn't exploded. That's why I was alive. The surgeon finished surgery. A nurse wheeled me out of the emergency operating room. I'd been conscious the whole time. I pointed to a pen in the nurses uniform pocket. The nurse gave me a pen and paper. I start scribbling wildly, got control over my fingers then wrote slowly, legibly I start writing notes, handed them to the nurse who took the note from me then read it aloud, "'All in all, I'd rather be in Philadelphia'."

The doctors in the room shuffled around uncomfortably. The nurse took another note out of my fingers and read it aloud, "'Send me to L.A. where I can see the air I'm breathing.'" Doctors start whispering to one another. I smiled at the nurse. She took another note from me and read it aloud, "'Does Nancy know about us?'"

The nurse turned to the doctors, "I think he's trying to be funny."

Ed Meese crowded in close to me, "He is being funny!"

It felt good to hear Ed's voice. It got darker, I closed my eyes finally at rest.

Washington D.C., hospital room

I awoke in a bed in a hospital, Nancy walked in, appalled by darkness filling the room, she tried to draw the heavy curtains open, but couldn't ...the curtains were nailed shut. She got afraid, then angrily glanced at my Secret Service agents in the room, "Un-nail these curtains right now or you're fired! Ronnie's an outdoor type, he needs sunshine. He's claustrophobic. Don't make me plead."

"Sorry, Mrs. President," an agent said, "it's too dangerous, someone could get in another shot, got to keep him closed-off."

"I know, I'm sorry, I'm so upset." Nancy sat down in a chair beside my bed, noticing me going in and out of sleep and took my hand. I felt confused.

I watched Nancy and smiled.

Nancy took my hand in hers, "What happened?"

"I forgot to duck, Honey."

She laughed, "You're gonna be fine, Honey, as soon as we get out of here, I'll take you home, get you in the sunshine." Nancy watching over me comforted me, I fall asleep.

After a few days my daughter Maureen, from my first marriage to Jane Wyman, was allowed to visit. Maureen was born a happy, bubbly type, seeing her cheered me up ...but, took some of the starch out of her.

Maureen was concerned, "I've brought you a gift to cheer you up."

It was a marionette with my face painted on it. I was surprised. I laughed, "It only hurts when I laugh."

Maureen brightened up, "I saw the ghost in the Lincoln Room at the White House, again. This time, Paul Robeson's ghost was with him. The spirits are contacting us."

I felt confused ...I was going to have a brainstorm, but the feeling passed, I forgot what I was going to say. The phone by my bed rang.

Maureen answered it, "It's Bill Casey. He says, 'not to worry', he knows what to do. He'll take care of everything."

<>

That day, Mar. 30, 1981 rubber-neckers drove by three neighboring estates, Bush's estate, John Hinckley Sr's estate, and his next-door neighbor's estate where Hinckley Sr. and his wife hid all day as 170 reporters set up camera gear on Hinckley Sr's front lawn.

CHAPTER 5

Mike Deaver called me up, "The official government line, accepted without challenge by media, is the assassination attempt was no conspiracy, it nothing more than the senseless act of a deranged drifter who 'did it to impress Jodie Foster.'"

"Yeah, Mike," I said, "The whole family's watching the news anchor say the exact, same thing." We watched George H.W. Bush being interviewed on TV by a reporter, "In reference to whether the current president, George W. Bush, knew the would-be assassin, John Hinckley, Bush said at the time, 'It's certainly conceivable that I met him or might have been introduced to him. I don't recognize his face from the brief, kind of distorted thing they had on TV and the name doesn't ring any bells. I know he wasn't on our staff'. Neil Bush used a similar line in denying he knew John Hinckley. 'I have no idea,' he said. 'I don't recognize any pictures of him. I just wish I could see a better picture of him.'

I switched the set off, and told my family what Mike said to me.

Between what Mike said and what the TV said, Nancy was besides herself, "U.S. District Judge Paul Friedman wants to let John Hinckley Jr. out of the nut house to visit his parents, but the Reagan and Brady families say, 'No'."

Even Patti, Ron Jr., Michael, and Maureen were on the same side for once, agreeing with Nancy. It was something to see. I felt loved.

"But," Nancy said, "the Bush's go way back with their neighbors, the Hinckley's ...in oil ...politics ...and, CIA ... all the way back to the 1960s, the days Dulles had Casey have Ronnie refuse to extradite suspects out of California for Jim Garrison's Kennedy assassination case."

I cleared my throat to get attention, "Everyone in the country supported the new Halliburton, Kelly Brown & Root regime with Johnson as the figurehead, I wasn't going to rock the boat." Nancy was getting ready to go off and I tried to smooth it over, "Look, I agree with you and the kids. Just because I prayed for Hinckley Jr's soul in the hospital after he shot me, doesn't mean I didn't want to fry the bastard ...he murdered several people, destroyed Jim Brady's life, the bastard almost killed me! ...But, those damn Bush's, they're like rattlesnakes, under every rock, spit or pee and you hit a Bush."

Patti went off first, "Hinckley's been in St. Elizabeth's Hospital in Washington since he shot you, he can rot there."

Even Michael sounded sharp today, "How that damn Edward Bennett Williams won the case arguing that creep gets acquitted by reason of insanity because he wanted to impress actress Jody Foster ...what kind of Twinkie defense is that?!"

Ron Jr. lost his ballet-trained composure, "The part that gets me, is Hinckley Jr's brother Scott was scheduled to have dinner at the home of your vice president's son, Neil Bush, the next day after the assassination attempt."

Maureen was fired up, "And, Vice President Bush and Oliver North had FEMA drills planned that day in case you were assassinated ...it's all over Hollywood. Mom, what did our astrologer psychic say, I can't remember."

Nancy was always helping the kids, "She said, 'Ask Paul Robeson's ghost about it.'"

Maureen wondered, "Did you?"

"No, that's up to your father, that's who Paul Robeson visits, not me."

Maureen was impatient, "Well, Dad? ... did you?"

I wasn't sure, "I don't remember ...Paul's Earthly story wasn't a happy ending, y'know."

Patti was excited, "Tell us the story, Dad."

All the kids agreed, they all wanted to hear. Nancy didn't like the kids taking over her, "Now, wait a minute. This is your father's time, not Paul Robeson's."

I calmed Nancy down, "Nancy, Maureen just saw Paul Robeson's ghost in the Lincoln room, Ron Jr's been asking me for years, I know Michael's curious, Patti's not the only one."

"Okay," Nancy agreed, "then get back to this Bush, Hinckley business."

I went along with her, "Fine, Mommy ... ... you see, back in late 1950s, early 1960s when we were getting all those dead Kennedys, Martin Luther King, Malcolm X assassinations ... J. Edgar Hoover was prancing around in women's clothes in drag, according to later newspaper accounts ... I never saw Edgar when I did drag acts in after-theatre parties for friends ...J. Edgar thought Paul Robeson would threaten national security, too, just like those other assassinated people ... that is, after he spoke with Allen Dulles back in the mid-1940s. You can't blame J. Edgar for doing his job, after all, I was on his payroll as an informer when I was president of Actor's Guild. We believed in anti-Communism, back in those days. Of course, when Paul Robeson went to Russia to perform and sing and talk to Russian officials, that opened the gate for the CIA director at the time, who was ... who knows?" I said. I loved playing guessing games and trivia games with my family, always did.

Nancy was out of patience, "Ronnie, it was Richard Helms, you can't expect the children to remember. We're having snack at four this afternoon. Please get on with your storytelling so we can have snack on time."

I didn't want Nancy on the warpath, "Yes, Dear. Well, Paul Robeson's ghost has been visiting me since they wheeled me into the hospital after Hinckley shot his wad."

Nancy frowned, "Ronnie, please watch your language around the kids."

Michael shrugged, "Oh Mom, we're not kids anymore, I'm almost 60!"

Ron Jr. had that look on his face like he was hearing a story from a story book, "Dad, so you think Allen Dulles, Richard Helms, and J. Edgar Hoover did something?"

"Oh, I don't know, I doubt it, there's never evidence against them."

Patti wasn't satisfied, "Then why's Paul Robeson's ghost haunting you?"

"He's not haunting me, he visits me."

Maureen was besides herself, "We're not getting anywhere!"

Nancy saved the day, as usual, "Look, everyone. I'm going to read you an article about Paul Robeson by his son in *The Nation*, so we can get back to this Hinckley mess ... In the morning of Mar. 27, 1961 Paul Robeson was found in the bathroom of his Moscow hotel suite after having slashed his wrists with a razor blade following a wild party that had raged there the preceding night. His blood loss was not yet severe, and he recovered rapidly. However, both the raucous party and his 'suicide attempt' remain unexplained, and for the past twenty years the U.S. government has withheld documents I believe hold the answer to the question ...Was this a drug-induced suicide attempt? In June of that year I met Dr. Eric Olson in New York ...we were both struck by similarities between the cases of our respective fathers. On Nov. 28, 1953, Olson's father, Dr. Frank Olson, a scientist working with the CIA's top-secret MK-ULTRA 'mind control' program, allegedly 'jumped' through the glass of a thirteenth-floor hotel window and fell to his death. CIA documents have confirmed a week earlier Olson had been surreptitiously drugged with LSD at a high-level CIA meeting. MK-ULTRA poisoned foreign and domestic 'enemies' with LSD to induce mental breakdown or suicide. Richard Helms was CIA chief of operations at the time of my father's 1961 'suicide attempt', responsible for MK-ULTRA. In 1967 a former CIA agent to whom I promised anonymity told me in a private conversation my father was the subject of high-level concern and Helms and then-CIA Director Allen Dulles discussed him in a meeting in 1955. The events leading to my father's 'suicide attempt' began when, alarmed by intense surveillance in London, he departed abruptly for Moscow alone. His intention was to visit Havana at Fidel Castro's personal invitation and return home to join the civil rights movement. My father manifested no depressive symptoms at the time, when my mother and I spoke to him in the hospital soon after his 'suicide' attempt, he was lucid and able to recount his experience clearly. The party in his suite had been imposed on him under false pretenses, by people he knew but without the knowledge of his official hosts. By the time he realized this, his suite was invaded by a variety of anti-Soviet people whose behavior was so raucous he locked himself in his bedroom. I confirmed my father's story by interviewing his official hosts, his doctors, the organizers of the party, several attendees and a top Soviet official. However, I couldn't determine if my father's blood tests had shown any trace of drugs, whether an official investigation was in progress or why his hosts were unaware of the party. The Soviet official confirmed known 'anti-Soviet people' attended the party. When I returned to New York in early June, my father appeared to me to be fully recovered. However, when my parents returned to London several weeks later, my father became anxious, and he and my mother returned to Moscow. His well being was restored and in September they went back to London, where my father immediately suffered a relapse. My mother, acting on ill-considered advice of a close family friend, allowed a hastily recommended English physician to sign my father into the Priory psychiatric hospital near London. My father's records from the Priory, which I obtained recently, raise the suspicion he may have been subjected to the CIA's MK-ULTRA 'mind depatterning' technique, combining massive Electro-Convulsive Therapy with drug therapy. On the day of his admission, my mother was pressured into consenting to ECT, and treatment began thirty-six hours later. May 1963, I learned my father received fifty-four ECT treatments, I arranged his transfer to a clinic in East Berlin. Did the CIA, in collusion with the British intelligence service, orchestrate his subjection to 'mind depatterning'? The release of the information will improve national security by helping to protect the American people from criminal abuse by the intelligence agencies supposed to defend them.'"

Patti was all ears, "That sounds about right."

"Then, just one more by St. Clair and Cockburn you'll like better, and we'll call it a night." Nancy read on, "Paul Robeson, the Black actor, singer, and political radical, may have been a victim of CIA chemist Sidney Gottlieb's MK-ULTRA program. We have previously noted Gottlieb's death and outlined Gottlieb's career of infamy. In spring 1961, Robeson planned to visit Havana Cuba to meet with Fidel Castro and Che Guevara. The trip never came off because Robeson fell ill in Moscow, where he had gone to give several lectures and concerts. At the time, it was reported that Robeson suffered a heart attack. But in fact, Robeson slashed his wrists in a suicide attempt after suffering hallucinations and severe depression. The symptoms came on following a surprise party thrown for him at his Moscow hotel. Robeson's son, Paul Robeson, Jr., has investigated his father's illness for more than 30 years. He believes that his father was slipped a synthetic hallucinogen called BZ by U.S. intelligence operatives at the party in Moscow. The party was hosted by anti-Soviet dissidents funded by CIA. Robeson Jr. visited his father in the hospital the day after the suicide attempt. Robeson told his son that he felt extreme paranoia and felt the walls of the room moving. He locked himself in his bedroom and was overcome by a powerful sense of emptiness and depression ...before he tried to take his own life. Robeson left Moscow for London, where he was admitted to Priory Hospital. There he was turned over to psychiatrists who forced him to endure 54 electro-shock treatments. At the time, electro-shock, in combination with psycho-active drugs, was a favored technique of CIA behavior modification. It turned out that the doctors treating Robeson in London and, later, in New York were CIA contractors. The timing of Robeson's trip to Cuba was certainly a crucial factor. Three weeks after the Moscow party, the CIA launched its disastrous invasion of Cuba at the Bay of Pigs. It's impossible to underestimate Robeson's threat, as he was perceived by the U.S. government as the most famous Black radical in the world. Thru the 1950s Robeson commanded worldwide attention and esteem. He was the Nelson Mandela and Mohammed Ali of his time. He spoke more than twenty languages, including Russian, Chinese, and several African languages. Robeson was also on close terms with Nehru, Jomo Kenyatta, and other Third World leaders. His embrace of Castro in Havana would have seriously undermined U.S. efforts to overthrow the new Cuban government. Another pressing concern for the U.S. government at the time, was Robeson's announced intentions to return to the U.S. and assume a leading role in the emerging civil rights movement. Like the family of Martin Luther King, Robeson had been under official surveillance for decades. As early as 1935, British intelligence had been looking at Robeson's activities. In 1943, the Office of Strategic Services, World War II predecessor to the CIA, opened a file on him. In 1947, Robeson was nearly killed in a car crash. It later turned out that the left wheel of the car had been monkey-wrenched. In the 1950s, Robeson was targeted by Senator Joseph McCarthy's anti-communist hearings. The campaign effectively sabotaged his acting and singing career in the states. Robeson never recovered from the drugging and the follow-up treatments from CIA-linked doctors and shrinks. Robeson's case has chilling parallels to the fate of another Black man who was slipped CIA-concocted hallucinogens, Sgt. James Thornwell. Thornwell was a U.S. Army sergeant working in a NATO office in Orleans, France, in 1961 ...the same year Robeson was drugged, when he came under suspicion of having stolen documents. Thornwell, who maintained his innocence, was interrogated, hypnotized, and harassed by U.S. intelligence officers. When he persisted in proclaiming his innocence, Thornwell was secretly given LSD for several days by his interrogators, during which time he was forced to undergo aggressive questioning, replete with racial slurs and threats. At one point, the CIA men threatened 'to extend the hallucinatory state indefinitely, even to a point of permanent insanity'. The agents apparently consummated their promise. Thornwell experienced an irreversible mental crisis. He eventually committed suicide at his Maryland home. There was never any evidence that he had anything to do with missing NATO papers."

"Now, I'm getting into it to where I can't stop," Nancy said, "Here's some Eustace Mullins from 1983 to clear things up ... Since the 1920s social engineering psychology in the U.S. was influenced by British Army's Bureau of Psychological Warfare. London's Tavistock Institute of Human Relations has the modest goal of social engineering human behavior of American citizens. Because of artillery barrages of World War I, many soldiers were permanently impaired by shell shock. In 1921, Marquees of Tavistock 11th Duke of Bedford, supported a group planning rehabilitation programs for shell shocked British soldiers, taking the name, 'Tavistock Institute'. British Army General Staff decided it was crucial they determine the breaking point of soldiers under combat conditions. Tavistock Institute was taken over by Sir John Rawlings Reese, head of British Army Psychological Warfare Bureau. A cadre of specialists in psychological warfare was built up. In fifty years, 'Tavistock Institute' appears twice in the Index of the New York Times ... yet, according to LaRouche and others, Tavistock organized and trained the staffs of Office of Strategic Services (OSS), Strategic Bombing Survey, Supreme Headquarters of the Allied Expeditionary Forces, and other American military groups during World War II. During World War II, Tavistock combined with the medical sciences division of the Rockefeller Foundation for esoteric experiments with mind-altering drugs. The present drug culture of the U.S. is traced in its entirety to this Institute, which supervised the Central Intelligence Agency's training programs. The 'LSD counter culture' originated when Sandoz A.G., a Swiss pharmaceutical house owned by S.G. Warburg & Co., developed a new drug from lysergic acid, called LSD. James Paul Warburg ... son of Paul Warburg who had written the Federal Reserve Act in 1910 ... financed a subsidiary of Tavistock Institute in the U.S., called, Institute for Policy Studies ...whose director, Marcus Raskin, was appointed to the National Security Council. This subsidiary set up a CIA program ... MK-Ultra ... to experiment with LSD on CIA agents, some of whom later committed suicide. MK-Ultra, supervised by Dr. Gottlieb, resulted in huge lawsuits against the U.S. Government by families of the victims."

Patti had a realization, "Mom, are you saying John Hinckley Jr. was an assassin conditioned by MK-Ultra?"

Nancy winced, "Of course, not. No one in their right mind would ever say anything like that, if they expected to stay alive."

<>

I was struggling to stay awake, everyone's attention was on Nancy, "Nancy, are we almost done with this Hinckley stuff? I'm sleepy."

Nancy nodded, "Yes dear ...There was stuff about you on TV."

Hearing that perked me up, "Great."

Nancy picked up a newspaper, "This is a before, during and after. *Family destroyed by assassination attempt*, Associated Press,

April Fool's Day, 1981, John Mossman ... The parents of John W. Hinckley, Jr., 'just destroyed' by their son's alleged assassination attempt on President Reagan, hope to see him 'as soon as possible', their attorney said, issuing a brief statement expressing their 'deep concern' for President Reagan and all those involved in Monday's shooting, including their son, John. It was confirmed the Hinckleys retained the law firm of millionaire defense attorney Edward Bennett Williams. The Hinckleys reiterated through Robinson they have provided psychiatric care for their son in the past, adding that 'recent evaluations alerted no one to the seriousness of his condition'. In Washington, an aide to Vice President George Bush disputed a *Houston Post* report the Hinckleys made large contributions to Bush's presidential campaign. The aide, Shirley Green, said no record of such a contribution could be found. The senior Hinckley is described by associates as a devout Christian who belonged to a weekly Bible reading club and recently did work in Africa for a Christian service organization. A statement from counsel for Vanderbilt Energy Corp. said the elder Hinckley had temporarily relinquished his duties as chairman for the Denver-based firm because of a tragedy involving a member of his family. John Hinckley, Jr., 25, who was arrested seconds after Reagan was shot in Washington, and being held Tuesday at a Marine base in Quantico, Va. The corporate statement didn't mention any change for Scott Hinckley, vice president of operations for Vanderbilt and brother of John, Jr. The father's move came amid confirmation the Department of Energy was reviewing Vanderbilt's books. *Washington Star* quoted an unnamed 'White House official' confirming DOE auditors asked for an explanation of an overcharge when oil price controls were in effect between 1973 and 1981. The *Star* said DOE auditors told Scott Hinckley there was a possible penalty of 2 million dollars for the overcharge.'"

Nancy was on a roll, "And now, the during. This is Nathaniel Blumberg's, *The Afternoon of March 30* ... When it happened it was beyond grotesque. For seconds Jonathan Blakely was stunned. John Chancellor, eyebrows raised, informed viewers of NBC Nightly News the brother of the man who tried to kill the President, was acquainted with the son of the man who would have become President if the attack was successful. Chancellor said in a bewildered tone, Scott Hinckley and Neil Bush were scheduled to have dinner together at the home of the vice president's son the next night. Neil Bush, who worked for Amoco Oil, told Denver reporters he'd met Scott Hinckley at a surprise party at the Bush home Jan. 23, 1981 ...approximately three weeks after U.S. Department of Energy began what was termed a 'routine audit' of the books of Vanderbilt Energy, the Hinckley oil company. In an incredible coincidence, the morning of Mar. 30, three representatives of U.S. Department of Energy told Scott Hinckley, Vanderbilt's vice president of operations, auditors uncovered evidence of pricing violations on crude oil sold by the company from 1977 through 1980. The auditors said the federal government was considering a penalty of 2 million dollars. Scott Hinckley reportedly requested 'several hours to come up with an explanation' of the serious overcharges. The meeting ended a little more than an hour before John Hinckley Jr. shot President Reagan. Although John Hinckley Sr. was characterized repeatedly by the national news media as 'a strong supporter of President Reagan,' no record was found of contributions to Reagan. To the contrary, in addition to money given to Bush ... a fellow Texas oilman ... as far back as 1970, the senior Hinckley raised funds for Bush's unsuccessful campaign to wrest the nomination from Reagan. Furthermore, he and Scott Hinckley separately contributed to John Connally in late 1979 when Connally was leading the campaign to stop Reagan from gaining the 1980 presidential nomination. Bush and Hinckley families, according to one newspaper, 'maintained social ties'. Evidence at the time made clear many connections between the Bush and Hinckley families. The official government line, accepted without challenge by media, was the assassination attempt was nothing more than the senseless act of a deranged drifter who 'did it to impress Jodie Foster'. To understand how that came to pass, it's essential to examine the trial of John W. Hinckley, presided over by Judge Barrington D. Parker. May 2001, Barrington D. Parker was one of the first eleven nominees for appointment to federal appeals courts by President G. W. Bush. Parker, a Republican appointed to the federal bench by President Nixon, was a man with an established reputation for politically partisan decisions and notable reversals on appeal. For example, when Edwin Reinecke, then lieutenant governor of California under Governor Reagan was convicted of lying to the Senate Judiciary Committee, Judge Parker could have imposed a five-year jail sentence and a $2,000 fine, but gave Reinecke an 18-month suspended sentence and one month of unsupervised probation. More importantly, not for nothing did Parker achieve notoriety as 'the CIA's judge'. Orlando Letelier, an influential opponent of the Pinochet dictatorship in Chile, was assassinated in 1976 in broad daylight on a street in our national capital. The judge at the trial was Barrington D. Parker. Director of Central Intelligence was George Bush, father of George W. Bush. Judge Parker refused to allow the defense to present any testimony concerning the widely suspected involvement of CIA. Parker came through again in 1977 when a former director of CIA, Richard Helms, pleaded no contest to charges of lying to Senate Foreign Relations Committee when he testified CIA had not covertly supplied money to opponents of Salvadore Allende in a secret effort to block his election as president of Chile. Judge Parker gave Helms a suspended two-year sentence and a $2,000 fine. Shortly before this decision, the lawyer for Helms, Edward Bennett Williams, pleaded with Judge Parker for a lenient sentence. And how did Barrington D. Parker become the judge for Hinckley's trial? 'In another sharp diversion from regular courthouse procedure,' as the *Washington Post* flatly reported, Parker's name was secretly selected from a stack of cards that bore the names of 14 federal judges available. 'That selection process normally is carried out by a court clerk,' the *Post* continued, but this time the selection was made in private chambers of the senior judge,' Blumberg said."

Nancy kept rolling. "Here's the 'during' part ...by Tom Reno ... The Bush and Hinckley families go back to 1960s in Texas. When the Hinckley oil company, Vanderbilt Oil, started to fail in the 1960s, Bush Sr's, Zapata Oil financially bailed out Hinckley's company. Hinckley was running an operation with six dead wells, but began making several million dollars a year after the Bush bailout. Besides all of the family ties, Neil Bush lived in Lubbock, Texas much of 1978, where Reagan shooter Hinckley lived from 1974-1980. During this period, in 1978, Neil Bush served as campaign manager for the current president's unsuccessful run for Congress. Ironically, Scott Hinckley was called on the carpet by the U.S. Department of Energy on the day Reagan was shot. The DOE told Hinckley it might place a 2 million dollar penalty on his company. Scott Hinckley, John's brother, was scheduled to have dinner at the Denver home of Neil Bush, Bush, Sr.'s, son, the current president's brother, the day after the shooting. At the time, Neil Bush was a Denver-based purchaser of mineral rights for Amoco, and Scott Hinckley was vice president of his father's Denver-based oil business."

Nancy picked up an old San Francisco Examiner, "Now, here's the 'after' part, then cookies and milk at 4 p.m. ...Patti, this is from your friend, Dave Emory ... According to *San Francisco Examiner* of Mar. 31, 1981 John Hinckley was a former member of the National Socialist ... Nazi ... Party of America. He was expelled for being so violent his fellow Nazis suspected him of being a government agent. In Oct. 1980, Hinckley was arrested at the Nashville airport as then President Jimmy Carter was due to arrive. At the time, he had a .38 caliber pistol and two .22 caliber handguns in his possession, along with 50 rounds of ammunition.' The *Chronicle* reported the next day that Hinckley had attended a memorial march to commemorate American Nazi Party founder George Lincoln Rockwell.'

"*San Francisco Examiner*, Mar. 31, 1981 mentions Hinckley Sr's participation in a Christian Evangelical organization called World Vision is not a passing interest. World Vision served as a front for U.S. intelligence in Central America, employing former members of Anastazio Somoza's National Guard to inform on El Salvadorian refugees in Costa Rica, according to the *National Catholic Reporter* of Apr. 23, 1982 ... and that a number of the refugees were liquidated, after being identified as guerilla sympathizers by World Vision operatives.' *Christian Century Magazine*, July 4-11 1979 reported World Vision had functioned as a front for U.S. intelligence in Southeast Asia during the Vietnam War. Hinckley Sr's participation in World Vision, World Vision's connection to U.S. intelligence, and the closeness of the Bush and Hinckley families should be evaluated in light of the fact George Bush Sr. directed CIA a few years earlier. Hinckley Jr. was represented by the law firm of Edward Bennett Williams, one of the most powerful law firms in Washington D.C. The Edward Bennett Williams firm's previous clients included former CIA director Richard Helms, Robert Vesco, also connected to U.S. intelligence, Jimmy Hoffa and John Connally ... Nixon aide H.R. Haldemann's, *Ends of Power*, said 'the whole Bay of Pigs thing' was a code phrase in the Nixon White House 'for the assassination of President Kennedy'."

Patti popped, "Dad, Bush presidents and vice presidents are oil and energy brokers, along with friends and backers like Kenneth Lay of Enron."

This conversation continued for the next twenty-three years.

"Dad," Patti said, "I've been researching it for twenty-three years with all my friends. Back in 1979 and 1980, in the middle of you running for president, George W. Bush's first oil venture, Arbusto, got a $50,000 investment from Texan James Bath who made millions investing money for Khalid bin Mahfouz and Sheikh Salim bin-Laden ...Osama's brother. Salem bin Laden and Khalid bin Mahfouz were involved with BCCI, Bank of Credit and Commerce International, bin Mahfouz owned twenty percent of its stock. A decade later, Harken Energy, that bought out George W.'s crumbling oil and gas business, had its CIA connections, 17.6 percent of Harken's stock was owned by Abdullah Baksh, another Saudi magnate reported representing Khalid bin Mahfouz. Way back in the 1960s you see John Hinckley Sr's Vanderbilt Oil bailed out by Bush Senior's Zapata Oil while both companies are both sitting on dead wells ...and Zapata or Arbusto or whatever it's called that year is bailed out by the bin Ladens ...then George Jr's Arbusto is bailed out by the Saudis ...and Richard Helms' real Bay of Pigs is just a few weeks after MK-Ultra tries to murder Paul Robeson, and Dulles is networking Helms and the Saudis ...do you think that has anything to with what Paul Robeson's ghost has been trying to tell you all these years?"

Nancy still read me to sleep, and was wrapping it for the night, "Senator Frank Lautenberg of New Jersey just released a list of some bin Laden family members allowed by the Bush Administration to leave the U.S. in the week after 9/11. Two of the bin Ladens who departed were investigated for terrorist ties before 9/11. Omar Awad bin Laden, a nephew of Osama bin Laden, was allowed to leave even though his brother and housemate, Abdullah, was a long-time American head of the WAMY World Assembly of Muslim Youth.

WAMY is a suspected terrorist organization raided by the FBI this past spring. The Omar and Abdullah bin Laden apartment was a few blocks away from the listed address of two of the 9/11 hijackers ...and from WAMY headquarters. Also allowed to leave was Khalil bin Laden, who Brazilian police investigated for suspected terrorist ties."

It was at that moment the ghost of Paul Robeson appeared to us. Everyone was still. The ghost of Paul Robeson moved his mouth like he was trying to speak, "That's not it. That's not why I'm haunting you."

I was astonished, "Then why?! Why?" I said, but, the ghost vanished. I didn't know what to make of it ...it confused me ...I almost had an idea ...I forgot it ...I stared off at the sea.

<> <> <>

Washington D.C.,
hospital room bathroom

I was singing, happy to be alive after the assassination attempt, not to mention being able to get to the bathroom by myself. I was down on the floor with a towel mopping up water that had splashed out of the sink. A shadow fell over me, I was startled, turned and looked up. It was George Bush, with an amused look and some of that condescension shoved in it he'd learned from Bill Casey.

George remembered something his father Prescott said ...George was a kid again, back with his father in the family mansion, remembering the feeling of being a kid, being scolded by his father. Prescott was upset with George for cleaning up lemonade George had spilled.

Prescott looked down on George, "Don't you know what maids are for? We pay them good money. You want to take their jobs away? Where's your sense of social responsibility?"

George was embarrassed, humiliated, feigned a tough look on his face, but his sensitivity showed thru.

I saw George was daydreaming, "George, you're looking through me like I'm not even here, that's no way to treat your boss."

George stopped daydreaming, "Sorry, I guess my mind was lost someplace else."

"Keeping savings & loan deregulation and anti-terrorism on schedule for me?"

"Not to worry, that's what friends are for."

I appreciated that comment, "Thank you George, I hired you because you're dependable, I'm glad it turned into a friendship."

George felt flattered, "Me too, I took the job so you could depend on me. I'll take care of everything ...until you're back on your feet, of course."

I questioned what he meant ...he must have seen that in my eyes. "George," I said, "Don't stay out of the loop, don't let me down, George."

George smiled, "Stay out of the loop? I am the loop."

A few days later, Nancy visited me again in my hospital room. She propped a pillow behind me. I had a maze of I-V tubes hanging out of my arm. Nancy sat down on the bed beside me, "I don't think it's a good idea we go to our daughter's wedding, unless you're better."

I was surprised. "Not go to Maureen's wedding?! Nonsense. I'll be fine. It's three weeks away."

Nancy frowned, "But Jane Wyman ... your first wife will be there. Jane Wyman is Maureen's mother, not me."

I saw that stubborn look on Nancy's face. There was no use arguing with her. I gave in ...I felt good-natured about giving-in to Nancy. She was usually right, anyway, "If it wasn't Maureen's third wedding I might put up a little more fuss."

Nancy felt like she was going to pop. "It's not that so much, but Maureen's 40 ...her fiancée is 28! I can't just stand that!"

I leaned over towards Nancy and hugged her, wincing because the hug hurt my ribs where the bullet fractured and split them. Nancy felt bad that I felt hurt.

Nancy took a card out of her purse, "Here's a wedding card I bought. Here's a pen. Why don't you write a note inside. I'll send it to Maureen."

I wrote a note. I spoke the words I was writing aloud as I wrote them so Nancy could hear, "Dear Maureen, best wishes on this wonderful day. Sorry we can't make it. Love, Mom and Dad."

Nancy felt relieved and put the card into the envelope and sealed it, "I'm so glad we don't have to see her real mother."

Church in L.A., Maureen's wedding

The wedding march was being played by an organist at a church in Los Angeles where Maureen Reagan was marrying Dennis Revell. The couple exchanged wedding vows, reading them aloud. Maureen read her vows to her groom, "I love you because you're going to let me be me."

White House, upstairs living quarters

At Nancy's insistence, I'd moved back into the White House. Recuperating in bed, in my pajamas, Nancy lay beside me in her robe, reading ...she put down her book, "I'm sure glad I got the hospital to release you to come home early."

I was happy Nancy had done that, "Me too, Mommy."

Nancy drew back the curtains and was astonished as was she saw outside, "Well, would you believe that?! There's a circus out there set-up on the lawn?"

I didn't believe her, "A circus!?" I leaned up from my bed, looked out the window and laughed, it was a real circus, "It's nice to be home again, back in the swing of things."

<>

Patti taped a couple new newspaper headlines into her headline scrapbook. 'CIA seeks law for surprise searches of newsrooms,' a *New York Times*. 'Reagan wants to abolish consumer product agency', a *Washington Post*. 'White House seeks eased Bribery Act ... Says 1977 Law inhibits business abroad by U.S. corporations', a *New York Times*.

Jun. 16, 1981, press conference #3

Ed Meese III and Larry Speakes were together in the White House Press Briefing Room. Ed was talking to reporters. He was angry.

Alan from CNN walked over to Meece, "I understand Ernest W. Lefever withdrew himself from consideration as Assistant Secretary of State."

Meese was upset, "Ernie believed the U.S. should take a soft line dealing with friendly Far-Right dictatorships. Some liberal Senators crucified him for it. I think ACLU lobbied against Ernie's confirmation. American Civil Liberties Union is a criminal lobby!"

Larry shrugged in chagrin, turned to an aide, "Ed Meese wears the mantle for this Administration's most right-wing law-'n'-order man."

Deaver pushed the President's son, Michael, in front of the cameras."

Larry tried holding back Deaver's hand, "I'm not so sure about this."

Michael Reagan stood before the reporters, a Christian in a arena of lions.

Alan went for him, "You work for a military supply firm?"

Michael Reagan answered bitterly, he knew what was coming. "Yes. It's so silly. Somebody else can write a letter to military bases and say, 'Hey, I think Ronald Reagan's a great President'. I write a letter and say my Dad's a great President ...and I have the press on my doorstep. Now, I have to resign from the company."

Alan wondered, "What's been your father's reaction?"

Michael laughed in a snide way, "He told me, 'Don't write any more letters!'"

I came into the room, Deaver walked to my side. The reporters put their attention on me. Alan was first to feed, "What's your Administration's response to the Israeli attack on Iraq?"

"I can't answer that."

"What's your reaction to Israel not signing the Nuclear Non-Proliferation Treaty?"

"Well, I haven't given very much thought to that particular question, there."

"Any comment on Pakistan's refusal to sign the treaty?"

"I won't answer the question."

"What do you make of Israeli threats against Lebanon?"

"Well, this one's going to be one, I'm afraid, that I can't answer now."

"What do you think of the tactics of political action committees?"

"I don't know how to answer that."

"I feel skeptical about your Administration's grasp of foreign affairs."

"I'm satisfied that we do have a foreign policy."

Alan looked at Larry. Larry shrugged.

I looked through my note cards, "I regard voting as the most sacred right of free men and women."

"Then why won't you support an extension of the Voting Rights Act?"

I shrugged off the question. I looked at a different note card. I found one I liked. I smiled. "Vice President George Bush phoned President Ferdinand Marcos of the Philippines and said, 'We love your adherence to democratic principle and to the democratic processes'."

"Marcos is brutally enforcing martial law in Manila."

I tried another note card, "Max Hugel, appointed by William Casey to run CIA covert operations, resigned today. There were allegations of fraud against him in connection with financial transactions in the '70s."

"There are reports Casey omitted stock holdings, and a $10,000 gift from his income tax returns."

"I don't know anything about that. As you know 12,000, air traffic controllers in their union violated a no-strike clause in their contract and walked off the job. I warned them to honor their contract or face dismissal. I'm firing them. I've ordered military personnel into airport towers to keep commercial planes flying."

Treasury Secretary Donald Regan stood at another podium. Larry signaled Don Regan with a wave. Then, Larry introduced him. Treasury Secretary Regan spoke to me in front of the press, "Mr.

President, I'd like to invite you to join the negotiating session where your tax-cut bill is being shaped."

I smiled, "Heck no. I'm not going. I'm going to leave this to the experts. I'm not going to get involved in details. It's Nancy's birthday."

"How old is Mrs. Reagan?"

I knew I'd get this right, "Twenty-eight."

"Mr. President. America's in the worst economic recession since 1930. Unemployment's risen to over 10%. That's the highest unemployment rate since the Second World War. There are dramatic increases in business failures, farm foreclosures, personal bankruptcy, and homelessness. Over 11.5 million Americans have lost their jobs. Another 10 million others are forced into lower paying work. What's the Reagan Administration going to do to fix this?"

I looked through my note cards. I found a card labeled, 'unemployment'. I read the card to myself. I faced the press, "Well, one thing we're going to do is change the way we figure unemployment. Before, we used to actually count how many people were unemployed. But, from now on we're just going to count how many people get unemployment insurance ...and, after it runs out ... we're not going to count the people who aren't working who no longer can collect unemployment insurance ...that should help. The recession is a problem we inherited from Carter. So is the growing budget deficit. I was in Cincinnati at a fundraiser luncheon recently."

Mike saw, I was starting to ad lib. He was frantic.

I continued, "I told my audience, 'I know you've all paid $2,500 a plate to be here. I thank you for that. I received a letter from a blind supporter. He wrote in Braille to tell me that if cutting his pension would help get this country back on its feet, he'd like to have me cut his pension. Next question.'"

"Is the constant feud going on at the White House ...inside the White House Staff ...and, inside the Cabinet ...and, between the Staff and the Cabinet ... hindering the smooth working of the country?"

I thought, this an easy one, I'll just deny it. "There is no bickering or backstabbing going on. We're a very happy group."

Reporters in the room broke out laughing. Alan kept questioning me, "Are you aware of Budget Director David Stockman's new book, and what he's saying about you?"

"No. I stand by the White House staff and Cabinet completely."

<>

Stockman stood in a corner of the room with reporters, "My last visit to the Oval Office for lunch with the President was more in the nature of a visit to the woodshed after supper. He wasn't happy about the way all this has developed. The President blames this whole flap on the media."

<>

Larry seeing things were now out of hand and needing to tighten the press conference up, spoke into his microphone, "Here's one you'll like. Justice Department is investigating a $1,000 payment given to National Security Adviser Richard Allen from a Japanese magazine after he helped arrange a brief post-inaugural interview with Nancy Reagan."

Richard Allen stood up and addressed the floor, "I didn't accept it. I received it. It would have been an embarrassment to the Japanese to return the money."

Alan caught the scent of blood, "Mr. President. Will you let Richard Allen stay on the job?"

"On the basis of what I know, yes."

"I want to ask GOP Finance Director Rich DeVos about charges Reagan economic policies are unfair."

Larry nodded his approval to Richard DeVos. Richard DeVos stood up, "When I hear people talking about money, it's usually people who don't have any."

Larry was feeling grim, "On a lighter note, President Reagan's going to accept the annual White House Thanksgiving turkey. We thought you'd get a kick out of this."

I received the gift. It start squawking, wildly flapping its wings. I looked through my note cards and found marked, 'Thanksgiving

Turkey'. I thought I'd try that one, and read the card to reporters, "I remember a Thanksgiving long ago. I was carving a turkey and I noticed what seemed to be blood oozing from it. I thought the bird was undercooked. Then, I realized I'd sliced open my thumb."

Some reporters laughed. Alan smirked, "I have a question for House Speaker Tip O'Neil. How do you rate the President's budget know-how?"

Larry nodded to House Speaker Tip O'Neil.

Tip O'Neil faced the reporters, "The President vetoed a stop-gap spending bill. This veto forced the federal government to temporarily shut down ... for the first time, in history. The President knows less about the budget than any President in my lifetime. He can't even carry on a conversation about the budget. It's an absolute disgrace."

Larry looked angrily at Mike. Mike shrugged. Mike looked at Larry, "He wasn't supposed to say that, Larry."

Barbara Walters was patiently waiting to ask me a few questions. I gave her the high sign, "Mr. President, what kind of man were you, as a father?"

Mike sighed in relief. Larry started to smile.

I smiled at Barbara Walters while fumbling through my note cards. I couldn't find the one labeled, 'family'. I knew I'd have to improvise, "I don't really know. I tried very hard, and worked at spending time with the family."

"What kind of adjectives," Walters asked, "would you use to describe yourself?"

I smiled, "I'm a soft touch, I really am. Sometimes, I'm stubborn, I hope not unnecessarily so, but I really can't answer that question."

Mike felt worried. He pointed at his watch and tried to catch Larry's attention.

Barbara Walters had a few more questions, "I understand Nancy's Social Secretary, Muffie Brandon, reported the White House is experiencing a terrible tablecloth crisis. 'One set of tablecloths,' she said, 'to my complete and utter horror, went out to the dry cleaner, and shrunk'."

I laughed, "I don't think that we have a crisis here. I think we'll manage. I don't see this as a frightening thing."

Mike waved his hand in Larry's face to get Larry's attention.

Larry got the message, "Ladies and gentlemen of the press. This press conference is over."

May 17, 1981,
Notre Dame, assembly hall

The Dean of Notre Dame was presiding over a ceremony, "I'm pleased to award this honorary degree from Notre Dame, to President Reagan."

I smiled absently, "I was here 41 years ago acting as a football hero in the film, Coach Knute Rockne, All American. That's when I first said, 'Win one for the Gipper!'"

The Notre Dame Dean had a few drinks to brace himself for the ceremony, "Your vision, now as then, has a compelling simplicity about it."

"I'm smart. I admit it."

The Dean looked like he was holding his breath, underwater.

Dec. 12, 1981,
White House Situation Room

CIA Director Bill Casey, Vice President Bush, and me were meeting in the White House Situation Room. Bill Casey felt relieved, "Well, it took the Senate four months of investigation into my business dealings. Now, the Senate Intelligence Committee decided, I'm not what they call, 'unfit to serve'. I'm still CIA director, after all."

George was glad his intelligence mentor had made it past Senate investigation, "That's great, Bill."

Bill nodded in agreement, "Now, this is over, I want to widen the intelligence role of CIA. We have foreign spy power, I want domestic spy power, too. I want it officially announced, in the press. That'll keep anyone from knowing where the bodies are buried."

I listened carefully. "You've got it." I turned to George, "What's this about Muammar Qaddafi threatening to get me assassinated."

George felt deflated, "It's a sad state of affairs."

I put on my actor's face, "George, I don't know about how you feel about it. But, I think I'll just call Qaddafi and meet him out there on the Mall."

Britain, U.S. Economic Council meeting, 1982

Great Britain was chosen as location for a U.S. Economic Council meeting. I appointed George Shultz, president of Bechtel, to head up the economic council. George Shultz liked to make decisions on behalf of the U.S. to benefit Bechtel Corp. directly or indirectly, sooner or later and the buck usually stopped with him, anyway. As all of us in office learn, the business of the U.S. is the business of the U.S., but the business of the U.S. is partnered abroad. Investment and merchant bankers, international bankers and central bankers came to meet with development, engineering, and construction firms from the U.S. and Europe, all sat in chairs with four-inch high national flags stuck in little bowls of sand and corporate logos pasted onto nametags on their table place settings. Shultz naturally radiated a diplomatic savoir-faire while addressing the gathering, "While I'm head of President Reagan's economic council, I remain president of Bechtel ...this gives me a leg up against Bechtel's biggest competitor's ...including, bin Laden Construction of Saudi Arabia, Brown & Root out of Houston, and Halliburton ...but, it's window dressing when the FED, Bank of England, Bundesbank, Export-Import Bank, IMF, World Bank, and Band of International Settlements throws reconstruction contracts to us or to them ...often it appears to depend on ...campaign contributions ...who's elected ...who's got more players on Wall Street ...who's got the most Congressman ...we call them Conmen, for short, handling the Administration ...steering CIA, Joint Chiefs of Staff, and the White House. But, you've got to ask yourself ...who does CIA work for? ...when? ...which bank? ...and where? ...who tells them what to do? For whom does the bell toll? ...Bechtel tosses its hat into the ring along with Kelley Brown & Root, Halliburton, bin Laden Construction ...I mean, who's calling the shots? ...a host of players with their own intelligence networks and freelance mercenary armies securing oil pipelines and oil contract negotiations? But, we do agree on one thing ... overall, we let the taxpayers in each country pick up the tab, through the mechanism of the government contract."

<>

A phone began ringing, an aide to Bechtel's President Shultz carried the phone to him, "Mr. Shultz, it's the President of the United States."

On the other end of the line I waited impatiently. Shultz finally picked up. I took my shot, "George, I'd like you to be my State Secretary."

"I accept the job," Shultz said, "give me a week to resign from Bechtel and make arrangements."

Dec. 17, 1981, Press conference #6,
White House press briefing room

Mike Deaver reviewed the videotape of my last press conference while rehearsing me for the next, he wanted me to look forward to giving press conferences, but they were a mixed blessing for me. I liked the attention ...but, I didn't want to say the wrong thing. I stood up in the White House Press Briefing Room, facing the press.

CNN's Alan asked, "President Reagan, do you agree with Justice Department's efforts to overturn Supreme Court's Webber ruling?"

I shuffled through my note cards. I couldn't find any card for that. I felt this was going to be one of those days, when nothing goes right. I looked at him, "I can't bring to mind what it pertains to and what it calls for."

"It allows unions and management to enter into voluntary affirmative action agreements?"

"Yes, of course I agree."

Ed Meese waved frantically at me. Mike Deaver hurried over. Mike put his hand over the microphone. Mike whispered to me, "Mr. President, say, 'No, I don't agree.'"

I corrected myself, "I mean, I do not support the Webber ruling."

Larry Speakes was amused but kept a poker face. Alan watched in silence, shaking his head. Larry continued briefing the reporters gathered for the press conference. Larry faced the press, "The White House is seeking to ease rules on rest homes. Proposals include repeal of regulations on sanitation, safety, and contagion. Christmas is approaching. President Reagan authorized the distribution of 30 million pounds of surplus cheese to the poor."

Alan laughed, "A government worker told me the cheese is over a year old. It's reached something called, 'critical inventory situation'. It's moldy. On PBS, the President said elements of FDR's New Deal resembled Fascism ... so, is this fascist cheese?"

<>

I was upset. I leaned in front of Larry Speakes into the microphone, "Move over Larry. I'll handle this, myself. Young man, New Deal proponents espoused fascism."

"You're distorting history. What about your wife's higher-than-usual disapproval rating?"

That didn't go so bad, "I just heard earlier today, and maybe Larry can tell me if this is true, I just heard that some poll or something has revealed, she's the most popular woman in the world."

Larry frowned, "I haven't seen any poll like that."

I kept speaking. "I want to make a statement to celebrate Voice Of America's 40th Birthday. I used to work in radio. I made up a lot of exciting details while I was announcing games, by reading wire copy without actually being at the games. Now, I submit to you ... I told the truth when I enhanced routine plays, like shortstop-to-first grounding outs. I don't know if the player really ran over towards second base and made a one-hand stab ...or, whether he squatted down and took the ball when it came to him. But, the truth got there and, in other words, it can be attractively packaged."

Patti was in the back of the room cringing, but was waiting for Alan so they could go out to dinner after the press conference ended and Alan had written and submitted his stories.

Apr. 2, 1982, Falkland war
press conference

Alan spoke first, "Several days ago Argentina invaded Britain's Falkland Islands. Hours later, U.N. Ambassador Jeane Kirkpatrick attended a dinner at Argentine embassy. The British fleet is on its way to Falkland Islands. Which side are we on?"

I scratched my head. "We're friends of both sides. The Falklands Islands war is a dispute over sovereignty of that little ice-cold bunch of land down there. England has always been proud of the fact that English police didn't have to carry guns. In England, if a criminal carried a gun, even though he didn't use it, he wasn't tried for burglary or theft, or whatever he was doing. He was tried for first-degree murder and hung, if he was found guilty."

The reporters in the room fell silent.

Alan spoke out, "That's not true."

Larry quickly spoke into his microphone, "Well, it's a good story. It made the point, didn't it?"

I felt good Larry was defending me, that's what he got paid for. I faced the press, "I've checked statistics ...and trees really do cause more pollution than cars. There's no recall for missiles fired from silos. Those that are carried in bombers, those that are carried in ships of one kind of another, or submersibles, can be recalled ...if, there's been a miscalculation. We're going to strengthen three military divisions in Western Europe, two of which are in Geneva ...and one, I believe, still in Switzerland. I'm going to end this press conference with a little story. I spoke to students at a Chicago High School. I told them why Ed Meese's revised tax exemption policy could not possibly have been intended to benefit segregated schools. I told them, there must be some kind of misunderstanding. I am unalterably opposed to racial discrimination in any form. I told them, besides, I didn't know there were any segregated schools. Maybe, I should have known. But, I didn't. I warned the kids, make sure I didn't tell them any lies. Don't let me get away with it, I said. Make sure, what I told you checks out and is true. Don't be the 'sucker generation'. The other day, I got a letter from Pope John Paul II. He said, he approves what we've done so far against U.S.S.R. The other day, I was at a National

Security Council meeting with CIA Deputy Director Bobby Inman. We were talking about Soviet weapons. I said, isn't the SS-19 their biggest missile? So Inman says, no, that's the SS-18. I say, so they've even switched the numbers on their missiles to confuse us. I thought that was pretty good. Then, he tells me the numbers are assigned by U.S. intelligence. Defense Secretary Caspar Weinberger explained the Pentagon position on what they call, 'protracted nuclear war'. We don't believe a nuclear war can be won. But, we're planning to prevail if we're attacked. With great regret, I've accepted the resignation of Secretary of State Al Haig. I'm nominating as his successor, and he has accepted, George Shultz ...to replace him."

Alan spoke up, "The jobless rate is the worst in 42 years, 11 million people are looking for jobs."

"In this time of great unemployment," I said, "Sunday's paper had 24 full pages of employers looking for employees. Unemployment must be caused by a lot of lazy people who'd rather not work. We're trying to get unemployment to go up, and I think we're going to succeed. You can put some of the blame for the recession on me ...because, for many years, I was a Democrat. It's the big spenders who cause inflation. They even drove prayer out of our nation's classrooms."

Alan interrupted, "Who are 'they'?"

I smiled, "They know who they are. One more thing. All those mistakes you reporters said I made at last month's news conference, the score was five to one in my favor."

White House Spokesman Larry Speaks spoke into his microphone, "That concludes the Press Conference."

Several reporters start shouting questions at me, "Sanctions against Argentina?"

I waved, "I can't give you an answer on that."

"What about the Israeli invasion of Lebanon?"

"This is a question, again, where I have to beg your tolerance of me."

"Isn't this departure of Haig a bit mysterious?"

"Once again, you ask a question upon which when I accepted his resignation I made a statement that I'd have no further comments on that or take no questions on it. We've got a 120 billion dollar deficit coming. You know, a young man went into a grocery store and he had an orange in one hand and a bottle of vodka in the other. He paid for the orange with food stamps, took the change and paid for the vodka. That's what's wrong."

Larry shook his head tiredly. Bill Barnes felt his mouth fall open. Mike sighed. Alan got in another question, "Interior Secretary James Watt warned the Israeli Ambassador, that if liberals of the Jewish community oppose Watt's plans for offshore drilling they'll weaken our ability to be a good friend of Israel."

I smiled and waved, "Watts is an environmentalist himself, as I think I am. Watts is going to open up a billion miles of California shoreline for offshore drilling. Watts speaks in black-and-white terms without much gray in his life. He sees problems without the complexity that is confusing to a lot of people."

Alan jumped at it, "Watts says, environmentalists are a left-wing cult dedicated to bringing down the government!"

Larry shook his head, "Ladies and Gentlemen, this Press Conference is over."

Another reporter got in a question, "Will you be visiting the new Vietnam Veterans memorial?"

I waved to the reporter, "I can't tell you until somebody tells me. I never know where I'm going. Y'know, I was in Texas the other day and asked someone what Pac-Man is ...and, somebody told me, it was a round thing that gobbles up money. I thought, that was Tip O'Neil. You can't drink yourself sober, you can't spend yourself rich, and you can't pump the prime without priming the pump. You know something? I said that backwards. You can't prime the pump without pumping the prime." I felt exhausted. I waved and smiled at the reporters. Mike walked with me away from the podium. I smiled at Mike, "Send 'em away laughin'. The show must go on."

Larry felt exhausted, "That's it. It's over."

<>

Alan wasn't satisfied. He wanted more, "What do you mean, it's over. I thought it was a double feature."

Larry wasn't in the mood, "You don't tell us how to stage the news, and we don't tell you how to report it. But, I'll give you this. Come Thanksgiving, I'm going to announce the White House is considering a proposal by Ed Meese to tax unemployment benefits. This, in my opinion would make unemployment less attractive. Ed told me, he knows that generally when unemployment benefits end, most people find jobs very quickly."

Alan was furious ...but, said nothing. He didn't want to lose press privileges.

< >

Mike led me out of the room away from the feeding frenzy, escorting me upstairs to the second floor of the White House to my bedroom, so I could sleep. Mile smiled at me, "You were on your toe marks, Champ. You were right on the money. Good job."

"Thank you, and good night." I looked out the window, "Sometimes I look out there at Pennsylvania Avenue and see people bustling along, and it suddenly dawns on me that probably never again can I just say, Hey, I'm going down to the drugstore to look at the magazines."

Mike closed my bedroom door behind him ...stood in the hall ...took his flask of vodka out of his coat pocket, put it to his lips and drained it.

White House 2nd floor
bedroom, 1982

Me and Nancy woke up in our master bedroom suite in the White House, I was amusing Nancy and myself by playing with the marionette that had my face painted on it that Maureen gave me to cheer me up when I was in the hospital, "Good morning Mr. Marionette, would you like to be shot today? I hope you like ruling the United States as much as me."

Nancy wasn't amused, "Don't kid yourself, Caesar. Mark Anthony's out there."

"I saw that movie, that starred Lawrence Olivier or Error Flynn?"

"Ronnie, it's not funny. When you got shot ...John Kennedy, Robert Kennedy, Martin Luther King, George Wallace, I thought about them, all those CIA coups murdering a country's president to put in a new leader that will do what special interests tell CIA to tell him to do for their financial portfolios ...all the children of those murdered leaders, their kids want revenge. I don't know who scares me more ...multi-national corporations trying to buy the Presidency ...or, those who hire mercenaries and assassins ...or, kids of the ruling families the CIA conquers. The U.S. had a civil war once ...is it ongoing? ...hidden behind smiles ...behind handshakes ...behind elections, in every country?"

"You're confusing me, Mommy."

"Listen. Kennedy wanted to disband CIA, he wouldn't support CIA banana republics, but you support banana republics. Kennedy wanted to get rid of the Federal Reserve Banking system and have the U.S. Government print its own interest-free money again, instead of having to buy it or rent it from the Fed when they print it up and claim face value, but you support the Fed. Kennedy wanted to end Vietnam, but you support foreign and colonial wars, you support CIA, Contras, the Deutschemark, Yen, the dollar and let Bush, Casey and Shultz dictate fiscal and military policy and make the decisions ...so, why would anyone want to kill you? Where's the percentage in it? You're already far-right, there's nothing to gain ...unless, they had something really evil in mind."

I felt small, "Nancy, you hurt my feelings. I let people pull my strings, it makes me look innocent, feel innocent and be innocent ... I know I'm not in charge, no president is, it's acting."

Nancy forged ahead, "I'm not talking about that! I'll find out who was behind this assassination attempt on you, one way or another! I'll fire them, kill the messenger, that's how it works! There won't be any more bad tidings, I'll sort through all the scapegoats. I've been talking to my astrologer! There's those 800 CIA agents Carter fired, a lot of hungry operatives out there."

I got over my hurt feelings, "But, they're on my side because of Casey and Bush."

Nancy's eyes flashed, "You keep Casey and Bush on your side."

I sighed, "What choice do I have? At least I can count on George Shultz. Bechtel's had him coaching me on foreign policy and taxes since I got into politics, I never did get support from Brown & Root, they backed Johnson against Kennedy, so when Kennedy was killed Brown & Root got the international development and recolonization contracts, not Bechtel. Nancy, help me with this. One, given Casey's previous jobs running government, running OSS Intelligence, running Export-Import Bank and sitting as director on his own banks ...and two, Bechtel's revolving door between Bechtel, the CIA and the Cabinet then back to Bechtel ...and three, given Bechtel was friends with Shultz and Dulles and Casey ...and four, given Shultz works for Bechtel as president of the company and works as head of my Economic Council, and now he's accepting my appointment to be U.S. Secretary of State ...and five, Casey was known as a Republican fundraiser ...and six, Bechtel is a fundraiser too ...and seven, Bechtel employees work with and for CIA ... and eight, like I say, Shultz worked for Bechtel ... then, one, does Shultz work for CIA as an asset, too? ...Two, how do we follow the Foreign Policy trail giving taxpayer dollars to foreign national states who then hire U.S. private enterprises and pay them with taxpayer money ...and three, where are Congressional kickbacks happening? ...and four, are those kickbacks immoral because they go into private pockets, or moral in the name of stopping Communism?"

<>

Nancy threw her arms up into the air in dismay, then held her head in her hands, "Ronnie I don't know why you ask me questions like that, I'm not a walking encyclopedia, it seems right ...but, moral too? There've been so many Bechtel Cabinet employees or consultants in Washington over the years like Dulles, Casey, and McCone ... influencing each administration. The '50s were simpler, kinder, and gentler ...and, such a long time ago ...looking back from now."

I was animated, "Remember the '40s, that was World War Two, the coups in Syria, Iran, Korea, Guatemala, Nicaragua, what goes around comes around. But, who's in charge of the whole thing? ... Me?"

Nancy laughed, "I don't think so."

I kept driving my argument home, I really had a brainstorm this time, I was determined not to lose track of it, to hold it tight. "No, I'm not controlling anything. I follow leads I'm given by my backers ...and, they follow their consultants ...but, everyone breaks the rules ...that's what they're for, to tip the scales in their own favor. Does that mean criminals, mafia, terrorists, central banks, those ruling families are running the show? But, which ruling families are the bad apples?"

Nancy looked over her shoulders then back at me, "You can't count on anyone but me, remember that."

I saw Nancy was worrying, I hugged her, I kissed her. "I know Sweetheart, I know."

Nancy felt better. "We're going for the gold."

"An Oscar! Golly, Nancy, I trust you more than anyone in the whole world, I love you."

CHAPTER 6

Some say, President Kennedy's decision on Oct. 2 to begin withdrawal of U.S. forces from Vietnam led to his assassination fifty days later, because stopping the war would decrease the national debt.

< >

Others say, when Kennedy fired Allen Dulles as DCIA he sealed his own fate, since both Dulles brothers were partners in Sullivan & Cromwell representing the Nazi portfolio in America, and Allen was a director of Henry Schroder Co. bank, a major Fed stockholder.

< >

Back at the ranch after my Presidential retirement, Nancy helped me do research so I could understand how to play my characters better, for the good of the script and the final product. I wanted that Oscar. I needed to get into the heads of my Warburg character. In 1902, Paul Warburg and his brother Felix left Germany and came to the United States. Brother Max Warburg stayed in Frankfurt to run the German branch of the Warburg family bank, becoming a military intelligence advisor for the Kaiser. In 1968, while I was Governor of California, attempting a tentative run for the presidency, publicly supporting presidential nominee Richard Nixon ...George H. W. Bush was entering the Texas Air National Guard, Antony

Sutton's, Western Technology & Soviet Economic Development, was published by Hoover Institute, on Stanford University Campus ...showing how the Soviet state's technological and manufacturing base, at the moment supplying North Vietnamese weapons and supplies to destroy American soldiers, was built by U.S. firms, paid for by U.S. taxpayers without their knowledge...

<>

...including the largest Soviet steel and iron plants, automobile manufacturing equipment, precision ball-bearings, computers ...the majority of large Soviet industrial enterprises were all built with U.S. financing, or technical assistance. Sutton's work led him to questions. Why did U.S. built-up it's alleged enemy, Soviet Union, while at the same time the U.S. transferred technology and financing to Hitler's Germany?

<>

It was starting to become clear to me back in 1981 when I was President, it was high time for me to understand central banking as much as God would let me. I took a report from the Oval Office bookshelf, Vera C. Smith's, *Rationale of Central Banking*, Jun. 1981, for the Committee for Monetary Research & Education. 'The primary definition of a central bank ... is a banking system in which a single bank has either a complete or residuary monopoly in note issue. A central bank is not a natural product of banking development. It's imposed from outside, or comes into being, as the result of Government favors,' Vera wrote. That wasn't terribly difficult. I kept reading. 'A central bank gets its power and commanding position from a government-granted monopoly of note issue, establishing a direct inflationary impact because of the fractional reserve system, which allows the creation of book-entry loans and thereby, money, a number of times the actual 'money' amount the bank actually has in its deposits, or reserves.' Vera said, '...its stock, owned by private stockholders who use the credit of the U.S. for their own profit ...

control the nation's money and credit supply... a bank of issue to finance the government by 'mobilizing' credit in time of war, at all times charging interest, paid yearly by income tax payments.'

I was getting sleepy and put the book back up on the shelf, I'd look at it another day. Heck, I never knew, til the last year of my life, that taxpayers paid from 200 billion dollars to 300 billion dollars each year in interest, on a total debt of six-to-eight trillion dollars ... accumulated since day one of Federal Reserve Operations, in 1913. Not a bad profit, for printing U.S. money and lending it to us. And, that 200-300 billion dollars a year in interest payments was not a bad profit for 90 years work by the major shareholders of the Fed, not to mention the outstanding eight trillion dollar taxpayer debt in the first place.

1913 & 1918
Allen Dulles' masquerades

-- 1913 --

Allen Dulles knew how to throw a party. He liked the attention and respect he got from people afraid of his power. Insider trading, everyone sold out, the game was finding the right price. This party included the families Dulles, Harriman, Rockefeller, Warburg, Schroder, Walker, Hoover, Rothschild, Brown ...dressed-up in Halloween masquerade gala as pirates, devils, fortune tellers, military officers, thieves, murderers, pimps, whores ... in Dulles' parlor! Dulles felt on top of the world, "Let's enjoy ourselves!"

His guests applauded. Dulles led a group of guests out of the ballroom, into a dark game room. He fumbled for a light switch ...but, used a match instead, lit a torch. He signaled musicians to begin. In the flickering light, call girls in shadows played 'strip billiards'. Opium pipes dangled from their lips. Blue clouds of opium in puffs streamed from their nostrils, spinning in circles in clouds. They were stoned. As he walked by them, Allen Dulles ran his fingers over their naked bodies. The opium seemed to coax their bodies onto his fingertips. He start chasing a stripper hiding behind a pirate flag. Hugging it, he wrapped her up in it ...then, sat her on his knee, "Were you here for our party five years ago in 1913? ...when we financed Kaiser Wilhelm."

Her eyes flared angrily, "I was with you, it was a two-week party. I'm still drunk from that cocaine opium soda you gave everyone. It was summer, 1913, one year before the war. Me and the girls played 'strip pool', smoked opium. You and your friends snorted cocaine, drugged our drinks ...you thought, we didn't see."

Dulles turned towards his guests at his dinner party. He tapped an empty wine glass with his spoon, "Gentlemen and 'ladies', German General Staff, I have an announcement. Max Warburg's going to head German Secret Service during the coming Great War ...while, his brother, Paul Warburg, just founded the Federal Reserve for us, isn't that special?"

A call girl Allen Dulles was flirting with reached out behind the curtains, letting her hand roam over Dulles' behind. Dulles felt surprised, but, trained as a double- and triple-agent, his feelings didn't show on his face and he kept speaking without betraying what was going on, "Some U.S. and Russia banking families are allied against us and the Kaiser ...but, in name only ... a temporary and cosmetic inconvenience for the duration of the war. It's not personal, regardless of the war's outcome."

A German businessman spoke indignantly to one of the guests, "Sheis. Dumkov. Who loses the war pays interest on the loans made to finance it. The winner gets reparations from the loser. The winner finances rebuilding the cities and factories. What could be more personal?!"

Allen Dulles overheard the comment and appeared to ignore it, pulling the call girl out from behind the curtain. A laugh of amusement spread through the party, "A spy, no doubt!" Dulles said, "I've learned from my uncles, who were foreign secretaries of the United States for several generations ...a spy in the hand is worth two in the bush. Tonight, we set the pieces in order ...and, select who'll be the first board of directors of our first American central bank, the Federal Reserve Bank."

Dulles was applauded. He was pleased and goosed the call girl.

His audience broke into laughs. A German international banker approached him, "What about Kaiser's approaching war?"

An English merchant banker smiled at the German, "How will we disguise our friendship, with our countries at war?"

An Italian international banker asked, "Who'll make the most in arms sales?"

Allen Dulles spoke louder than everyone else, "Who'll make the most in interest charges on loans? Loyalty to each other ... comes before loyalty to one country or another. This way, we profit in war or peace as a one world government ...and, preserve our relative positions for our dynasties in a new world order." He start auctioning-off his call girls ...negotiated, brokered and bartered to his heart's content. Afterwards ...he felt like talking.

-- *1918* --

Paul Warburg talked with Allen Dulles, "I was successful in immigrating from Germany ...and, in a few years did what no one in America was able to do, I established a Central Bank. I took economic and financial control of America." Everyone clapped. He continued, "My brother Max, head of Warburg & Co. in Germany, was in charge of the Kaiser's Military Intelligence for World War I ...he'll represent Germany at the Peace Conference in 1918-1919. Max and I have worked together bankrupting and buying up each others' countries at every opportunity, as our family bankers have done in Bank of England, the Fed, the Reichsbank, Bank of France, in Russia, in Italy and all through Europe. Our family financed all sides of each war ...primarily as Rothschild bank agents. Now, that Kaiser and German General Staff have lost the war, it's time to win the peace. The time's right for America to buy up German industry. In Germany, my brother's on the board of I.G. Farben, the biggest chemical and pharmaceutical cartel in the world. Here in America, I'm on the board of American I.G. ...and we've chosen Allen Dulles of Sullivan & Cromwell attorneys to represent the Farbin portfolio ...selling and trading shares of Farbin stock in America.

< >

"As to your portfolio losses in World War I, we'll make these cosmetic only, Max and I will adjust Fed and Bank of England interest rates, inflate the currency in Germany relatively deflating rates in other countries ...so, use the deflated currencies to buy up German stocks ...buy up German stock at pennies on the dollar. And, we'll default loan schedules ... to your benefit, till everyone regains their losses. Russia defeated enemies of the United States. Now, Russia's enduring this 'revolution' of hers. She's ordained and christened herself a new name, the U.S.S.R., Union Of Soviet Socialist Republics. Soviet, means workers' governing groups. For business reasons, the United States must now betray Russia, her ally."

I had researched all this stuff for my acting roles. At the time, when the Communist Revolution seemed in doubt, Wilson sent his personal emissary, Elihu Root, to Russia with 100 million dollars from the Special Emergency War Fund to save the toppling Bolshevik regime.

Okay, that went smoothly with two Warburgs ...but, I've got a scene playing all five brothers coming up. Now, let me get back to the election of Hoover to the Presidency influenced by Warburg Brothers, directors of Kuhn Loeb Co. bank ...who financed Hoover's campaign.

In exchange, Hoover promised to impose a moratorium on German war debts. The history books I read to develop my characters, wrote of months of hurried and furtive preparations in Germany, and in Wall Street offices of German bankers setting up the Moratorium ...Germany had to be flooded with American money. Within eight months of Hoover's inauguration, the stock market crashed, officially beginning the Great Depression, the most severe economic crisis in U.S. history. Hoover was the George W. Bush of his day.

< > < > < >

Behind the scenes, Schroder through Bechtel, had helped me become President ...so, I promised to be the best Cold Warrior in town ...but, I didn't know till later, after my Presidency ... Bechtel was a Schroder subsidiary ...if I had known, it wouldn't of changed a thing. I didn't know then, Schroder was a major shareholder of the Fed ...if I'd known, so what?

I was my own man.

We were Cold Warriors.

We had a job to save America, at least I did. I wasn't a banker and didn't want to be, so the details escaped me.

White House Press Briefing Room

At the next White House press briefing, I restated my hardline position on Soviets and terrorists. After the press briefing, as was my custom, I returned to the Oval Office and flipped over the next page on my desk calendar.

Washington hotel ballroom

At the same time I was across town at a press conference talking about my hardliner position against Soviets and terrorists, Nancy had a routine to deliver, as well. Nancy was on the other side of town ...in a hotel ballroom, popping speed uppers ...and, Miltown downers ... while giving another performance of her, 'Just Say No' to drugs speech. Nancy addressed world heads of state, "It's consumers' own fault ...being addicts ..if people didn't use drugs ...if they didn't buy drugs, ...there'd be no demand ...the drug market would fall ...go belly-up." Nancy kept smiling, waiting for applause to die down.

Mario Alarcon sat in the audience, not far from Monzer Al-Kassar, Bill Casey, and George Bush, everyone was clapping. Nancy waved, start walking offstage, stumbled, caught her balance and, teetering dizzily, managed not to fall.

Ambassador Roosevelt's White House office

In her White House office, Ambassador Selwa Lucky Roosevelt

was busily planning parties, receptions, luncheons, casual dinners, formal dinners, and state gala events. She looked up and saw several of Meese's and Deaver's munchkins storm in. Lucky cringed. The Deaver munchkin start barking orders at her, "Deaver says you're the new protocol chief ...so, get me duplicate copies, starting now, of each official gift the President gives to anybody."

Lucky was offended, "No. I don't like your attitude. You may leave my office."

The Deaver munchkin barked, "I'm ordering you to, in Deaver's name!"

The Meese munchkin was not to be outdone, "I'm ordering you to, in Meese's name! And, I want your navy blue water cooler, for our mauve one!"

Lucky was angry, "No. You little munchkins have big attitude problems. I'm having trouble coping with you Meese and Deaver munchkins with your attitude problems. You frustrate me, get out of here."

Air Force Two over
Central America & Argentina

Lucky flew on Air Force Two to Argentina and Central America with Deaver's advance team. Part of the reason she went, was to see why her staff hated Deaver's advance team. Lucky was ignored on the plane. In the limo, Lucky felt Deaver's advance team were ashamed to be seen with a female diplomat. Later in the day, she walked into a meeting with the Latinos. The Deaver advance team leader wasted no time. Deaver's advance man was pissed off, "Let's cut this cordial crap, get down to business!"

Lucky cringed. She knew what was next. She watched Mario Alarcon get angrier and angrier, tried to smooth things over, but felt it was futile as despair overtook her she addressed the Latino leaders, "Now, just calm down, I'm just as frustrated by Deaver's advance team, as you are ...these damn munchkins are in my face every minute, every day. I came on this trip to see why my staff hates to go abroad with Deaver's munchkins ...now, I know. I see, the munchkins do not follow State Department Ambassadorial protocol procedures, to respect your culture. The California munchkins make up their own rules ...they are nouveau riche. I must be patient with them, perhaps you might consider allowing for their natural shortcomings, as well?"

Back in D.C., Lucky waited outside by the White House Diplomatic Entrance, until the right moment, then waved to the band leader, signaling the ceremony to begin. Lucky's staff of senior protocol officers walked with foreign ambassadors and ambassadors' families, that streamed out of a long line of limousines stretching around the block. Everyone walked towards Lucky. She smiled, as a flourish of trumpets greeted each Ambassador and their family ...each group was met by military aides wearing crisp Marine Honor Guard uniforms, smartly saluting each group, as it passed. The Ambassadors and their families dressed in their national costumes, as was customary for Ambassadors going to meet the President for the first time. African ambassadors and their families dressed in magnificent blue, purple, and yellow robes, and white feathered headdresses, trimmed with gold ...Asian ambassadors and their wives wore bright orange and pink silks from Thailand, Burma, Philippines, Malaysia, and Brunei ...Arabs of the Gulf States wore handsome desert garb, black abas, and white kaffiyehs, trimmed with gold.

Back in her office, Lucky was writing in her diary. 'The most unpleasant part of dealing with White House staff is the constant personal humiliations they take pleasure in inflicting. Alexander Haig was their prime victim.' Lucky thought it was because Haig offended the munchkins, and Mrs. Reagan ...when he said, after the assassination attempt on the President, he personally was 'in charge'.

Lucky was told how it went down. Everyone was in the White House Situation Room, watching the press on T.V. One of the reporters in the crowd outside the Situation Room asked, Who's in charge?

Larry Speakes insisted, "Vice President Bush."

Well, State Secretary Haig was watching TV from the Situation Room, too ...and, saw and heard Speakes say that on TV.

Haig start yelling at everyone in the Situation Room, "Bush isn't even here!"

Then, on TV, one of the reporters asked Speakes, is the country going to be put on Red Alert, for a possible nuclear war attack on us.

Haig jumped out of his chair, stormed out of the Situation Room, left behind Cabinet members and White House Staff he was with, who'd been discussing what to do about the assassination attempt on President Reagan. Haig rushed out in front of live TV cameras he pushed Larry Speakes out of the way. Haig faced the cameras, "We're not putting the country on Red Alert Status. I'm in charge, as of now."

Lucky kept writing in her diary. The way it was told to me, she wrote, back in the Situation Room everyone was watching the live TV coverage take place in the room outside, Deaver turned to Weinberger and smiled, Weinberger nodded negatively, frowning. Deaver smiled at Meese the munchkin king, who was picking his nose.

Deaver watched Meese and cringed. White House Head of Staff James Baker III saw Deaver cringe, "Haig's not in charge, he better read his Constitution. If the President is assassinated, or hurt and can't fulfill presidential responsibilities ...then, the Secretary of State's not in charge."

Haig came back in the Situation Room. Defense Secretary Weinberger was furious, he rushed over to Haig, "You're not in charge!"

"The hell I'm not, read your constitution!"

It was Lucky's observation, Deaver's and Meese's munchkins hated Haig. They hated Haig for saying he was in charge when the President was almost assassinated ...they hated Haig for being rude pushing Speakes aside in front of TV cameras. But Haig, who was after all, her boss, said he never meant what he said to be taken the way it was taken. His relation with the White House Staff went from bad to worse.

Lucky was shocked to see staffers treat Haig so cavalierly. On the trip to the Versailles Summit, munchkins deliberately kept Haig off the President's helicopter so Secretary Haig and his wife couldn't arrive with the President ...and, assigned the Haigs to a cargo helicopter that landed in a cow pasture far behind the Presidential party so the Haigs had to run to catch up ...then, had to desperately search to find a limousine to ride in the motorcade. Barbara Bush told Lucky, the reason munchkins hated Haig was because he was pro-Israel ...munchkins were pro-Arab ...because, they were kissing the butts of the President's backers.

White House Situation Room, 1981

If the Situation Room could talk, a lot of people would listen, especially if someone played the tapes from bugs CIA had in the room, a lot of people would get sober. In one of the meetings, CIA Director Bill Casey, and Vice President Bush, got their heads together on what Bush later called, 'the Lebanon thing'. Bill succeeded in getting George to agree, send Les Aspin and Bill Buckley, who were a couple CIA operatives, on a CIA covert-ops team to liberate a mosque held by PLO terrorists.

Bill looked into George's eyes, "The Mosque is held by PLO terrorists. I want to send Les Aspin and Bill Buckley over there, in charge of enough mercenaries to terminate our terrorist problem. We have a lot of oil money in the Middle East, the World Bank, and IMF, over-lent there and I have my responsibility to my own investment bank as well as my international banking consortium's involvement. As DCI, I can't look weak."

George nodded, "Let's settle this terrorist thing."

Weeks later, there was a little political fallout after their hit team killed terrorists that held the mosque because, Les Aspin and Bill Buckley posed for photographs of them torturing terrorists and executing them, that got published in the alternative press. In following up, Situation Room hosted Bill and George, again. Bill mumbled, "Buckley and Aspen did good killing those terrorists at the mosque. I want to send Buckley back to neutralize more of them ...or, kidnap them, and their families."

"Families of PLO terrorists?" George said, "they're innocent."

Bill mumbled, "So's my stock portfolio. Terrorists impact the market globally for my investment banking consortium. Being DCI's about swinging the market back in third quarter. Keep Reagan out of the loop so he can have plausible deniability."

Bud McFarland, National Security Agency director, came in the room.

George briefed him, "We're sending a covert-ops team in to protect investments in the Mid-East, you won't be involved but we're positioning the operation under National Security Agency for deep cover. If anything goes wrong, you take the heat, not me, not Bill, not the President. That's how we play the game ... you knew the scapegoat pecking order when you bought into office, it's your turn."

Bud McFarland fiddled with a pill bottle.

Bill and George both noticed.

George whispered, "Antacid?"

Bud shook his head, "Valium."

Lieutenant Colonel Oliver North came in, saluted smartly.

A slight smile appeared on Bill's face. George greeted Ollie North, "At ease, North. I'm dispatching you to the Contras ... as a communications courier. Report back to me, when you return."

North left the room.

I walked into the Situation Room, "George, got some paperwork for me to sign for your new Special Situations and Preventative Crisis Planning taskforce? ...that pre-emptive retaliation stuff?" I took the stacked papers George handed to me, "Too much to read, what does it say."

Bush reported, "Our Contra and anti-terrorist milestones are on schedule. Paul Nitze says, Full-Court Press against Soviets is on schedule, too."

I sighed, "I take on moral responsibility for all innocent people if I let any country in the Americas fall to the Commies. Thank God, He sent Jesus to take on our sins or I could never send people to their deaths."

Bill twitched at the mention of God. Bill, a devout Catholic, was recognized by the Knights of Malta, a Catholic laity organization serving the ruling class way back in the days of the crusade, and today. Bill mumbled, "Faith isn't enough, Ronnie, to send people to their deaths when survival, covert-ops, and war are involved. There's no salvation in it, you got to think in practical terms. These are good acts we must do, to save mankind ...any good people killed in error go to Heaven, bad ones, who cares where they go."

In my heart, I agreed. "Sometimes, when I watch reruns of my old Westerns it's so simple, good guys, bad guys, right and wrong, good and evil. I want what's best for God and country but who are the special interests that run America, that I'm protecting? ...I don't even know. Sometimes, I look in the mirror, I think, 'If God gives me free will then that makes me a little god myself.'"

George understood, "We all have that, Mr. President. It's called, executive privilege."

We all chuckled. I lightened up, "George, on a lighter note, how are you doing deregulating the Savings and Loans?"

"S&L deregulation is on target."

"I trust you, I always have."

George felt his face flush. I studied Bill's eyes to discern a reaction to what me and George were talking about. Bill was smiling at some kind of inside joke only he got, like his mumbling. I looked at George, "I know you'll do a bang-up job, as usual. Let me tell you all a few stories behind the scenes in some of my movies I starred in, in Hollywood. Did I ever tell you the one about ..."

I had a captive audience.

Not long after, Bill and George met in the Situation Room, again. Bill wasn't happy, "CIA Agent Buckley's been kidnapped in Beirut, he's a hostage, they took him into Kholmeini's Iran."

George was upset, "What if Buckley talks, what if he says it was my idea, what am I supposed to do, now?!"

Casey looked in a condescending way at Bush, "Get him out of there."

"How? ...he was our expert."

Bill motioned George to come closer. Both men habitually looked over their shoulder, to make sure no one was coming in. Bill whispered, "Call Margaret Thatcher, see if we can use her MI-6 covert-ops people to pull Buckley out."

George nodded, picked up one of the phones in the room, dialed British Prime Minister Margaret Thatcher, spoke with her and hung up, turned to Bill and smiled, "On our behalf ...the British will use Leslie Aspin to approach Monzer Al-Kassar ...Monzer Al-Kassar will approach the Palestine Liberation Organization for us ...Thatcher will have MI-6 have Aspin go through Monzer Al-Kassar to meet their demands. Thatcher says, MI-6 says will trade arms through Monzer Al-Kassar to Kholmeini's regime, to get our hostages back. For God's sake, how'd we get into this mess?"

Casey mumbled, "I'm not saying I got us in it, I'm not saying you did ...or, who said what ...covert-ops is secret. Tell one person, if you have to ...its your word against his ...you were DCI, you know the score, take it through the Oval Office ...but, keep the President out of the loop ...so, he has plausible deniability ...we cite National Security reasons ...then, there's no accountability, no way to get us."

National Security Director Bud McFarland came in. Bush turned to him, "It's time to level with you, Mac. When Buckley went to Lebanon to kidnap terrorists as preventative medicine, it backfired. He got kidnapped."

Bud was anxious, he swallowed a valium to avoid having a panic attack, "Who sent him?"

Bush sighed, "Let me explain. Bill, call Ollie North in here. Mac, you back into the dark side of the room, so North won't see you."

Bud nodded, he backed into the shadows. Lieutenant Colonel Oliver North entered the room, saluted briskly, "Yes sir."

Bush smiled, "At ease, Colonel. I'm sending you over the pond to British Intelligence to help MI-6 with a little covert-ops for us, to bring back British agent Les Aspin. MI-6 wants Aspin to be our liaison with the Iranians, who are holding Buckley after he was kidnapped in Lebanon by PLO terrorists ...then, they moved him to Iran. MI-6 says Aspin will trade U.S.-made weapons to the Iranians, to get our hostages back. Hell, the allies are sending billions of dollars of weapons to the Iranians anyway, what's a few million dollars more, a scratch, we have to be practical ... dismissed."

Lieutenant Colonel Oliver North saluted, left the room. Bud McFarland walked out of the shadows, gulping another valium.

Bud was flustered, "This is illegal!"

Bill and George closed-in on Bud.

At that moment, me, Admiral Poindexter, Defense Secretary Caspar Weinberger, Presidential Counselor Ed Meese, and White

House Chief of Staff James Baker III together walked in the Situation Room.

Bill turned to me, "Mr. President, Bill Buckley the CIA Lebanese Division Chief, and six American bystanders have been kidnapped by PLO terrorists."

I was shocked and dismayed, "They never let up, do they? Spare me the details, get our hostages out from the PLO, save our people! Everyone here, go to Bush's Special Situations Crisis Management Group meeting ...that's his baby, spare me the details, bring me the solutions. This Administration doesn't compromise with terrorists, they're dead meat."

"I want Buckley back alive, he's my friend."

George nodded in agreement.

I suddenly felt I had to speak, "I've been preaching a hard-line, the White House doesn't give-in to terrorists, giving-in encourages more kidnappings, if I give in, I'll look like a hypocrite to the American people, not like a John Wayne hero."

Bill gestured to Poindexter, Weinberger, Meese, and Baker to leave the room, waited for them to leave. Bill looked at me, "Ronnie, we all have to lose our virginity. I lost mine to Allen Dulles and Bank of International Settlements. You're losing yours to terrorists, just bend over and take it, you've fought the good fight."

I took out my pocket Bible I always carry with me, "I know that one, 2 Timothy, 4:6 ... I have fought the good fight, I have run the course to the finish, I have observed the faith."

George smiled, "We all have, there's no blame, we can't be over-rigid, no one wants to negotiate with terrorists, not you, not me, not Bill." George took the pocket Bible out of my hands. He flipped through it, then read it, "Ephesians 6:12-13 ... We have a wrestling, not against blood and flesh, but against the governments, against the authorities, against the world rulers of this darkness, against the wicked spirit forces in heavenly places.' Terrorists are wicked spirit forces."

I took the Bible back, "2 Corinthians 11:22-27 ... Are they ministers to Christ? I reply I am more outstandingly one ...in labors more plentifully ...in prisons more plentifully ...in blows to excess ...in near-deaths often."

Casey cast a furtive glance at Bush, then smiled. Bush nodded back.

I continued to read, "By Jews I five times received forty strokes less one ...three times, I was beaten with rods ...once, I was stoned ...three times, I experienced shipwreck ... "

Bill listened and start thinking about the military covert-ops missions Ollie North and his team member, Richard Secord, had done over the years ...to Bill, it seemed like the Bible passage I was reading, was a word-for-word description of North and Secord's missions that, in serving the U.S., North and Secord endured the trials and tribulations of the Apostle Paul. Casey kept listening.

I kept reading, "...A day and a night I have spent in the deep ...in journeys often ...in dangers from rivers ...in dangers from highwaymen ...in dangers from my own race ...in dangers from the nations ...in dangers, in the city ...in dangers in the wilderness ...in dangers at sea ...in dangers among false brothers ...in labor and toil ...in sleepless nights often ...in hunger and thirst ...in abstinence from food many times ...in cold and nakedness." I stopped reading, "Well, if Paul could put up with all that, I guess I can put up with losing face. I can back-down on my hard-line position, you negotiate with the terrorists. Just, don't tell anyone, I'm backing down."

Bill smiled at George. George smiled back.

I felt confused then had a realization, "Can we go through a third party, so we're clean-looking?"

Bill nodded to George. George went to the door, opened it ...went out ...then, came back in the room with Ollie North. Richard Secord waited outside in another room.

Lieutenant Colonel Oliver North saluted me. I saluted back. Bill nodded to George. George smiled at me, "Ronnie, Lieutenant Colonel Oliver North is the answer to our prayers, on this one."

"I understood. I took out a pen, I autographed the pocket Bible, handed it to Oliver North. North put it in his attaché case, "Mr. President, in Nicaragua, it's too late to back out now, we're beating the Communists."

Bill mumbled something, catching North's attention, "Ollie, you're not going south of the border on this one, you're going to Israel. Israel's Mossad intelligence covert-ops teams are going to do the actual training of the Contra's for us, to give us deep cover. I want you there, to supervise, report back to me."

That bothered me, "Congress cut-off U.S. Contra aid. Are foreign nationals offering to illegally help us, by sending money?"

Casey mumbled so words never carried far, "The oil sheiks agreed but it's going to cost World Bank percentage points down-the-line, on other deals. The Israelis agreed so Israel keeps getting U.S. foreign aid, they'll do what we want."

Director of the Office of Budget Management David Stockman walked into the Situation Room, along with Defense Secretary Caspar Weinberger.

Casey turned towards them, "Weinberger, you're Defense Secretary even if you hate the Israelis, you keep weapons flowing to them."

Weinberger had a short fuse, "I don't hate them ...if we want to keep interest rates down, we have to keep the Arabs happy."

Stockman reacted, "This is another installment on our continuing saga. Weinberger ...you're sick, you're going to bankrupt the U.S. with phony military spending. Who's making all the profits? That's what I want to know."

George had taken Oliver North into a corner of the room so no one could hear them. George whispered, "Ollie, I'm dispatching you to Saudi Arabia to the oil sheiks to launder money for BCCI."

In another corner of the room, in front of a full-length mirror, Mike was brushing lint off my shoulders in preparation for a press conference. I zeroed in on him, "Mike, are you skimming-off Contra money from my campaign fund, behind my back?"

No one in the room wanted to hear the answer so everyone hurried out. Mike followed behind them as George Shultz walked in. My eyes lit up when a I saw him. I shook his hand enthusiastically, "I'm glad Haig is gone as State Secretary and you accepted the position and came onboard."

State Secretary George Shultz smiled graciously. I talked to him a long time to fill him in, then brought the conversation to a close. I looked at Shultz, "What I've just described to you is the way relationships work between Bill Casey, George Bush, Bud McFarland, and Oliver North."

Shultz didn't show surprise. As President of Bechtel, having had a leading role in the President's Economic Council, Shultz had a supply of intelligence reports flowing to him bigger than mine and for all I knew, maybe was telling the same men what do to long before I came on the scene and addressed them, and probably, long after I'd retire.

Shultz smiled, "I'm sorry, Mr. President, I'm not down with the program. What Bush, and North, and Casey, and McFarland cook up is on them. They can deceive and manipulate each other or themselves, or you ...it seems to me within a moment's notice and within a moment's thought. Are you sure you trust them enough to know? ...will they put national interest above their own private interest?"

I chuckled, "Hell no. I trust them to do just the opposite, to be exactly who they are, I depend on that. As long as they serve themselves, they serve America. They are America. That's not betraying me, they're just doing the jobs I hired them to do, whether I understand what they're doing, or not ...whether I approve, or not ...the more self-serving they are, the more I trust them. So, they have no reason to betray me. They're the most qualified men in the country to do whatever the hell it is they're doing. As long as I let them, America's safe. I support them, they are America."

Shultz frowned, "It's your neck if you hiccup."

I wondered what he meant by that and was dismayed, irritable, "You and the other Bechtel boys advised me my entire political career, since the early '50s. I've never seen you be so negative, before."

Shultz was confident of his own knowledge, knew his own abilities, was one of the most capable businessmen in the world, and one of the most influential, "Mr. President, it breaks down like this ...we have the financiers with their loans and interest rate, we have the arms makers and their provocations to increase sales, we have countries destabilized by CIA acting on behalf of the Central banks and investment bankers waiting to loan money to countries that need it, we have the big construction firms, Bechtel, Brown & Root, Halliburton, Bin Laden Construction, rebuilding countries after Bank of England's MI-6 and Fed's CIA tears countries apart ...but, when we lose intelligence operatives who are team players and they become rogue players and free agents on us ...there's no order left in the new World Order, anymore ...is there? ...it turns into a nuclear free-for-all ...doesn't it? I'm afraid Bush and Casey aren't team players for Democracy, they're free agents in it for themselves. Casey's looking after his banking interests, swinging his Central bank investment consortium into Deutchmarks, Yen, and Kugerands. Bush's looking after his oil interests in the Gulf, crapping bricks to get back his Cuban oil, and get African oil out of Angola and Sudan before his British and Chinese competition does. Deaver's on the take with the WACL death squads and Contras who, I think, are not freedom fighters at all but mercenaries protecting cocaine operations that help fund the CIA black budget ... now, I don't call all this, being 'negative', Mr. President, it's being realistic, brutally realistic. National borders are blurring, national interests breaking down into diverse money-issuing portfolios challenged by diverse ruling family portfolios all worshipping fourth-quarter profits. Stockman's right, we're bankrupting America, we better grab all we can before the country is taken over by German, Japanese, and Arab banks. I'm afraid we may be looking at the rise and fall of America, in our lifetimes."

My Irish temper was flaring, "The White House is not going to fall apart with me at the helm. Hell, we'll all make enough money we can live in any country we want to, but not me. I believe in America. Come, look at my old Hollywood movies with me, again ...you'll see, I'm the original American hero. Nothing's falling apart while I'm in charge."

I meant it.

Blair House, the White House
guest house, 1982

Blair House was falling apart. White House Protocol Ambassador Lucky Roosevelt's job for the U.S. included finding accommodations for foreign ambassadors and dignitaries visiting the White House. Blair House, the official White House guest house, was located across the street from the White House. That's where foreign visitors usually stayed. Blair House was in bad shape.

Lucky considered remodeling Blair House one of her pet projects. Lucky watched, Foreign Secretary George Shultz walked up to the porch, towards her. She smiled at him. A long, comfortable silence passed between them. The wind softly moaned. The door of Blair house blew open. Lucky and George Shultz looked a bit spooked when the door opened by itself, in the wind. Shultz recovered his composure, "Lucky, are you glad I put you in charge of fixing Blair House up?"

"Oh yes, it'll be beautiful again. And, I'm taking you up on that bet. I'm betting Blair House will be remodeled before this Administration leaves Washington."

Shultz noticed how smooth Lucky's voice sounded. He gestured they go they inside. They walked into Blair House. Lucky flipped the light switch on and off, several times. The lights didn't work. Lucky frowned.

Shultz frowned, "The electrical system needs overhauling. Tell me about protocol."

Lucky had a disarming smile, "Of course, would you like a glass of water."

Shultz nodded, "Yes, that'd be nice."

They walked into the kitchen. Lucky took two paper cups from a dispenser, went to fill the cups at the sink, turned the water tap on. No water came out.

Lucky frowned, "Maybe we could get water when we go back to the White House."

"That'd be fine."

Lucky smiled warmly, "Protocol is good manners, making the other person feel at home. State visits ...for chiefs of state such as Queen Elizabeth of Great Britain..."

Shultz noticed the wall thermostat, ripped off the wall, was hanging by electrical wires. He turned the thermostat control dial up with his thumb, he listened ...but, couldn't hear the thermostat click, or the furnace turn on.

Lucky continued, "...or President Mitterrand of France ..." Lucky said. Lucky flipped on the air conditioning while she spoke. Shultz looked along a far wall. The air conditioning unit was laying on the floor, in a pile of dust. Lucky noticed Shultz was very observant.

She kept speaking, "...usually last a week ...the President gives a state dinner..." Lucky watched as Shultz discovered the fire sprinkler systems were dripping water on the wooden floors and carpeting. "...An official visit is for heads of government such as British Prime Minister Margaret Thatcher, or, German Chancellor Helmut Kohl ...that's the same as a state visit ...except, reigning monarchs and presidents get a 21 gun salute, prime ministers only get 19 guns. Now, for ceremonial arrival at the White House ..."

Shultz wrinkled his nose, "I smell a small gas leak. Lucky, please note we'll have to get someone in here to fix that, too."

Lucky made a mental note, "There are about ten state and/or official visits a year. An official working visit is long on substance, short on ceremony, a two or three day stay gets no state dinner ...but, there are lunches and or dinners for you to host as State Secretary ...or, for the vice president to host. You personally go to the airport to greet visitors who come on state visits ...for working visits, we send the helicopter, bring them to Washington Monument ...and, you greet them there. It used to be, the President himself greets chiefs of state at the airport, security doesn't permit that, now," Lucky said. Lucky noticed that Shultz kept looking up at a chandelier, swinging back and forth,...the chandelier let go, crashing to the floor. Lucky and Shultz jumped back.

Lucky watched George Shultz react with dismay, "I don't believe it."

"I didn't either, the first time I came into Blair House."

"Please continue what you were telling me."

"In many countries in the Middle East, and Far East, the formal welcome is more important than the substantive discussions." As Lucky spoke with Shultz, they noticed Blair House guests had brought their own chefs along with them, to do native cooking ...several chefs of differing nationalities were walking in and out of Blair House. Lucky thought, Shultz found that amusing or remarkable because of the wondrous looks passing over his face. "During the Eisenhower Administration, the state visit of King Ibn Saud of Saudi Arabia almost got canceled, the King refused to come unless Eisenhower met him at the airport." Workers unloaded truckloads of food in and out of walk-in refrigerators. "King Hassan of

Morocco is heading an Arab League delegation to Washington soon and sent word, he won't come unless you meet him at the airport."

"Please remind me later at the right time."

"Okay. When Blair House closes for remodeling our guests may choose their hotel, we pay for all rooms and expenses for principals and entourage of twelve." They continued their inspection of Blair House, found the curtains torn, stained by water damage, the bedroom carpeting was dirty, bedspreads were torn and stained, soiled linen and towels were scattered about. Lucky could tell by the look on his face, Shultz had enough of inspecting Blair House for one day but she said nothing of it, and continued explaining protocol, as Shultz had asked, "If the entourage is over twelve then the principals pay for it, themselves. It's a good thing too, because many visitors feel the bigger their retinue the more important they are and come with 747s full of retainers. Generally, the smaller the country, the larger the entourage. We only pay for five limousines, no matter how large the entourage."

Shultz admired Lucky's thoroughness, "Lucky, you sure know your stuff. I'd like to continue chatting but I have an engagement. Thanks for explaining protocol to me."

Lucky was exuberant, "You're welcome." She was satisfied with their meeting at Blair House and that they shared an understanding for what needed remodeling. As Lucky and Shultz spoke, chef's assistants led five goats on leashes into the kitchen ...and, unloaded several crates full of chickens. Lucky noticed the bewildered look on Shultz's face.

Lucky tried to put him at ease, "Fresh eggs ...our Middle Eastern visitors like fresh eggs ...fresh goat milk ...fresh goat meat."

Shultz took it in stride, "Lucky, at State Department dinners I like round tables, seating ten, absolutely, no reporters at my table, nothing to inhibit conversation."

Lucky was startled, "My God! ...that man brought in a box of meat infested with maggots! I'm calling Department of Agriculture, immediately!"

Shultz noticed Lucky's boiling point, too. He watched Lucky walk to the phone. Dialed, put the phone to her ear, frowned then hung up and looked at Shultz, "Blair House phone doesn't work."

"It figures." Shultz looked at his watch, "Lucky, I've designed a menu card, as a souvenir for guests to take home with them. I don't like veal, it's too common, I hate squash."

They continued their inspection on one wing of Blair House, they found one monarch brought in his own vibrating bed and had eighteen mattresses spread on the floor for his bodyguards. Shultz and Lucky turned away.

"Lucky, I guess I've seen it all, now."

Lucky smiled and had seen enough for one day, too.

"Lucky, no tall flowers for centerpieces, they block conversation and keep me from eyeballing guests."

Lucky felt tired and managed a smile, "You've got it, boss."

At that moment the water heater in Blair House broke, filling Blair House with water.

CHAPTER 7

Versailles Summit Gala

At the Versailles Summit, Deaver's front men pushed Lucky and the U.S. Ambassador to France out of their way. The U.S. Ambassador to France complained, "You staffers and advance men have no business attending the dinner and keeping Lucky out, she's part of the official delegation ...you can't keep Lucky out, she's indispensable, Lucky must be included or I'll protest to the President."

As soon as Lucky saw a telephone, she phoned Deaver back in the U.S. She was furious but controlled her anger, "You keep your munchkins off me! ...and, off State Department. This is my first trip abroad with the President, please rein-in your munchkins so this won't happen again! I've had enough of your pushy munchkins, to last a lifetime!"

Deaver put her on hold. Standing there, in the phone booth, Lucky remembered back to 1952. Lucky and husband Archie were in Madrid, where Archie was CIA Madrid Station Chief. Archie was talking with Nazi Spanish Security Chief Otto Skorzeny ...years later Archie told Lucky, Skorzeny helped Bormann organize the postwar Odessa Nazi underground in Argentina then came to Spain to help the fascist Franco organize and train death squads to defeat anti-Fascist partisans in the Spanish Civil War ...and, that the

Dulles central bank consortium financed Franco's side of the civil war and their enemies, the anti-Fascist partisans fighting for Democracy. The other man in the conversation was Nazi Werner Naumann, who organized the postwar Nazi underground headquarters government-in-exile in Madrid back in 1943, nine years earlier. Werner Naumann planned a Nazi coup d'état to take place in Berlin in 1952 ...it was exposed at the last minute and failed.

Lucky remembered the scene Naumann created. Naumann threw his hands up in the air and the entire Nazi-run Spanish embassy was thrown into chaos by the arrival of the 'We-like-Ike' advance team there to make preparations for President Eisenhower's impending visit. The advance team frantically passed out 'We-like-Ike' lapel buttons, ignored Spanish ambassadors and State Department people, ordering around their hosts. The advance team's behavior compromised Archie's covert relations with Spanish security and intelligence services run by Otto Skorzeny, who stormed off angrily with Neumann. Lucky remembered, after Archie became CIA Britain Station Chief, Archie was treated just as rudely there by the Kennedy presidential advance teams when Lucky and Archie were stationed in London.

<>

Back at the ranch after my presidential retirement, Nancy continued researching what had gone on behind the scenes while we were in Washington, to find out who was pulling our strings. She read me the work of Mae Brussells, a college radio talk show host, who had an article published, *Nazi Connections to JFK*, in *Rebel Magazine*, commenting on Otto Skorzeny and Klaus Barbie. Nancy started reading, "By 1952, Klaus Barbie had arrived in Bolivia via a stop in Argentina. He had been spirited out of Germany by CIA, with a hand from the Vatican. Soon, he teamed up with SS Major Otto Skorzeny, now affiliated with CIA ...thanks to Reinhard Gehlen, who's whole Nazi anti-Soviet intelligence outfit had been hired by CIA. Dr. Fritz Thyssen and Dr. Gustav Krupp, both beneficiaries of McCloy's amnesty, bankrolled Skorzeny from the start. Barbie and Skorzeny were soon forming death squads, such as ...Angels of

Death in Bolivia ...Anti-Communist Alliance in Argentina ...and, in Spain with Stephen Della Chiaie, Guerrillas of Christ the King. In 1952, Otto Skorzeny, released from American custody in 1947, moved to Madrid. He created what is known as, 'the International Fascista'. CIA and Gehlen's BND dispatched Skorzeny to 'trouble spots'. On his payroll were former SS agents, French OAS terrorists and secret police from Portugal's PDID. SS Colonel Skorzeny's CIA agents participated in terror campaigns waged by Operation 40 in Guatemala, Brazil, and Argentina. Skorzeny was also in charge of the Paladin mercenaries, whose cover, M.C. Inc., was a Madrid export-import firm. Dr. Gerhard Hartmut von Schubert, formerly of Joseph Goebbels' propaganda ministry, was M.C. operating manager. The nerve center for Skorzeny's operations was in Albufera, Spain. It was lodged in the same building as the Spanish intelligence agency, SCOE under Colonel Eduardo Blanco ...where there was also a CIA office."

Nancy told me, Henrik Kruger's, *Great Heroin Coup*, talked about International Fascista, too. "It fulfilled the dream of Skorzeny ...but, also of his close friends in Madrid, exile Jose Lopez Rega, Juan Peron's grey eminence ...and Prince Justo Valerio Borghese, the Italian fascist money man who'd been rescued from execution from the hands World War II Italian resistance fighters by future CIA counterintelligence whiz, James J. Angleton." Nancy had turned into a great researcher. Nancy returned to the Mae Brussells article, "A subcommittee on international operations of Senate Foreign Relations Committee prepared a report, *Latin America, Murder Incorporated*, still classified. The title repeated Lyndon Johnson's remark three months before he died, 'We were running a Murder, Incorporated in the Caribbean'. Murder Incorporated concluded, 'The United States had joint operations between Argentina, Bolivia, Brazil, Chile, Paraguay, and Uruguay. The joint operations were known as, Operation Condor. These are special teams used to carry out 'sanctions' ...the killing of enemies.'"

Aug. 3, 1979 Jack Anderson's column carried the head, *Operation Condor, An Unholy Alliance*. "Assassination teams are centered in Chile. This international consortium is located in Colonia Dignidad, Chile. Founded by Nazis from Hitler's SS, headed by Franz Pfeiffer

Richter ...Adolf Hitler's 1000-year Reich may not have perished. Children are cut up in front of their parents, suspects are asphyxiated in piles of excrement or rotated to death over barbecue pits. Otto Skorzeny had code-named his assault on American soldiers in the Battle of the Bulge, 'Operation Greif', the 'Condor'. He continued Condor with his post-war special teams, imposing 'sanctions', meaning the assassination of enemies. Skorzeny's father-in-law was Hjalmar Schacht, president of Hitler's Reichsbank."

Nancy returned to Mae, "CIA's, Skorzeny's and Gehlen's death squads with headquarters in Madrid were additionally funded by Martin Bormann when the Evita Peron-sheltered Nazi flight capital funds were distributed after 1952."

<>

By the time Lucky was off hold and Deaver was back on the line, Lucky had a few more thoughts to share with him, "Mike, your advance team brings out the worst in everyone ...each one has a private, personal business agenda to take care of. Why don't you learn some lessons from Secret Service? ...they can be demanding, too ...but, they manage to do so without causing heartburn, or heartache. They're brave, incorruptible, discreet, good-natured and, totally professional. Why can't you and your advance teams act like them? ...would you like me to arrange to get a training person from Secret Service over to you, to train you and your staff, and advance team?"

Deaver ignored Lucky, "Okay. Lucky, help me out back here in America. I've got a photo-op set up with the President and King Ibn Saud. Will you call and have the Arabs lose their robes ... don't let 'em dress in those, 'I'm-a-rich-oil-sheik-wearing-sunglasses-fuck-you-outfits', okay? We don't like the domestic impact of that image. It hurts the President."

White House

When Lucky returned to the United States, she hardly had a moment's rest. She immediately caught heat from the protocol chief of Morocco, Moulay Hafid el-Alaoui ... a relative of the King of Morocco, King Hassan. Then, Morocco was in the middle of a bloody civil war where the King, a fascist, was defeating his democratic opponents by killing off his civilian population.

"Ambassador Roosevelt," Moulay Hafid el-Alaoui said, "... don't you agree? It's disgraceful, this rich country of America is ungenerous ...counts pennies with the King of Morocco? My king is hospitable to American officials who visit ...his Majesty provides you with any number of limos you ask for in Morocco ...but here, you humiliate us with only five stretch limos."

Lucky seethed inside, but handled matters gracefully, "Oh, Moulay Hafid! My face is blackened! Everything you say is true, your king is indeed a man of legendary generosity, no one can match his hospitality, his munificence ...but, you must understand ... my President Ronald Reagan is also a true prince, a man of great heart who wants to receive your king who is accountable to no one ...but, my President, alas, is accountable to the legislature for financial matters ...please, please, Moulay Hafid, let us hear no more about this awkward matter ...you're a gentleman ...and will not wish to embarrass me further." Lucky waived her hand in a gesture of dismissal.

The next morning, when Lucky arrived at the White House main gates, she saw a troop of oddly-dressed men wearing pantaloons and striped vests, red fezzes and pointed bedroom slippers carrying silver teapots, Bunsen burners and picnic baskets full of Moroccan mint tea leaves, escorted by the Secret Service taking out their handcuffs. The tea makers were indignant and one protested, "King Hassan of Morocco expects us to make tea for Mrs. Reagan." His tone of voice indicated he'd be in great trouble if he didn't do as he'd been told, Secret Service man handcuffing him had no regard for him, "I don't care if he's the biggest heroin dealer in North Africa, you're going to jail."

Lucky watched the scene repeated everywhere she looked and hurried over to the Secret Service man who handcuffed the tea maker, "These funny-looking guys in pantaloons and striped vests, red fezzes and pointy bedroom slippers carrying silver teapots, Bunsen burners and picnic baskets full of Moroccan mint tea leaves really are King Hassan's tea makers, they're definitely not terrorists, leave them alone, they're with me."

Lucky led the tea makers into the White House and immediately, the White House curator panicked as tea makers plopped down onto the red-carpeted floor of the main hall and began making tea. Their alcohol stoves shot out bright blue and yellow flames. The King's aide in charge of pomegranate juice was busy making the juice with a special fruit juice squeezer for the Cabinet meeting King Hassan was to attend. An entourage of servants and aides accompanied King Hassan as he approached Lucky, including the king's servant in charge of holding the king's coat and hat, the servant in charge of holding his eyeglasses, the servant to serve the king cigarettes, servant to serve coffee, servant to serve water, and several veiled belly dancers dancing around to music made by the Moroccan King's musicians who accompanied the entourage playing their instruments.

A Moroccan intelligence officer introduced himself to Lucky, "We flew in plane-loads of live lambs, our chefs and our kitchenware are to be used at a dinner the King has planned."

Lucky rolled her eyes, "I knew it! What next?!"

Bekka Valley poppy fields, Lebanon

Monzer Al-Kassar was a state-sponsored drug lord, weapons trafficker, narco-terrorist, and respected multinational businessman surrounded by belly dancers he kept on heroin, relaxing on a blanket spread in the middle of his opium poppy fields, enjoying life in the Bekka Valley in Lebanon watching his cargo of heroin being loaded onto his plane. Then, he boarded the plane, took off, and a few minutes later landed at an airport in Syria.

There, an Al-Kassar family celebration with Monzer's three brothers and his sister, a several day event celebrating his sister's wedding with her fiancé Prince Haidar Assad son of King Assad of Syria was under way. Monzer noticed his sister and future brother-in-law constantly flirting with each other, infatuated. That made Monzer happy. According to custom, when his sister and her fiancé saw Monzer watching them flirt, his sister acted shy and innocent, blushing. Monzer approved of this marriage, "How's my favorite sister?"

Monzer's sister laughed, "Your only sister."

"And, Prince Haidar Assad most powerful son of King Assad of Syria, still enjoying being head of Syrian intelligence?"

Prince Haidar was happy, "I'm making a fortune, did you bring another shipment of Bekka Valley heroin with you?"

"Let's talk business, later."

King Assad of Syria joined them, "Monzer! Welcome to this wonderful wedding!"

"Yes, it's great," Monzer said, "...the Al-Kassar family and your royal family intermarries."

King Assad took Monzer Al-Kassar aside, whispering, "I've been planning revenge on CIA since 1949, when they toppled my family monarchy, and installed their puppet regime ...my mother and father would be alive today if John McCone, Bechtel, and Bush didn't arrange that coup slaughtering my loved ones. I swore to Allah this day would come, and it's near."

Monzer and King Assad mingled with wedding guests while wedding musicians played. Monzer noticed Prince Haidar, who was standing too close to the band's loudspeakers, cover his ears with his palms, then move away.

Prince Haidar was desperate, franticly trying to block the sound from his ears. Prince Haidar Assad, Intelligence head of Syria was remembering, reliving a day he spent in Moscow in the basement dungeon of the Union of Soviet Socialist Republic's intelligence service, GRU. KGB was there, too. Prince Assad was there for training exercises, being personally trained how to interrogate a subject using torture by an instructor wearing mirror sunglasses. Prince Haidar Assad held his hands against his ears as his victim screamed, then Haidar grabbed another one of his victim's fingers, bending the finger back until the bone snapped through the flesh with a cracking sound. Haidar then held his ears because the subject's screams were shrill. When the subject stopped screaming, Haidar bent back his subject's ring finger until the bone snapped, then twisted it off, watching the subject's wedding band fall to the prison's metal floor.

Today, at the wedding, Monzer smiled as the wedding vows were being exchanged with a Moslem religious cleric presiding over the ceremony, "Take the rings and repeat after me, with this ring I thee wed."

Prince Haidar held his bride's hand, "With this ring I thee wed."

The prince slid the wedding ring over his bride's ring finger ... at the same time oddly remembering his subject's ring falling through the air towards the metal prison floor, hitting the floor as Prince Haidar placed a wire noose around his subject's neck, tightening it to suffocate his subject and the veins swelled purple, tightening it until the subject's screaming stopped and blood spilled from his subject's mouth onto the wedding ring on the metal floor of the prison. Then, Prince Haidar released the noose so his subject could breath again and not die.

Haidar gazed into his bride's eyes, repeating his vow, "With this ring I thee wed."

Prince Haidar remembered slipping the wire noose off his subject's neck, picking up a tube with an air bladder attached to one end of it then forcing the bladder and tube down his subject's throat into his subject's stomach and turning on the air pump attached to the tube, making his subject scream again while the subject's wedding ring lying on the metal prison floor was slowly engulfed in a puddle of blood flowing around it.

The Muslim religious cleric continued the ceremony, "To honor and love till death do us part."

Haidar remembered the look in the eyes of his subject's wife stretching one arm away from her captors, reaching her hand straining to shield her children's eyes, her children were horrified and crazy with fear and wildly crying ...Prince Haidar smiled because he felt so powerful, "To honor and love till death due us part."

"To honor and love," his bride replied, "...till death."

In Prince Haidar's mind, he saw the image of his subject with the air hose forced down the subject's throat into the stomach exploding the subject's stomach, the subject's wife screaming, Prince Haidar had to press his hands against his ears, his face rigid.

The wedding orchestra played, 'Here comes the bride', the sound of *Ouuu's* and *Ahhhh's* and applause of wedding guests filled the air.

The sound of the applause reminded Prince Haidar of the day he received the Soviet Intelligence Medal of Achievement from his instructor who wore sunglasses, for graduating from the torture school. Haidar kissed his bride.

Wedding reception,
palace, Damascus Syria

At the gala Royal wedding party for his sister, Monzer Al-Kassar introduced Lieutenant Colonel Oliver North to Syrian King Assad. As instructed, Lieutenant North give King Assad the pocket bible autographed by 'President Ronald Reagan' and a set of matching pistols, then saluted King Assad, noting the king was pleased. The men embraced, there was discussion between North, Monzer and the King ...North walked from the courtyard to a helicopter waiting nearby, and departed.

The wedding reception featured live entertainment. The main attraction was Prince Haidar torturing Bill Buckley. The Al-Kassar and Assad ruling families watched as Haidar forced an air hose down Bill Buckley's throat into Buckley's stomach, Haidar turned on the air pump. Using torture, he forced a confession out of Buckley.

Monzer was curious, then repulsed, but continued videotaping the tortured confession.

Bill Buckley screamed, "I swear it! Let me alone! I'm begging you! Please! It was Bush's idea to kidnap and neutralize PLO terrorists and their families, not mine!"

Monzer watched Haidar look to King Assad for confirmation. King Assad was pleased. Monzer felt pleased too and nodded to King Assad, who walked over beside Buckley, "You're in Syria, Buckley ...not, Iran ...not, Lebanon. I finance PLO with Monzer's help, and our poppies. Do you think PLO is right, or wrong?"

Buckley was weak, he felt terrified, "You're right! PLO's good! CIA ordered me to do it! CIA's bad!"

King Assad looked at Monzer's video camera, "The PLO are not terrorists, they are 'freedom fighters' fighting to get British and American troops out of the Mid-East, fighting to get Israel out of Jerusalem. PLO does not care Israel is the biggest customer for U.S.

and British arms. PLO knows U.S. foreign aid to Israel is used to buy weapons from America."

Monzer continued videotaping Buckley's torture and confession, with King Assad providing his monolog, then finished, took his video camera into the palace audio-visual lab, edited out Buckley's death so the footage showed Buckley still alive, and pleased with himself, Monzer inserted the edited tape into a tape duplicating machine, made several copies ... called in a British MI-6 agent from an adjoining room and handed him two copies, "Give these tapes to Margaret Thatcher and tell her, give a copy to Bill Casey."

Buckingham Palace,
British Royal ruling family

Early next morning, Monzer Al-Kassar's British MI-6 liaison arrived at Buckingham Palace in Great Britain, met Margaret Thatcher and handed her the videotapes, passing along instructions as told ...then, everyone went to 16 downing Street to an MI-6 office viewing room, where British Prime Minister Margaret Thatcher and British intelligence MI-6 chiefs watched Buckley's confession and torture on videotape and drank tea.

White House Situation Room

Several days later in the White House Situation Room, Monzer Al-Kassar's MI-6 liaison handed a copy of the videotape to DCI Bill Casey, who called in Vice President Bush, Foreign Secretary George Shultz, National Security Director Bud McFarland, Lieutenant Colonel Oliver North, and me. Bill started the tape.

I threw up immediately.

Bud McFarland stressed-out, having a mental breakdown and start yelling, "I can't take this job, anymore! You can shove it! I resign!" McFarland yelled into the phone, "Operator! ...get me to a mental hospital! I'm going in!"

Bill looked at George. George watched McFarland. Secret Service men rushed in with ambulance orderlies, strapping McFarland onto a portable ambulance gurney. McFarland stared then yelled, "Can you believe this shit?! I didn't do it! I'm innocent! They did it! It's not my fault!"

Casey mumbled, "That figures." Bill had expected it out of McFarland all along and looked at George. Bush looked back at Casey and shrugged his shoulders.

Mental hospital, Washington D.C.

National Security Director McFarland committed himself to a Catholic mental hospital with icon pictures on the wall of Jesus Christ, heart exposed pierced by a spear from which a single drop of blood formed, reminding the faithful Earth was a place of suffering. McFarland was stressed out, reached for his pants folded on a chair beside the bed, took out a bottle of valium pills, poured all the pills into his palm, gulped them into his mouth, took a drink of water and putting his hand on his heart, waited to die. Bud McFarland had decided to go home.

Nancy's White House office

Sitting in her office at the White House, Nancy felt nervous. Suspecting the worst, she phoned Mike Deaver, "Mike, Ronnie's in trouble, I just know it. What did they do to McFarland? Why's he trying to kill himself? What did they say to him? Is it Casey? Or Bush? I should fire someone but I don't know who, to protect Ronnie. Should I fire McFarland?"

Mike didn't know what to tell Nancy, when she was like this. He stalled, "It may not look very good if the President's wife goes on the rampage, the press will call it 'another firing spree'. Nancy, would you really fire the head of the National Security Agency after he tried to kill himself in a mental hospital?" Deaver was pleased how he expressed his point without Nancy blowing up.

Nancy didn't feel any calmer, "I have to protect Ronnie, I have to get rid of everyone who wants to hurt him! Don't you get it!?"

White House Situation Room

Bill and George sat in silence. Casey spoke first, "I'm not too upset."

"I'm freaked," George Bush said, "my dick's in the wringer. What we gonna do?"

Bill mumbled, "We'll shut down the operation."

George got upset, "If they shut down operation, the hostages will be killed!"

Bill gave George a look of disbelief, "Who gives a fuck about the hostages? I've got my consortium portfolio to protect!"

George put his hand on his forehead, "Contras will be killed if they don't get their weapons, my investments and your loans to our juntas down there will go to Hell and they're go with the Bundesbank not the Fed!"

Bill stared at George, "Screw the Fed. I'm diversified. I've got loans I can make in Africa and China. Hell, we're in the middle of destabilizing the Soviet Union and Eastern Europe with our 'Full-Court Press'. Do you think I can afford to care about lives of a few hostages? ...can you?"

"I guess not," George was dismayed, "when the one world government investment portfolio is at stake ...our British and German investors would kill us, hostages are going to die sooner or later, anyway. I just never know who they're gonna be, it puts a stain on my cover."

"Don't blow the President's cover, if he goes down, so do you."

"What about you?"

"I've been in the game too long George ... I know where the bodies are buried. I've been a player in Wall Street banking as long as your father, I was there when Wall Street started the whole intelligence racket, no one can get to me."

George didn't like the condescending tone in Bill's voice, "You should know where the bodies are buried, you put them there."

Casey got angry, yelled through the door into the waiting room, "North! Come in here!"

North came in, saluting sharply, "Yes sir."

Bill got a kick out of how seriously North took himself.

"McFarland's in the nut house, we need you. I know you're handling arms-for-drugs negotiations with the Contras ferrying our arms down there and shepherding back their cocaine shipments into the U.S. using CIA and diplomatic immunity. Vice President Bush wants you to go to Iran, to negotiate more arms-for-hostages deals."

North looked at the vice president. George nodded. North nodded back, "Yes sir ...am I being drafted into CIA?"

George frowned, "No, Ollie ...that's getting to be an old joke, don't you think?"

North stiffened, "Yes sir."

George sighed, "This is private enterprise. Bill and me are running it for U.S. national security, burying the operation in National Security Agency paperwork so you're officially working for NSA, the same cover we use for your Contra activity. Let me assure you, what you do for Bill and me goes higher than NSA or CIA."

Days later, Ollie North in civilian clothes, disembarked from a 747 in Iran.

Reagan dress rehearsal,
White House press room

In the White House Press Room, Mike Deaver rehearsed me on an anti-drug speech. Looking distracted, he flipped open his wallet, pulled out a few bills. Mike hated being behind on his bills ...to make it worse, he only had about 1,700 dollars in his wallet. Behind Mike, a Contra in a brown military uniform held a briefcase, waiting. Mike glanced at the Contra and the briefcase, smiled in relief, took out his flask form his inside coat pocket and had a nip of vodka. Mike waved at me, "Ham it up, Ronnie! This is something you believe in, remember? Be convincing as hell."

"I'll turn up emotional involvement on this one." I start delivering my speech in earnest, suddenly adding anguished emotional overtones, as if the speech I was giving mattered to me.

Mike nodded an okay to me, motioned the Contra over, took the briefcase, opened it and saw it was full of money and taking out a couple stacks of hundred dollars bills, put them in his briefcase while I continued rehearsing my anti-drug speech.

Exclusive men's club, Washington D.C.

A few days later, I was delivering the same speech Mike had rehearsed me on, in an exclusive men's club in Washington. I considered myself animated, a hardline cold-warrior. I walked to the podium, began my anti-drug, anti-terrorist, anti-Communism speech to the elite group of businessmen there especially for my presentation.

Exclusive men's club, London

A few days later, I flew over the Atlantic to London for a meeting with Britain's MI-6 intelligence leaders. I gave my anti-terrorist, anti-Communism speech again ...for me, it was giving the same speech over and over again. I'm glad I had good speech writers. In a room on the other side of the building, Oliver North, Les Aspin, Monzer Al-Kassar, and a MI-6 handler were cutting weapons deals, considering various weapons-for-hostages scenarios that would be a win-win situation for everyone involved in negotiations and trades ... and ensuring the Bank of England, Fed and Bundesbank would launder approximately three trillion dollars each year in illegally derived heroin drug money.

The MI-6 intelligencer opened a briefcase showing it was full of money, put a few stacks into his pocket then pushed the briefcase to Aspin. Aspin pocketed a few stacks of money then pushed the briefcase to Monzer Al-Kassar, who tossed some money stacks to North. North had a look of doubt on his face. Monzer Al-Kassar smiled coldly, "I want to stuff some of this money in your uniform between your shirt buttons, it's not for you, it's for your Contra support efforts."

North had a question, "Is it true what Aspin said, we can make 125 million dollars profit on a 250 million dollar arms deal selling U.S. missiles?"

Monzer Al-Kassar nodded, "In a heartbeat ... welcome to the ruling family world of terrorist financing and big business ...there's profits to fund your Contra war and all Casey's private wars, enough profit for your black budget operations and to kickback all your Congressman's campaign funds."

Leslie Aspin was troubled, "I'm worried about my brother, he worked with U.S. Customs Intelligence, he's the one that informed CIA's Wilson and Terkil sold 100,000 stinger missiles to Libya through Kaddaffi ...I don't trust him."

Leslie Aspin remembered the arguments he and his brother Michael got into.

Aspin home, London

In his London home, Leslie Aspin was in another argument with his brother, Michael ...over money, "Michael, I'm telling you, this is a sweet deal, 125 million dollars in profit cut three ways, just the first one of many!"

Michael Aspin already lost patience with his brother, "You're crazy! You're in bed with British, American, Syrian, and Soviet intelligence ... you're gonna get crucified by all those double- and triple agents! I won't let you do it!"

Leslie stared in disbelief at his brother, "You did it with CIA in Libya! You middled their arms and drug deals! You made a fortune! Now, you won't let me?!"

Michael was more upset, "It almost cost me my life! I was a cut-out, a set-up! So are you! You're blind as a bat!"

Michael flipped his Leslie an obscene gesture so Leslie would bugger off ...Leslie left the room. Michael picked up the telephone, dialed and waited, "Is this U.S. Customs Intelligence? Give me the director. Hello. Michael Aspin here, remember me? I gave you Wilson and Terkil. Now, I'm giving you North, MI-6, Monzer Al-Kassar but you have to get my brother out alive."

Nancy's White House office

In her White House office, Nancy reached over to get her lines from her speech writer, Peggy Noonan. Nancy rehearsing her lines different ways trying on different emotional angles, sad, angry, concerned, impatient, happy, thoughtful. Nancy looked at Peggy, "Now, this is the speech for the crack-baby ward, about the toddlers and kindergarten-age kids at the hospital born addicted to crack?"

Peggy agreed, "That's right." She tried not to anticipate First Lady Nancy Reagan's reactions, apprehensively waiting to hear Nancy's approval or criticism.

Nancy questioned her, "This line here, 'I've just come from seeing crack-babies at the hospital, I've seen things so terrible I can't even describe them.'"

"Yes?"

"I'm not even scheduled to go to that hospital maternity crack-baby ward until after the speech!"

Peggy was tossing pearls before swine, "It's a good line, it'll draw people to you."

"Oh ... I'll keep it, then."

Peggy had approval and relaxed. Nancy was getting in the flow of the speech Peggy wrote for her, rehearsed more lines, "How does it sound, this way?"

Exclusive women's club, Washington D.C.

In a Washington D.C. exclusive women's club, First Lady Nancy Reagan walked to the podium, ready to deliver the speech Peggy Noonan had written for her. Nancy took pride in being a fashion plate, she liked to make the best appearance possible, she liked earning the attention of her audience by delivering her same, 'Just Say No', anti-drug speech, time and time again. Each time Nancy delivered her, 'Just Say No', speech she made it sound brand-new, fresh, like she'd just thought of it. Nancy and Ronnie were actors, both knew how to deliver lines to an audience, both knew how to play then hold a house.

GRU counterfeiting room, Moscow

While First Lady Nancy Reagan delivered her speech at an exclusive women's club in Washington D.C., half a world away in Moscow in a GRU-KBG printing shop, Monzer watched 18" x 24" sheets of counterfeit American $100 bills roll off the printing press, signaled to his men who then went over to the trimming machines and trimmed then stacked packs of trimmed bills into cardboard boxes, put the boxes on dollies and wheeled them onto the loading platform beside Monzer's private jet. Monzer told the pilot to go first to Iran, then Bahrain. At Bahrain, Monzer Al-Kassar took the boxes full of counterfeit money to BCCI to have them laundered, exchanging dirty boxes for clean boxes of legal American currency.

In the U.S., Nancy continued giving her, 'Just Say No To Drugs', speeches at every opportunity just as if they mattered or made a difference.

Bekka Valley poppy fields, Lebanon

Monzer Al-Kassar arrived at his Bekka Valley poppy fields in Lebanon in his Soviet handler's helicopter, landing near his own jet where they were greeted by belly-dancers from Monzer's harem who'd just fixed on heroin moments before the helicopter landed. Monzer got off, watched the Soviet helicopter fly away, and within minutes two other helicopters set down ...one had a British flag painted on it ...the other, an American flag. From out of the British helicopter, stepped Leslie Aspin ...from the American helicopter, Oliver North stepped out. Both men were greeted by drugged belly-dancers.

Outdoor brunch speech
by Nancy, Washington D.C.

Throughout Washington D.C., Nancy preached her, 'Just Say No To Drugs', anti-drug speech to different audiences at different locations, daily. Habitually, she took methamphetamine pills to bring her up that made her so excited her eyes sparkled, then start giving her, 'Just Say No' speech at an outdoor brunch, looked up into the sky and watched a 747 and thought for a moment it was a giant bird and, realizing it wasn't, got upset, reached into her purse and grabbed a few Miltown tranquilizers in her hand, popped them in her mouth, drank some water from a glass on the podium felt dizzy, felt shaky and, wanting to come down, took another pill.

A murmur passed through the audience as more and more people noticed what Nancy was doing. Nancy kept taking pills and she wasn't sure if she was taking the right pills, or not. So, she took a couple more of each. Nancy felt desperate. She didn't notice the murmur growing in the crowd. She didn't notice the people seeing what she was doing but she knew that night she'd have to take several Miltown downers to cancel out the speed uppers in her system so she could crash and sleep. Nancy felt giving her 'Just Say No To Drugs' speeches every day was becoming demanding, boring, too much to ask. Yet, Nancy was able to find strength to continue giving them because Nancy believed in her cause ... it made good press and that helped Ronnie and knew everyday Americans believed in her. Nancy looked up into the sky and thought, "It's not a bird, it's a 747."

Onboard Air Force Two

The 747 flew high over Nancy, as she gave her 'Just Say No To Drugs' speech at the outdoor Washington D.C. brunch ...the 747 was Air Force Two. Onboard Air Force Two, Leslie Aspin and Oliver North sorted *Playboy Magazine* center-page foldouts ...behind them, their aides sorted kilos of cocaine and kilos of heroin into several stacks on a lounge couch on the plane. Les Aspin and Ollie North were getting off on contact highs from the smell of the drugs in the air and each man was boozing it up. North smiled. He was the one who thought of taking the centerfold pictures out of the magazines onboard Air Force Two.

North's aide was sweating, "Heroin from Monzer Al-Kassar to the Contras goes here."

Leslie Aspin looked at a centerfold, "Right."

Oliver North tried to concentrate but he felt too relaxed to bother thinking. North's aide kept working, "Cocaine from the Contras, to the Syrians via Monzer, goes there."

Leslie Aspin yawned, "Got it."

"Cocaine from the Contras," the aide continued, "...and heroin from Syria via Monzer Al-Kassar goes to pay off the Azima brothers in Kansas for guns Azima brothers ship to the Contras and for the missiles Azima brothers ship to Monzer Al-Kassar who gives the missiles to Afghanistani Muhajidin for CIA."

"Got it," Leslie Aspin said, not really paying attention.

North busily sorted centerfolds, "One for you and, one for me. One for you and one for me."

North's aide put a few kilos aside in separate piles, while far below them on the ground beneath Air Force Two, First Lady Nancy Reagan finished her 'Just Say No To Drugs' speech at the outdoor brunch feeling woozy, sat down on a lawn chair drinking another glass of water, tilted her head back to watch the 747 fly by, swallowed another pill and feeling dizzy, fell off the chair onto the lawn.

<>

I was at a garden party Katherine Graham was giving in her Washington D.C. mansion ...Katherine published the *Washington Post*, a CIA media asset. I was giving my anti-drug, anti-terrorist, anti-Communism speech. I raised my eyes over my audience in the garden, looked up into the sky, and watched Air Force Two fly by overhead, tipping its wings.

<>

In Air Force Two, North and Aspin were busy ... their aides sorted kilos of coke, smack, and bills of laden. North listened to an announcement the pilot made over the cabin speakers, "We'll be arriving Kansas in 90 minutes, 90 minutes, Kansas the land of freckle-faced blondes, gapped teeth, red checkered shirts and blue denim coveralls, barefoot in waving field of grain who grow up to be centerfolds."

Hours later, the pilot circled over a private landing strip Azima brothers built on their farmland in Kansas. The plane landed, taxied to a stop. Oliver North and Leslie Aspin got off the plane. Oliver North immediately saw Azima brothers throwing an outdoor picnic,

picnic blankets spread all around the grounds covered with kilos of cocaine and heroin, open crates of weapons, missiles, cardboard boxes full of money. Monzer Al-Kassar and several Contras walked to North and Aspin and started shoving stacks of money at them.

At Katherine Graham's mansion, I was animated delivering my 'anti-' speech ...every time I gave that speech, the audience loved me, cheered me on. It was Hollywood, all over again.

<>

In Kansas, Monzer Al-Kassar was determined to influence the arms-for-drugs-for-hostages deal his way, "I want more Stinger missiles for Afghanistani Muhajidin, I'm expanding into their opium and heroin trade."

North listened, noting the Azima brothers smiled in reaction to whatever Monzer said. Monzer handed North an attaché case full of money, took a few stacks of money out and put them in his pockets for 'business' expenses, closed the briefcase, handed it to a Contra who handed some kilos of cocaine to North who handed a Stinger missile and bill of laden for the Stinger missile shipment to the Contra. The Contra held the Stinger missile and bill of laden for the missile shipment up. Monzer gave several kilos of heroin to the Contra and the Contra handed the Stinger missile and bill of laden to Monzer. Monzer traded more kilos of heroin to the Contra in return for more kilos of cocaine from the Contra. Finally, Les Aspin and Monzer returned to a plane and took off. Ollie North and the Contras got into Air Force Two and took off.

CIA headquarters, Langley Virginia

At CIA headquarters in Langley Virginia in the communications room, CIA Agent Pollard intercepted a radio transmission. Unknown to CIA, Pollard was a 'mole', a double agent betraying CIA and on the payroll of Israel's Mossad intelligence service. Pollard intercepted a radio signal originating in the Mediterranean ocean, indicating unusual shipping traffic in shipping lanes used for drug and weapons trafficking. Pollard listened to the sound of his radio crackle then picked up his phone to report his findings. "This is Pollard, hello? Is this Mossad? Unusual traffic in drug and weapons trafficking shipping lanes off Greece in Mediterranean Sea towards Cyprus."

Mossad Israeli intelligence building, Israel

In Mossad intelligence headquarters in Israel, director of Mossad picked up his phone. He was CIA-Mossad double-agent Pollard's handler, recognized Pollard's voice immediately. Pollard was excited, "Unusual traffic in shipping lanes used to smuggle weapons to Arab terrorists. You better look into it, deposit my check in my Swiss account."

The Mossad intelligence director hung up the phone then called director of Greek intelligence, "Hello, this is director of Mossad, Greek intelligence please ... I've been tipped-off about possible arms-smuggling vessels off Cyprus, see what you can do to stop them, we don't need PLO terrorists with more weapons to attack Israel or Greece."

Onboard weapons-smuggling ship, off Cyprus

Onboard the ship smuggling weapons, a seaman fastened down a tarpaulin the wind had blown off several weapons crates stamped with the Azima brothers shipping logo, firmly securing the tarpaulin as a Greek Navy coast guard cutter intercepted the ship and boarded it, finding the weapons crates. But, all the Greek Navy found inside the crates were 60 Czech machine pistols Leslie Aspin was smuggling to Iran to test the security of the smuggling route. But, Greek Navy also found 250 tons of weapons no one could account for.

When Leslie Aspin learned of the bust, he phoned, "Monzer, they busted our gun shipment. I lost 60 Czech machine-pistols I was smuggling in to test the route ...I didn't even know about 250 tons of weapons onboard. I presume you were secretly piggy-backing my smuggling route."

Monzer felt betrayed, "Get off the phone, Aspin. Bust's are the risk of doing business ...deal with it ...it doesn't matter, I'm insured through Lloyds of London. I'm not upset."

White House Situation Room

Bill finished talking, hung up the phone, "Well, they busted your first underground arms shipment to terrorists."

George Bush was surprised, "My load?! We're in this together."

"MI-6 told me, it was insured through Lloyds. I'm not too upset about it."

"That makes one of us."

"Business-as-usual in this racket."

George stayed upset, "Don't get the president's dick caught in the wringer."

Bill was frustrated, "We can't deal direct through MI-6 now, we need a scapegoat. I think Israel should take the blame."

I kept quiet as long as I could, then turned to State Secretary George Shultz, "They told me they had good ideas to try out, you know my management style. I hire people to make their own decisions."

Bill looked at me. I looked back at Bill then George Bush, "What are you guys trying to do to me? I didn't do anything wrong."

Shultz spoke flat out, "Congress said, no more Contra aid. Sending Ollie North abroad to get foreign national support for the Contras ...not to mention authorizing sale of weapons to a terrorist country ...might be an impeachable offence."

I was vulnerable, "You're all twisting it around! You know, I don't like details! I manage my people, I don't do their work! I didn't tell him, do that! I'm being taken advantage of! You're using me! I don't like it!"

Shultz spoke calmly, "It came out of the Oval Office, that makes you responsible."

I pleaded, "I'm innocent I tell you! I don't know what to do. I trusted you guys. Now I don't. You misled me. You sold me out. It's not supposed to be this way, my approval rating's gonna suck, we'll all be hanging by our thumbs in front of the White House if anyone finds out ...should I take a chance, go on TV, tell my side of the story to the American people or, play it safe and hide?"

Bill seemed to enjoy me squirming, "That's your choice, time to close-up shop, do damage control, pursue alternative routes, plant disinformation cover stories. I'll set up Israel as our arms-for-drugs scapegoat to take the blame for us ...put us in the clear."

I felt myself racing emotionally over the top, "I don't want to know! I'm going to keep trusting you, do your jobs. I'm going to pretend none of this is happening. I'm going to focus on my Summit meetings with Gorbachev and the Russians, enjoy this presidency for a change! Paul Weyrich and the Free Congress Foundation are running a Full-Court Press to destabilize the Soviet Union and Eastern Europe ...coordinating our anti-Soviet foundation fundraising activity ...disseminating the money to our Eastern European nationalist apparatus ...along with the money they got from money-issuing family investment consortiums in Britain, France, Italy, Germany, Israel and Saudi Arabia. Gorbachev will have to have the commies go bankrupt to finance fighting all the insurgencies we've started in Eastern Europe and in Soviet Union ...he'll have to negotiate. You take care of the Iran-Contra business, just solve it. Leave me out of it. I have to fight the Russians ...I can't be bothered with details, do your jobs!"

Bill was sleepy, his head felt heavy, his eyelids were closing, he dozed off, starting to talk in his sleep, "Get a piece of Russia, use Iran, Iraq, Afghanistan, Turkey, India, China, a Cold War picnic ...use death squads, as usual." Bill laughed in his sleep.

It was amusing. I turned from Bill to Shultz, "Bill's not a bad guy ...when he's asleep." Everyone laughed. I felt good, I'd pleased everyone. "Leave 'em laughing," I said, leaving the room with State Secretary Shultz.

As soon as we had left, Bill opened one eye, looked around, watched the door close, opened his other eye, turned towards George Bush, "Is he gone?"

"Yes."

"He's the one who falls asleep in meetings, not me. That's what my media assets tell me. I'm using the same assets to set-up Israel to take the blame ...it's all worked out already."

George was surprised, "You amaze me, Bill, you're the intelligencer extraordinaire, I respect the hell out of you, when you're like this."

Bill was pleased, "MI-6 will have Israel run a parallel arms-for-hostage operation ...I will then inform on it ...bust them and me at the same time. I'll hire a hundred freelance operatives to hire people, make bogus deals ...I'll tell all of them to say they have the 'go-ahead' from Vice President Bush, himself."

George didn't expect this in a hundred years, "From me? I'm not giving any go-aheads."

Bill smirked, in his smug way, "Of course not ... I'm going to lie. I'll pretend they have go-aheads ...I'll tell everyone, they have your approval to make deals ...I'll tell them, they can run operations on your say-so ...that they have your approval to set-up and run arms-for-hostages deals. I'll dateline it. Then, we bust everyone who says they're working for you ...there'll be legal confusion and congressional investigation teams will claim its hearsay when everyone says they had your approval. If Aspin or North or Al-Kassar get busted and say they're working on your authority ...nobody will believe them because, everyone and their uncle's been 'crying wolf'. I'll plant a couple dozen disinformation stories in the press, have the press focus on our fall-guys to take attention off you."

George knew he didn't have a choice, "Like you planted those October Surprise disinformation stories to discredit Carter."

Bill felt flattered but was defensive, "I never said, I did that."

"You didn't have to, your fingerprints were all over it, it's the touch of the master."

Bill smiled his reptilian smile, "The 'old boys' call that, 'the Midas touch'. Now, what we'll do first, is arrange to have an 'Anti-terrorist Summit' in London during the day ...at night, we get together in private to work out trades between North and Monzer for hostages, kapeesh?"

Café in open bazaar, Turkey

In a Turkish bazaar café, Monzer Al-Kassar addressed a meeting he'd called of all the terrorist leaders of the Middle East, feeling proud, powerful they regarded him as the supreme narco-terrorist in the world. Monzer looked at his friends, "As your leader, I welcome you, freedom-fighters of the Arab world ... here today to get your orders, from me. They call us terrorists ...but, we're not terrorists because they made war on us with their coups in Egypt, Syria, Algeria ...they're the terrorists ...the colonialists enslaving us ...we're victims fighting for our freedom. The United States is the invading power in the Mid-East, they've robbed us ...we'll drive the invaders out with help of Allah!"

Texas Ranch

Monzer's private jet cut through Mexican airspace, to Texas airspace then landed on a Texas ranch owned by one of the largest landowners in Texas, where Contras were trained. Monzer got up from his waterbed onboard his jet, left his harem girls and dressed. Monzer had his crew unload crates of kilos of heroin, telling them, exchange them for crates of kilos of cocaine the Contras had brought to the ranch. Monzer and the Contras also exchanged crates of weapons at the Texas ranch.

Private airstrip in Kansas

Monzer then flew to Kansas to meet with Leslie Aspin, gave Aspin money which Aspin gave to Azima brothers, who continued to use a vegetable exporting front to mask their international arms dealing. Supervised by Azima brothers and Oliver North, crates were packed with rockets and rocket launchers ...disguised with cabbages put over the hardware. An Azima plane was entirely loaded with crates, marked 'cabbages'.

North felt victory in the palm of his hand, "More cabbages for the Contras! Great. We've got the cabbages, do you have enough cabbage launchers?"

London daytime
anti-terrorist Summit

Bill, Leslie Aspin, and MI-6 reps went to the anti-terrorist Summit in London that Bill arranged. The summit was attended by official state reps during the day. Bill was the first speaker at the private, day-time summit. Bill mumbled, "Have Israel ship the arms for us to the PLO ...we already have them train and ship arms to the Contras for us."

A British MI-6 director nodded.

Bill kept speaking, "I want Israel to take the heat when the whole shabang blows up in the press."

The MI-6 agent was amused, "That's what Israel's for."

But ...at night, behind closed doors, they held their own private terrorist summit, where they planned and negotiated arms-for-hostages deals, capturing larger shares of the heroin and cocaine money-laundering traffick, rated the Bormann organization based in South America on how cooperative they were last quarter, and argued Bank of England's arguments for raising or lowering the Fed's interest rates to reduce or increase the value of billions of dollars of U.S. treasury bills owned by China and Saudi Arabia.

London evening
terrorist summit

In a nutshell, in the day they held their anti-terrorist summit and during the night they held their terrorist summit. Bill attended private and secret terrorist meetings, where he was met by Monzer Al-Kassar. He shook Monzer's hand warmly, "Monzer, how are your BCCI accounts growing?"

Monzer was pleased with Bill's civility, "Good, Bill. Did you have a good anti-terrorist meeting today with Margaret Thatcher and MI-6?"

"Yes. She does a good job for House of Windsor, keeping 1001 Club, P-2, Vatican Bank, Opus Dei, and Knights of Malta inbound on recolonization of Africa and South America. She's a little shabby on recolonization of Eastern Europe but plays a good game of catch-up and does well in Asia." Bill enjoyed speaking knowledgeably ...he knew how much he could safely say and walking the line amused him so he felt enthused, "As I said, she's a little sloppy with economic counter-intelligence on the destabilization of Soviet Union and Eastern Europe. By the way, I have a warehouse full of those Stinger Missiles you wanted, but half must go to bin Laden and his Muhajidin to support our World Anti-communist League 'Full-Court Press' to destabilize Soviet Union and Eastern Europe on Russia's southern flank on Afghanistan and Pakistan poppy and Baku oil fields."

Monzer smiled, "No problem, as long as you continue to give my Middle East heroin shipments CIA protection and keep giving me diplomatic immunity in and out of the U.S."

"Fine." Bill poured Monzer and himself another gin-and-tonic out of an iced pitcher.

Monzer smiled, "How many percentage points did you pick up in your portfolio when you and the Pope destroyed the labor unions in Poland?"

"Recently? ...or in World War Two."

"Not when you built your portfolio using the Office of Strategic Intelligence," Monzer said, " I mean, now ...with CIA help ...when you, and the Pope had AFL-CIO sell out when you both 'turned' or killed off labor leaders in Poland."

Bill wasn't going to let out a thing, he knew when to keep his mouth shut, "You mind your central bank, I'll mind mine."

Monzer's laugh was condescending.

Bill noticed the aire of superiority in Monzer Al-Kassar's laugh. Bill wasn't offended by it. He kinda liked resentment of authority.

White House press briefing room

Not having attended the anti-terrorist summit in London and back in Washington D.C., I stood in front of a mirror practicing angles on my good looks. In a few minutes, I had an entrance to make to address newspaper and TV news press. I peaked through a window curtain, watching reporters pushing and shoving to get the best seats to interview me. I was sadly amused. White House Spokesman

Larry Speakes smiled, "Press conference time, reporters are waiting, time to go get 'em, champ."

I smiled confidently at Larry. I liked something about him, even if he was more East Coast than West Coast. I walked behind the briefing room podium then began to address newspaper and TV news reporters. I acted serious, "I'm disappointed, people think I know what's going on around here, in this Iran-Contra fiasco. Nothing's going on. I know nothing about any arms-for-hostages trade ...it's against stated White House policy to negotiate with terrorists. I'm shocked and disappointed, about these rumors."

When I finished my speech, Larry ushered me away from the podium then he briefly addressed the reporters, "Ladies and gentlemen of the press, that's it. No questions, not one. Sorry. Bye." Larry listened to the groans of the press fade as he ushered me between Secret Service guards into an adjoining hallway then to an adjoining private room. Larry smiled at me, "Good job, champ. We'll have the public approval poll results in a few minutes." The phone rang. Larry picked it up, listened for a few moments then hung up. The eager look of anticipation faded on Larry's face. He was sad, "That was Deaver, bad news. Your public approval rating's down, people don't believe you didn't know what was going on ...the public thinks you're lying."

I didn't think I could brave faking a smile, so I didn't even try. I felt sad, "That's awful."

Iran-Contra Hearings

Nancy and me attended the Iran-Contra Congressional Hearings when Admiral Poindexter and Lieutenant Colonel North testified. Nancy cowered, seeing they were trying to implicate me. That infuriated her. Nancy watched the congressional chairman pound his gavel. She jumped because the sound startled her, and took another pill to calm down.

The chairman addressed the hearing, "We strongly suggest in the future, the President consult with Congress. We outlawed additional U.S. aid to the Contras. The fact, Mr. North circumvented Congress is not to our liking. It's U.S. policy not to negotiate with terrorist states, Iran, Syria, Algeria, and Lebanon. Iran-Contra Congressional Investigation Committee commission finds Oliver North guilty ...however, we grant him immunity, because he agreed to testify. We didn't call Vice President Bush, or CIA Director Bill Casey to testify because we ran out of time. We allowed only three months for this investigation, because of upcoming elections. We started our investigation focusing on mid-1980s with the revelations, Israel was involved in arms-for-hostages negotiations with Iran, a terrorist state."

The spokesman smiled at Bill ...I felt indignant. Nancy watched Bill and George shake hands, each looked satisfied. Bill felt smug, amused. George stared at Bill with awe in his eyes, "Bill, how'd you pull this off?"

Bill mumbled, "Extortion."

The spokesman continued, "This Commission finds President Reagan probably didn't know the extent of his subordinate's arms-for-hostages negotiations. That's because of his management style of fully delegating responsibility. We find, the President had no mal-intent. We find the President genuinely did what he felt was best for the hostages, for America and for the American people. We find the President not guilty of any wrongdoing."

I felt relieved and the gloom lifted off me. I smiled into the cameras. I started to leave the hearing room. Nancy felt relieved, elated. She started to leave with me.

On my way out, I ran into Bill. I didn't like his cavalier, devil-may-care attitude, "I was feeling disappointed in myself. But, Congress exonerated me to the American people ...I see you with the devil-may-care look on your face, it stirs-up my Irish blood. It makes me mad as hell! Don't get me into something like this, again!"

Bill kept an eye out for trouble, "Mr. President, your Secret Service bodyguards are too far behind you, it's best you slow yourself down a bit, wait for them, you never know."

I sensed the threatening tone in Bill's voice. It frightened me, like he was sneering at me. I pushed through the crowd towards Nancy, we met and embraced. I felt good, I saw Nancy beaming with happiness, "Nancy, I still don't know, should I go on TV, tell the American people my side of the story or should I stay off TV ... play it safe."

Nancy smiled, "Whatever you think is best, Darling. Just tell the truth, like you always do, it'll be okay."

White House press briefing room

A few days later, in the White house in a private room adjoining the press briefing room, me and Mike Deaver were chatting ...soon, I was going to meet the press with a live, televised statement. I watched through the one-way mirror Secret Service used to monitor the press briefing room.

The room was packed with reporters. Mike felt the weight of being in charge of my public approval ratings and as usual, Mike was there beside me each time I appeared in front of TV cameras. Mike felt responsible for my public image, "Ronnie, I'm not sure you making a public appeal is the right thing. Will it raise your public opinion rating? ...or lower it? You refused to rehearse in front of our focus groups ...that leaves me out in the cold ...I can't guarantee this, one way or another. But, I respect your decision to go on the air, to tell the truth."

I felt positive, "Mike, I've nothing to hide. I did what was right. I'm going to tell the truth."

"Heaven help you, here's to you." Mike took a nip.

I walked into the press briefing room, standing in front of the TV cameras, smiling, "I've come before the American people to tell the truth from my heart. As you know, both the Iran-Contra committee and the investigation group I commissioned found me innocent of wrong-doing ...yet, it appears there was done without my knowledge, by Oliver North acting on behalf of National Security Agency, some arms-for-hostages bargaining that, was partially successful. I didn't know anything about this, while it was going on. But, this is my Administration, the buck stops here. It's been the policy of the White House, my Administration, my policy, American policy and policy of the American people not to negotiate with terrorists. But, some of this did go on. I want to say, in my heart, I didn't mean to trade guns-for-hostages. I didn't mean it, in my heart. I hope you understand.

I hope you forgive me, I didn't do anything wrong." I finished my statement. The camera technicians and reporters clapped, then the microphones were turned off.

I saw Mike open another bottle of vodka, refill his flask, take a nip. Mike greeted me, "A couple more seconds, the poll will be in. Here it is. You're public approval rating is up ten points! You did it, Ronnie! You did it! I learn something from you, once in a while. When right and wrong comes down to a public apology, then everything's okay. I wouldn't have believed it unless I'd seen it, myself."

I felt exonerated, forgiven, I felt like a winner, "Ten points! That's great! I'm vindicated! I've been forgiven by the American people! For something I didn't even do!"

Mike was relieved, "According to the polls, people didn't care if you did or didn't ...just that, you did it in Kholmeini's Iran."

I frowned, "I wish there was some way to get rid of Khomeini, he's a real pain in the ass."

CHAPTER 8

White House bedroom

The days went by, one party after the next. I flipped calendar pages on my desk calendar, seasons changed from summer to fall. One night in our White House bedroom, Nancy watched me fall in and out of sleep. Nancy was thinking fast. She whispered to me, "Ronnie, wake up! Shsss! Don't say anything, the room's bugged. Sleepy, wake up! We're going for a ride, to have a private talk."

"Can it wait til tomorrow?"

"No!"

I protested, "We've got speeches tomorrow."

Nancy was determined, "That's good ...they'll think we went to bed. We'll sneak out. You'll hide on the floor of the car."

Dressed in robes, we headed out our bedroom, down the stairs, into the kitchen ...but, had to get past a Secret Service guard.

Nancy approached him, "A midnight snack, you know how it is."

The guard smiled. Nancy could see he was hiding cookies behind his back. We walked past the guard, into the kitchen then sneaked out the back door. I watched Nancy's derriere as she walked ahead of me. Outside, we ran behind the trees til we got to the garage, entered a side door, got into our car. Nancy spoke quickly and quietly, "You know the drill." I got down on the floor of the car and hid, Nancy drove out the garage onto the streets of Washington D.C.

Washington D.C. streets

Nancy drove us through the streets of Washington D.C., knowing we could talk in private in our car. I looked out, we drove along. Nancy was apprehensive, "Jupiter, the head god is conjuncting Mars, god of war. Maureen's seen the ghost in the White House Lincoln Room again. She hasn't figured out what it's trying to tell her. Why hasn't it gone over to the other side? Joan Quigley says, it's dangerous."

"Outside the White House ...or, inside it."

"Huh?"

"Nuclear war with Russia? ...or, infighting between my staff and cabinet?" As we spoke, I relived some scenes from a war movie I starred in. The car heater was on, I dozed off, dreaming.

Nancy touched my arm, "Ronnie! Wake up!"

I was sleepy, "Where am I?"

"You're here, Ronnie."

Well, at least I was here, "I guess I dozed-off a few seconds, I'm okay. I was dreaming, fighting to save American lives. Trying to figure out what's going on? ...who's calling the shots?"

Nancy was all over the map, "I asked Joan to ask the stars. When she does our charts next week, she'll schedule our White House meetings to coincide with good celestial and planetary vibrations. The last time I was in her flat in San Francisco, we had a séance around a crystal ball." Nancy remembered the séance, well ...Joan's house was full of crystal balls, amethyst crystals, peacock feathers, chakra magic wands, eerie posters of magical, supernatural, biblical, and angelic scenes. Nancy sat with Joan Quigley at a card table. There was a crystal ball in the middle of the table.

In the dimly lit San Francisco flat, Joan Quigley looked inquisitively at Nancy then stared into the crystal ball between them, "The stars impel, they don't compel. I see danger. I cast your charts, made your schedules for the Russian and German summit meetings, and the G-7."

Nancy was thrilled ...now, she felt safe again, "Good. Is it safe for

Ronnie to go? I'm so worried, all this Russian, 'Evil Empire', stuff he's been saying to the cameras ...if I was Russian, I'd be pissed off, I'd want to get even."

Joan had plenty to say, "Ronnie's should cut out that 'Evil Empire' crap, it stirs up shit."

Nancy drove our car through the Washington D.C. streets, "Joan says the planets say you have to knock off the evil empire bit, it's like watching old reruns, bad for the box office, gets you more bad reviews than good ones."

I wasn't pleased, "Those are some of my best lines. I've got to please the far-right, Nancy, Weyrich's Free Congress Foundation and the 'Full-Court Press' people destabilizing the Soviet Union and Eastern Europe are okay with the 'evil empire' bit ...they're my inspiration for it. But, Republican National Heritage Committee Nixon set up because he owed Dulles, kicks in a lot of campaign money ...gets out the ethnic vote for us ...but, those people are a bunch of lousy Nazi's and fascists, killers, sociopaths. They scare me."

Nancy cringed at the thought, "Ronnie, aren't those Republican National Heritage Committee people the leaders of death squads Bill Casey's using to destabilize Soviet Union and Eastern Europe?"

"Yes, they're real Nazis and Fascists, just like in movies I starred in." I went into a daze reliving my times on the set I killed Nazis, shooting them, fighting hand-to-hand combat remembering the Hollywood crew kept backing the camera away from the action. Nancy glanced at me, saw the strange look on my face, wondered about my mental condition.

< >

On the other side of town, Bill Casey was asleep ...dreaming about his visits to Allen Dulles at Fort Hood in 1945, in lavish officer's quarters just at the close of World War II. Bill watched Allen Dulles give several Nazi SS officers U.S. Generals' uniforms to put on. Nazis changed uniforms. Allen Dulles shook their hands. The phone start ringing. Bill felt confused, he was in the same room with Dulles watching him, but, at the same time, Dulles was on the other end of the phone line, too! "Yes, Bill, everything's fine, you're worse than J. Edgar Hoover, don't worry."

Bill was upset as he spoke into the phone, "I've got as many central bankers up my ass as you do, I'm lending against my portfolios, too ...is it a done deal? ...have you hired Hitler's intelligence people to start the CIA? ...have you started them activating the Christian West Plan to overthrow our Russian allies? ...are they going to train American death squads? ...I see ...it'll be called, Special Forces, or, Green Berets? ...they're going to fight alongside Otto Skorzeny's Nazi Werewolf death squads, underground in Russia and Eastern Europe ...now? ...when World War II is scheduled to end?"

"Yes! ...your limited prospectus investment portfolio is safe, good bye!" Bill tossed and turned, mumbling.

<>

Nancy wanted to stop the car to look at my mental state, I was so involved with what I said.

I was angry, "Dulles, Casey and Eisenhower never should have brought Nazis and Fascist financiers and generals and spies into the U.S. I don't care how much the German and British and American central banks are in bed together ...I don't care, how much the Nazis and Fascists financed the Republican Party before, during and after World War II ...I don't care how much campaign kickbacks they give now!"

Nancy saw how excited and troubled I was, she didn't know whether to humor me, calm me down, or talk sense to me, but she stayed calm, "But, Ronnie, we were a part of that in the '50s, you were the main public speaker advocating CIA's Christian West Crusade For Freedom ...you take responsibility for that."

"I do! ...but, in the '50s it was different. When I helped them, I was a confused man in mid-life crises with stars and stripes in my eyes. Hell, do you think I can live with myself, now? ...do you think I like the Nazis and Fascists that fill my campaign fund now? I can't stand them! Even Bush can't stand them ...and his father is one!"

Nancy knew she had to do something quickly, to get control over the situation before it got out of hand. "Calm down, Ronnie. It does no good to complain. We made our bed ...we have to lie in it. Grab hold of yourself, calm down!"

I felt the concern in Nancy's voice, "All right. Am I getting carried away, again? It's just my pet peeve, Honey. By the way, Billy Graham stopped by the White House the other day, told me Daniel was put in the lion's den because you shouldn't believe astrologers are more powerful than God."

Nancy was relieved I'd changed subjects, "Ronnie, this is the real world. Get a life."

I didn't understand what Nancy mean. I knew she had my best interests at heart, I shrugged off her comment.

"Joan's a good astrologer. She was right about the assassination attempt on your life, she's been right about scheduling all your summits ever since. We're keeping her! ...no matter what Billy Graham says. What are Carter's Naval Intelligence people telling you is going on behind the scenes in your White House?"

I perked up, "They're wrong, Bush and Casey aren't setting me up as a patsy. No one knows what's going on behind the scenes. And, I'm the president! ...an actor walking around on stage saying this and that, it means nothing ...who's telling the people who tell me what to, what to do? What's going on? Who's calling the shots? Don't ask me, I just work here."

"My spies said it was North, Halper, Cline, and Casey."

I was surprised, "You have your own personal spy staff?"

"Yes, just like George Bush does with his interagency task forces. I want answers. I want you to be safe. We're in this pretty deep, aren't we?"

I was amused, "If it gets any deeper, we'll come out in China. George Shultz will take care of it, he's a good man."

Nancy wanted to know enough to take care of it, herself, "I know, I figured it out. Casey's using Bush, Bush's using Ollie, Ollie's using McFarland and Deaver, Deaver's using you. That means, Deaver's lying to me! He'll be sorry! Everyone set you up as Mr. Plausible Denial!"

I already knew that, going in, "I like being Mr. Plausible Denial, Nancy, it's a good part for me to play, I think I do it well, it worked for Iran-Contra, I'm in the clear, I like that."

"How long has this been going on?"

I broke it to her slowly, "From the beginning."

Nancy felt hurt, "Why didn't you tell me?"

"Two reasons, Darling. I wanted to protect you, and, I wanted to give you ..."

"...Plausible denial. Thank you, Darling, that was considerate. I've got some questions. What does Casey get out of it? What does Bush get out of it? What does North get out of it? My astrologer can't help us, unless I know enough to ask her the right questions. She's the one who got me in touch with my spiritual higher power, that's how I found out what I know. Gorbachev's assistant uses an astrologer, too. Hitler did. The Pharaohs did. All world leaders do ...it's natural."

"So, you followed our astrologer's suggestion and hired personal spies?"

Nancy was vindictive, "My spiritual higher power told me, do it. I'm so afraid ...there's so many people out there I need to fire to protect you, and there's so little time. Deaver says, I have 'firing fever' again ...he's right. Who made money from this Iran-Contra arms-for-drugs-for-hostages smuggling ring?"

I knew that 'get-even' tone in Nancy's voice, "I don't know ...it makes me question my basic values ...I wonder if the drugs were there to finance the Contras, or the Contras were there to protect the drug lords ...if it had nothing to do with anti-Communism at all, just a shadow government of big business drug-runners."

"Don't worry, Joan will fix us up with her Vedic astrology charts, they're better than European or American charts, by far." Nancy looked for a place to park. She pulled the car over, to look in my eyes while we talked. "You still angry about Iran-Contra?"

I loved Nancy could read me so well, "Yes. I gave Casey hell, today. But, I'm not angry at you. You always know what I'm feeling, I love you."

"I love you too, Darling ...what's really bothering you? What are you most angry about, Honey."

A worried look come over my face, I bit my lip thinking about what to say, "I'm angry because, I'm worried ... my whole White House staff, and my Cabinet's, corrupt ...how'd it ever get to be this way? ...was it always this way and I never saw it? I'm supposed to be saving America, not getting America sick. Am I losing my ability to judge character? ...losing my ability to lead America? ...am I getting too old? ...is my thinking fuzzy and messed up? ...I forget things, I get things all mixed up."

Nancy watched me carefully to see if I could handle it or was falling apart.

I kept talking softly, "Were the drugs there to finance the Contras, or the Contras there to protect the drug lords, which came first, the chicken, or the egg? Deaver's being investigated by a grand jury for lobbying for Contras, back-channeling foreign aid back into campaign fund chests for bribes. George Bush's son got Contras on Medicaid in Florida. Casey's got me bankrupting the country so his central banks can loan us more money ...he's buying up national debt bonds faster than his German and Japanese central bank buddies are. All the interest from the national debt goes to them! It's like that Errol Flynn movie with the spies, my whole staff and cabinet is corrupt except George Shultz and Lucky Roosevelt. What am I gonna do?"

Nancy sighed and relaxed to see my mind was working okay, we were talking intimately, again, "It'll be fine, Darling. You'll take care of it, you always do."

I felt funny but was serious, "Why am I so talented in picking out crooks to work for me in government? It'd be different if I knew they were crooks ...then, at least I could take credit for it. How's it gonna to reflect on my judgment? What will the American people think of me?"

"Our approval rating's gonna suck."

"How can I get people to approve of me?"

"I made a new list of people to ax, in the meantime if we want to stay alive and prevent more assassination attempts, we better 'go along to get along."

I felt desperate.

Nancy looked into my eyes, "If we want to stay alive, we better do the best acting we've ever done."

<>

We sat in silence in the dark. I broke the silence, "You're right, Darling. I'll ask Casey for help, and if he's being blackmailed. That'd help explain the confusion and intrigue around here. I've got to know, what kind of a guy is he? But, my mind, I feel it starting to go, Nancy. I'm so afraid."

Nancy doubted herself, it showed in her voice, "You're doing fine, Darling. Don't worry, everything'll be okay."

"Maybe it's not senility or Alzheimer's, maybe I'm being poisoned to death like President Roosevelt was."

"Stop kidding around, that's just a White House old wives' tale."

"No, I looked it up," I said. "His son said he was poisoned by two Byelorussians painting his portrait while they had tea, he collapsed, his son said they were spies, double agents working for German intelligence."

"Ronnie, the Russian spies are really working for German military intelligence, the German spies are working for Russian military intelligence, Israel's spies are working for British intelligence and British intelligence is working for American intelligence. American intelligence is infighting and competing like brothers and sisters for political funding and financial portfolio point growth for one client or another, the CIA's out to destroy Naval intelligence because it's patriotic, rogue ex-CIA agents are working against mainstream CIA agents, big business is against little business."

I held my head in my hands, trying to clear my thinking, "Nancy, stop, I'm not up to this. I can't feel anything for anyone anymore except you, nothing and nobody else matters to me ... I don't want to be old being taken advantage of, I want to be a young man again, swimming in the river, watching the clouds, I wish I never went into politics, I wish I'd never been an FBI spy, I wish I could undo my life, undo all the mistakes I made and live life all over again. I'd do things right this time. I want to forget it all, Nancy, except loving you."

Nancy felt tears in her eyes, "That's really sweet, Darling ... Ronnie! A car's followed us!"

I was scared by the fear in Nancy's voice, "Is it one of ours?"

"How would I know?"

I knew I had to protect Nancy, "I hope it's not a god-damn terrorist. Let's go back, Nancy."

"I'm trying to." Nancy started the car engine, put the car into gear, sped off down the street.

"Try to shake them!"

"I'm trying to."

We drove through the streets. The car behind us started to fall back. I felt better, "There's the White House! If we can just make it there!"

White House, Aug. 21, 1983

At the White House, Lucky was waiting for Corazon Aquino to arrive on a visit, watching Deaver's advance men rudely walk around. She had to correct one of them, "The campaign trail that qualified you as a Deaver munchkin, isn't a course in diplomacy. You're thrown off by your shadow, project your shadow on others that attack it, feel attacked by someone else's shadow when it's really you, attacking yourself and all hell breaks loose. Remember, Amir the King of Hell on Lotus Mountain bowed down with his shadow legions to Buddha."

Deaver's advance man didn't have time for this, "I don't know what you're talking about. Get out of my way, Lucky ...here comes our photo-op. Mrs. Aquino! Will Mr. Aquino be coming?"

Lucky and President Corazon Aquino of the Philippines, eyes wide, stared unbelievingly. "No, my husband will not be here," Corazon Aquino said, "he was assassinated last year."

"Oh, sorry," Deaver's advance man said. "Can you turn a little more to the right for this shot?"

Lucky took Cory Aquino aside into a Ladies room, "Oh, Cory, I'm so sorry. I'm so humiliated by Deaver's advance men!"

Economic Summit in
hotel, Williamsburg, VA

Arriving in Williamsburg, a day before the Economic Summit, Lucky checked into her hotel room, disturbed when she tried to use her special phone to the White House that the line was dead. Lucky called a White House communications aide to her room, held up the dead phone for him to see. He nodded, "It's dead, one of the White House staff told me, cut off your phone."

Lucky was shocked, "What?"

"Sorry, ma'am, White House staffers don't give reasons."

Lucky hated the munchkins.

Restaurant in Williamsburg

Lucky's boss, State Secretary George Shultz, invited her out to dinner, they were seated. Lucky didn't know where to begin, "I'm so angry with Deaver's White House staff, I'm keeping it in. I don't want them to force me out the way they did Haig. I'm an innocent, my mentors were men like my husband Archie, a CIA career man. He regards serving David Rockefeller as a privilege, calls serving his country an act of higher calling, that serving one's country is something one chooses to do rather than to make money, noblesse oblige. I never saw much of the breed who get presidents elected, the advance men, the media manipulators, the dozens of men and women who make the campaign successful then stand in line with their hands out ...expecting to be rewarded in a spoils system of political appointments."

Secretary Shultz thought Lucky was a sharp cookie, honest, forthright, smart, sincere, trustworthy, and very attractive. He was glad Lucky worked for him. Shultz tried putting her at ease, "In this administration, advance types and media photo-op people ended up being White House Staff. To them, they form the trappings of a court ...but, this is their first encounter with real power. For many of them, it's their stepping-stone to big money in the private sector. They think, conducting foreign relations is like being on the campaign trail. With mindsets like that, you get heroes ...or, bums. This White House Staff divides and reproduces itself like cancer."

Lucky felt good her boss saw it that way. She was disgusted with Deaver's munchkins, "They're little shits, mental mice."

Shultz chuckled, "Inelegant but descriptive. Mike Deaver deals from strength but he's overwhelmed, his staff smothers him ...he's the eternal advance man, nothing escapes his attention, he's the President's shadow. The President's surrounded by shadows. Deaver's a movie director, sets the scene, spins the scenario, gets his actors in place, for him its, 'lights, camera, action'."

Lucky wondered, if George Shultz what psychological shadows were, the dark side of man ...the personal fears deep inside unknowingly projected onto others who then become targets so you're shooting at the things you don't like or fear in yourself ...if that's what he was talking about.

She had a few things to say about Mike Deaver, "Mike Deaver's devoted to Mrs. Reagan, and the President. He winds them up, sets them like an alarm clock. No one else can deal with Mrs. Reagan's whims and desires, make her hidden agendas into dynamos, milestone them out, track them, make them happen, and all the time keep her hand from showing."

Shultz was still chuckling, "Deaver could be Reagan's closest friend, his dearest adviser ...but, he's your designated liaison with the White House, you're stuck with him. Deaver wields a lot of power, most of the time he influences the President in a positive way, he's pretty well-counseled, for a Staffer."

"I'll never forget the day I came to Mike's office after he persuaded Reagan to call Israeli Prime Minister Menachim Begin to demand the Israelis stop bombing Lebanon," Lucky said, "almost all my family lives there, I'll always be grateful to Mike for that."

"Everyone's human. Lucky, if you let them get your goat, they'll win. If you go public, trying to protect yourself, they'll do to you what they did to Al Haig ...turn everything around like it's your fault, say you're petty, worried about perks."

"Should I be direct with Mike? I'm afraid if I am, he'll stab me in the back."

"It's your call."

Lucky looked at Shultz curiously. Shultz smiled at her. He looked at his watch. Lucky left.

*Jefferson Room, State
luncheon, White House*

Lucky coordinated a State luncheon, with Secretary Shultz hosting the President of Portugal. She'd seated herself beside the Portuguese Chief of Protocol, a smooth-talker. One of Lucky's aides hurried over to her, whispering in Lucky's ear, "You like the way I put the luncheon together? ...eight round tables of ten each, vermeil vases, slim as candlesticks, flowers above the sight line so the Secretary can eyeball everyone."

Lucky cringed, "It's beautiful and too late to change it, you know Secretary Shultz doesn't like vases of flowers on his tables."

The aide shrugged, walked away. Lucky and the Portuguese protocol chief made small talk. Lucky heard someone hit a spoon against a glass, calling for everyone's attention. That surprised Lucky, no one was scheduled to speak. Secretary Shultz stood up to propose a toast, "Ladies and gentlemen, I hope you've had a chance to admire the beautiful flower arrangements in the center of each table. However, these luncheons are designed for conversation and eye contact, which the flowers impede. Therefore, I ask the waiters to remove the centerpieces, so we can get on with the luncheon."

Lucky was floored, in a long and awkward silence, embarrassed. Everyone knew it was her job to do things right ...now, things were wrong. Lucky noticed the Portuguese protocol officer's amused expression. He tapped her on the hand. Lucky didn't want to talk to anyone right now, she wanted to be invisible, "I want to disappear."

The Portuguese protocol officer pointed to the menu card George Shultz had designed as mementos to be taken home by his guests. Lucky saw the Portuguese protocol officer was pointing at the word, 'Schultz'. "I didn't know the Secretary spelled Shultz s...c...h, I thought it was s...h... I think that's another 'no-no', an unpardonable sin."

Lucky was humiliated.

White House formal dinner dance

That evening, was a formal dinner dance at the White House. Lucky read the name cards at the table ...she rolled her eyes, she was seated right next to her boss, Secretary Shultz. Seeing Shultz enter the room, she sat down before he got there. She tried to prolong a lack of contact between them. Then he said, 'hello'.

She had to answer, "Mr. Secretary, why don't you fire me now, get it over with, so we can enjoy the party." Lucky watched the twinkle in George Shultz's eyes, heard him chuckle, had the feeling he'd already forgiven her.

Secretary Shultz looked into Lucky's eyes, "I got your attention, didn't I?"

Lucky rolled her eyes. George Shultz asked her to dance. Next day, Lucky coordinated a luncheon for Mr. Eanes, a guest of Defense Secretary Caspar Weinberger. Weinberger waved Lucky over to his table, "Recognize those flowers? They're from yesterday, the ones your boss had taken off his tables. I had my Pentagon people negotiate with Shultz's State Department people for the vases and flowers Shultz didn't want. Like 'em?"

Lucky was bewildered and looked at the flower arrangements on the luncheon tables, how beautiful they were, "Yes, they are beautiful."

President's trip to Beijing, China

Lucky looked out the window at the ground below, as Air Force One circled the Beijing Airport runway. The plane landed, slowed to a stop. Lucky felt irritated, Mike Deaver made everyone wait in the plane except his advance team. She watched them go down the gangplank, to set up photo-ops. Lucky felt more upset, when Deaver ordered Cabinet officers and Ambassadors to exit the plane using the rear steps of Air Force One.

No one was allowed to leave the plane until, Nancy and me disembarked. Lucky knew Deaver wanted photos of me being first, to show to the American people on TV. Lucky and the Ambassadors followed Cabinet members off the plane. They walked along on the tarmac. Lucky saw one of Deaver's advance men. He was yelling at Secretary Shultz, who was walking in front of the delegation, with Chinese officials, "Mr. Secretary, move away from the President, we need a clean photo!"

Lucky got more upset, clenched her fists, stormed over to Deaver, "That's it! I promise, I'm not going on any more trips overseas with the President, if your munchkins run them!"

< >

When we got back in Washington, Alfred Bloomingdale, our confidant and the husband of one of Nancy's best friends Beverly Hills socialite Betsy Bloomingdale, was partying at a sadomasochism party. He picked up Vickie Morgan as a submissive woman, hired her, had her sign a slave contract in return for him signing a series of checks. He beat her, whipped her and played with her for sex however he wished and she had to obey ...then, he died of unrelated causes. His sex slave sued his estate. The newspapers loved it. Nancy's friend confided in her. Nancy stood by her friend through thick and thin. Her friend told the press, Nancy is a loyal friend, a beautiful person. Nancy was glad to read something positive about herself in the newspapers. I walked in on Nancy, and her girlfriend, who was crying. Nancy held her hand. "Ronnie, her husband's dead."

"I'm so sorry."

Nancy's friend had made peace with her husband's death, but not with his mistress, "He had an S&M mistress! She's suing me for millions!"

I gave Nancy a look, I didn't get it ...that, Nancy took to mean, 'What can I do?' Nancy knew, "There's allegedly a group sex video circulating, talk of blackmail ...but, the little slut who slept with him, her roommate beat her to death with a hammer."

I didn't know what to make of this, "... A smoking hammer?"

Nancy didn't find that amusing, "Can you get Bill Casey involved?"

That seemed to me a rhetorical question, "Sounds like he already was."

Nancy knew I was talking about the hammer murder ...the implication of Casey being involved shocked her. It shouldn't have. There's only one way you know where the bodies are buried.

1984 Normandy

Deaver came up with a photo-op for me that sent shivers down my spine. I'd be meeting with G-7 business leaders in Europe on the anniversary of D-Day. That was when Allied soldiers landed in France to liberate Europe, to end World War II. Deaver decided to stage the photo-op of my lifetime, when I made my 1984 visit to the Normandy battlefield. Deaver set my speechwriters to work. They found a letter sent by the daughter of a soldier describing her father's hope of someday returning to the battlefield to respect his fallen comrades. The day finally arrived. I stood on rolling grassy hills covered with thousands of white crosses in rows from horizon to horizon from sea to sky. I stood, surrounded by old veterans who'd actually fought against Nazis on the Normandy Coast in 1944. Deaver arranged for the woman who had written the letter about her father to be there. I moved closer to my toe-marks. I felt secure, once I found them ...I knew cameras would be getting the best viewing angles on my profile. I saluted the graves and spoke to my audience, "I've come here to salute the sacrifice of those who helped destroy Hitler and the Third Reich, liberate France, liberate Europe, to end World War II. Here, on the Normandy cliffs overlooking the Atlantic Ocean, forty years ago Private Peter Zanatta, whose daughter is standing beside me, landed on this beachhead. Peter Zanatta was an ordinary American citizen. He fought here, watched his friends die fighting the enemy. He did what he had to do, he kept on going. His daughter wrote him a letter. I want to read part of it to you today. 'Dear Dad, I'll never forget what you went through, Dad, nor will I let anyone else forget. And Dad, I'll always be proud.' That's what this patriotic woman wrote to her father. I'm telling everyone here today, and everyone at home watching this on TV, that yes, we're proud. We'll always remember. We will always be proud. We will always be prepared, so we'll always be free." I started to cry. I brushed a tear off my cheek.

Nancy started to cry. Deaver did too. There was not a dry eye in the audience at Normandy. Reporters swarmed around me for an impromptu press conference. CNN's Alan was there on assignment, "Mr. President, your speech was beautiful. It moved me. Would you describe your Administration's Arms Control Policies?"

I was partially deaf as I grew older. I turned my head to hear more clearly. Unexpected questions often confused me. I stood there with a blank look on my face. Nancy went into action. Nancy whispered, "Tell them we're doing all we can."

I smiled, "We're doing all we can."

White House

My Presidential tour of Europe featuring the Normandy photo-op, ended. Everyone was back at the White House. Deaver immediately start using camera footage of my Normandy photo-op in TV commercials designed to get me re-elected as President in 1984, for a second term of four more years. Deaver rehearsed me for the TV spots, "Remember, we want to keep Mom and apple pie flying the whole time. Get them to feel redemption, patriotism, and family."

I read my note card, "We see an America where every day is Independence Day, the 4th of July."

Deaver was satisfied, "Good. I'm cutting in a montage from footage of you at Normandy. That good piece, you wiping a tear out of your eye. I'm glad I told you to cry, when you hugged old geezers who fought there. I want to re-record what you said. The wind was blowing, fuzzied your words. It's the next note card. Let's do it. Take 1."

I read my next note card, "You're the best damned kids in the world."

Deaver felt things were going his way, "Great. Only one take. Now, I cut in footage of you standing at the border between North and South Korea, you stare grimly into Communist territory. Then, I cut-you-in at the Olympics hugging an American gold medal winner. We overdub it with a voice, that says, 'America's coming back!' Then, we get the Marlboro man. He brushes dust off his cowboy costume, starts rolling up his sleeves and says, 'We rolled up our sleeves, showed that working together there's nothing Americans can't do.' That's America."

Treasury Secretary Don Regan watched the rehearsals for the first time, with Larry Speakes, "You mean, every moment of every public appearance is scheduled? Every word scripted? Every place where Reagan's supposed to stand, taped with toe marks?"

Larry was amused, "Ronnie's been learning lines, making his face pretend he's feeling one way or another, hitting toe marks for half a century ... that's what qualified him to be President."

I overheard the first part of their conversation and felt compelled to defend myself from looking dumb, "You know, what makes me happiest? Each morning, I get a piece of paper that tells me what I do all day long. My job is acting a script. Characters come and go, the plot goes forward. A lot of people don't know if I'm a President playing an actor or an actor playing a President. For me there's no difference."

Deaver walked over to Don Regan, "It's true. I'm his stage manager, producer, director. I hire stage and sound crews. If they mess up, the scene doesn't work. We shoot more takes, til our focus groups laugh or cry, feel patriotic, or angry ...whatever, we want the public to feel ...then it's a wrap."

I was an expert on my home turf, "In show business, drama is when you suspend disbelief in the audience. You get them to believe in the illusion, to make-believe. If an actor believes what he's saying, the audience does. Remember that. It might help you out, some day."

Don Regan felt awkward, "Mr. President, James Baker and I decided to switch jobs. He's gonna to be, Treasury Secretary ...I'm gonna be your new Chief of Staff."

I was confused, "I didn't know that. That true, Mike?"

"News to me."

"We're gonna wait til you're re-elected," Don Regan said. "We want your okay."

"Okay. As long as Mike keeps giving me that piece of paper every day that tells me what to do. Are we done shooting, today? ...Mike."

Larry turned to Don Regan, "You don't get along with Nancy, do you? You're gonna have to figure out how to stay out of her way. Get on her wrong side, she's death on wheels."

Don Regan smiled, "So am I."

Mike looked at his clipboard, "Ronnie there're a couple more election photo-ops coming. In your last speech, you said corporations shouldn't be taxed, at all. I knew that'd need damage-control. The opinion polls agree. Tomorrow, I'm flying you to a working-class bar in Boston. I want you to drink beer with bar-flies. Make it look like a scene from, Cheers."

"Okay, you're the boss."

Ed Meese had something bothering him, "Your damn Education Secretary, Terrell Bell, got tired of us pressuring him to cut education budgets to schools, telling him to make teachers preach more discipline and morality. He put out some stupid, 'liberal' report to the press demanding we reform education. I'm gonna have our Conservative backers throwing gasoline on me and flicking their Bics."

Mike knew what Ed was talking about, "That's the, 'Nation At Risk', report. It demands more Federal funding of schools. It says, 'If an unfriendly foreign power attempted to impose on America the mediocre educational performance that exists today, we might have viewed it as an act of war'."

Ed fumed, "How you gonna fix it?!"

Mike took a nip of vodka, "Give me a second."

I cracked a joke, "Maybe we can get Nancy to fire him."

Ed took it seriously, "That's a good idea. After, we're re-elected."

Mike had a brainstorm, "This is what we do. We get a re-election campaign photo-op with Ronnie standing with Bell. Ronnie endorses the report. Ronnie makes a bunch of, 'excellence in education', speeches. We'll have a teacher-of-the year ceremony in the White House. I've been talking to NASA already. They're gonna give us a, 'Teacher In Space' program. That's damage-control."

Ed liked it, "Then, after we're re-elected, we fire Bell, get a 'conservative' in there."

I needed to get a laugh, "It's a take." No one laughed. I was deflated.

Deaver's face lit up an ideas, "That photo-op, where I had you pose at Handicapped Olympics. Leslie Stahl of CBS picked it up ...but, said you pushed Congress into cutting Federal support for handicapped."

"Shit!" Ed couldn't believe it.

Deaver frowned, "Stahl showed footage of Handicapped Olympics with Ronnie standing there, smiling ...surrounded by kids in wheelchairs and balloons and flags. I called Stahl. I thanked him for the five minute pro-Reagan spot. I told him, 'Haven't you people figured out yet, that pictures override what you say?'"

Don Regan was surprised learning how my White House Staff operated.

Deaver was all systems go, "Ronnie ...in these re-election spots, we're gonna limit and focus the public mind to you talking about a few issues. Cutting taxes. Being against abortion. Promoting Strategic Defense Initiative Starwars. You can see, how taxes hurt. You can see, how SDI can aim a laser beam to shoot down a missile. You can see, the fetus in the womb kicking away from the needle. That's what you want your audience to feel."

"Okay."

"We're gonna show you happy in a bunch of White House official ceremonies with other statesmen, waving from helicopters, reviewing parades, reviewing troops, enjoying yourself, having the time of your life."

"That'll be easy" I said, "...because, I am."

< >

In the 1984 presidential election, I was re-elected in a landslide over Carter's Vice President, Walter Mondale, winning forty-nine of fifty states, nearly sixty percent of the popular vote. My chances of winning weren't harmed when, during the week of the Democratic National Convention, I played to the audience with one of my favorite jokes, "My fellow Americans, I'm pleased to tell you today, I've signed legislation to outlaw Russia, forever. We begin bombing in five minutes."

< >

I always used that line for sound checks for my radio addresses. I spoke the lines when there was lots of tension between the U.S. and Russia. I guess, a lot of people have no sense of humor ...because, it left some people questioning my understanding of the realities of my foreign policy and international affairs. But, it was part of my scripted lines on the note cards, designed to show Russia ... we didn't take them seriously.

In 1984, the title year of British intelligencer Aldous Huxley's book, *1984*, describing British society run by Big Brother, I honored Whitaker Chambers posthumously with a Medal Of Freedom award as a champion of democracy.

< >

It wasn't till I retired, Nancy read me books all the time, that popped another of my bubbles. Whitaker Chambers, at Columbia University, made himself a name as a literary writer. Chambers later held jobs at, *The Daily Worker* and, *The New Masses*. He supported himself doing freelance translations. Some of his associates thought Whitaker Chambers was a Nazi spy. Edwin Sievers, another literary figure, met Chambers, had dinner with him at Chamber's house in Newark, New Jersey. Sievers walked in Chambers' apartment. On the wall he saw a life-sized portrait of Adolf Hitler.

A letter, Ms. Dorothy Sterling wrote to the *New York Times* was published in 1984. Ms. Dorothy Sterling was a *Time* employee from 1936 to 1949, assistant bureau chief in *Life Magazine* news bureau, from 1944 to 1949. She'd worked with Whitaker Chambers, when he was foreign news editor, at *Time*. In her letter published in *New York Times*, Mar. 11, 1984 ... she denounced Whitaker Chambers for distorting news and inventing war-related stories to fit his right-wing viewpoint. The letter was called, *Whitaker Chambers, odd choice for Medal of Freedom*. "To the editor ... many of my former colleagues at *Time* will share my feeling of consternation at the news that the Medal of Freedom is to be awarded to Whitaker Chambers posthumously. We still remember his reign as *Time*'s foreign news editor, which began in the hopeful summer of 1944, when Allied armies were marching across Europe. *Time*'s foreign correspondents, men like Charles Wortenbaker, John Hersey, Richard Laterbach, Storan Probitivich, and Percy Knauth, reported the emergence of popular governments backed by partisans who'd been fighting Hitler. The readers of *Time* never saw these dispatches. Whitaker Chambers suppressed them, rewrote them, distorted them, tailoring the news to make it conform to his own right-wing view of world affairs. From Paris, Charles Wortenbaker protested *Time*'s story of '*Red Riots*', which had been substituted for his cable describing France's orderly new local governments. Probitivich's reports from Yugoslavia, telling of the slaughter of partisans by Drosimer Hylovich, never saw print. So many of John Hersey's stories from Moscow were suppressed, he stopped sending political news and confided cables to accounts of Shostakovich's newest symphony and other cultural events. Reporting from China, Theodore H. White saw his criticisms of Chang Kai Chek's autocratic regime replaced with warm, glowing praise of Chang as a defender of democratic principles. When researchers in *Time*'s New York office protested the inaccuracy of the foreign news reports, Chambers habitually replied, 'Truth doesn't matter' ...facts were altered to fit his anti-communist crusade. Eventually the correspondents' protests resulted in an investigation, Chambers was made an editor of special projects, a position he held until 1948, when he named Alger Hiss as a communist. Whatever views one may hold about the Hiss case, there is no doubt, Whitaker Chambers perjured himself during a grand jury investigation, and changed his testimony repeatedly. During the first trial, when Lloyd Paul Striker said to him, 'Lying comes easy to you', Chambers replied, 'I believe so'," Dorothy Sterling said.

Waldolf Astoria, 1984

The Beijing China trip seemed to have happened ages ago. I had a speech to give at New York's Waldorf Astoria Hotel. Nancy felt paranoid, occasionally looking back over her shoulder wanting to make sure we weren't being followed or recorded. Feeling the coast was clear, she smiled at me. I was dismayed, "God, I wish I could trust my judgment, every time I appoint someone they embarrass me. Is it me, Nancy? ...is my mind going?"

Nancy had noticed, she was answering that question from me more often these days. She didn't like it, "No! That's foolish! It's not you, Darling. You can't be responsible for everyone, you can't be responsible for the whole country."

"You really think so?"

Nancy was upset, "If we get out of this job alive, that's enough for me. We can't beat Satan and his underworld any better than God can. I love you, Darling. Break a leg."

I appreciated that, we kissed. I went onstage to deliver my speech, "When a man or a country questions one's own ability to be a leader in the world, or in his own neighborhood, or in his own house, he measures himself by Bible virtues of hard work, honesty, and spunk. John Mariotta provided jobs and training for hard-core unemployed in the South Bronx. This businessman's faith in God moves mountains. He helps hundreds of people who'd almost given up hope. People like Mariotta are heroes for the '80s." I watched a spotlight scan the crowd, it stopped on my friend, John Mariotta. I was happy.

John Mariotta addressed the crowd, "The success of Wedtech, my defense contracting company, comes through a joint venture with our silent partner, God ...and the Ronald Reagans of our society."

Nancy noticed Ed Meese was jovial. Ed felt all-powerful, greedy for more of whatever he could get and met with me later that evening back at the White House. Ed noticed I seemed fidgety, "What's up, Ron?"

"I have to confront you about these 'rumors' of your criminal activities."

Ed laughed til he wheezed, "Really? Why? You always trusted me before."

"Why? ...because I put your name in to be head of the Justice Department then they made you head of the Justice Department ... because I trust you. This is for your own good, as well as mine. Did you file false tax returns?"

Ed shrugged.

I didn't let him answer, "Did you illegally retain stock in companies doing business with Justice Department? Get illegal payoffs from parties for government favors?"

"C'mon Ronnie, lighten up. I'm head of the Justice Department of the United States. Nofzinger's our military-industrial lobbyist, Mariotta's president of Wedtech. We're all partners in Wedtech! Isn't that a hoot?!" He laughed.

I was confused ...then, I laughed too, "You sly old dog, that's a good one, I hope you don't get busted and don't do time. Gonna get away with it?"

"Mr. President, I got 200 million dollars in orders from the Army and Navy."

"That's really great, Ed."

"We sold 75 million dollars worth of bonds to build up Wedtech! Sittin' in clover! Now, we're declaring bankruptcy, it's a dream come true. There's one born every day!"

I felt my happiness for Ed fade, "I don't want to hear any more about it, Ed."

"Lighten-up, Ronnie. I'm in charge of law and order for the whole U.S."

I felt pushed to the edge, "Ed, the only reason you got confirmed by the Senate to head Justice Department was because I recommended you and I have a high public approval rating. But, this foolin' around, what you're doing makes me look bad, reflects on my Administration, don't you see?"

"No way, don't you understand?" Ed said, "I'm head of Justice, I can find where the bodies are buried, no Congressman's gonna mess with me!" Ed laughed some more.

I didn't, "I want to be a hero, not a bum. You're Justice Department head, you're my friend. That makes a double moral and ethical responsibility on your part to watch out for me. You've seen my old 'Westerns', you've seen the Indians use a branch in the dust to sweep over their tracks so no one can follow them. Clean up your act or cover your tracks."

< >

Early on in my second administration, Assistant Chief of Staff Michael Deaver talked about leaving the White House. Deaver was overeager to cash in with lobbyists on his contacts with White House Staff, with Cabinet, with me, and Nancy. Deaver put together a plan to open his own public relations firm. Nancy heard rumors. There was going to be an investigation of Deaver's influence-peddling. Lynn Nofzinger left his White House job. Nofzinger went into the lobbying business. Months later, I watched a Senate Hearing pronounce a verdict on Meese, Mariotta, and Nofzinger of Wedtech. Meese, Mariotta, and Nofzinger stood before the Senate Hearing Committee. The Committee spokesman addressed them, "Mr.'s Meese, Mariotta, and Nofzinger of Wedtech all pleaded guilty to fraud ...we're convicting Mr. Nofzinger ...we're not indicting Mr. Meese, head of the United States Justice Department."

Ed had a 'holier-than-thou' grin on his face. I smiled when I saw Ed like that. A few days later, me and Ed talked privately in the Situation Room. Ed turned to me, "I told you, I can find out where the bodies are buried. Congress won't mess with me. I hate to tell you, Ronnie, but I told you, so."

I wasn't happy, "Knock it off, Ed. I don't like it."

Ed lit a cigar, "My aides in Justice are like you, they had morals, they quit on me. Who needs 'em? Nofzinger's already successfully appealed his conviction. We both got off, scot-free. I guess I'm the oldest person in the 'me' generation. I'm laughing, all the way to the bank."

What could I say? "Say hello to Bill Casey and George Bush when you get there."

<>

On our way out of the room, a reporter intercepted us just as Bill Casey walked up, and asked Ed and Bill, what was their experience of working with me. Ed answered first, "My experience of working with Ronald Reagan. He's always fair and loyal to me, bless his soul."

Bill spoke up, "My experience working with Ronald Reagan. Of course, everybody sees it differently because we have different priorities. I'm restricted by National Security policies and my Top Secret Clearance from sharing with you some of the details. But, there's a lot I can say."

Nancy walked up and led me away, back towards the Situation Room. I smiled at her and tried to make her laugh, "Nancy, I bet Coors is the first American beer into the Soviet Union and Eastern Europe, you can bet the Bechtel team will be busy there like they are in Libya, Saudi Arabia, and Communist China. They'll all be eating McDonalds' hamburgers and drinking Coors beer. But, what's in it for me? Why are they making me make all these appointments? I just do what I'm told, my 'kitchen cabinet' can't be beat, I'm in front of the camera all the time, we have all the public approval we need, that spells 'relief'."

Nancy smiled a little, but didn't laugh. Her smile faded, "Ronnie, I'm miserable because my Betsy Bloomingdale's husband Alfred died and I miss him."

"So do I."

"And he left all this sick sex stuff in the newspapers fooling around with that S&M mistress ...he was into 'blue' movies, kinky sex ...that spells, 'drugs'."

Nancy saw, I was tense. I didn't like talking about this stuff, "Nancy, I don't want to hear about it. I have to go onstage this afternoon, tell me later. This appearance I have to make, is like being emcee at Academy Awards." Later that afternoon, I walked up to the podium to deliver my speech to United States Chamber of Commerce luncheon guests, "I'm pleased to be here, this afternoon, as emcee at the United States Chamber of Commerce Luncheon ...to introduce some of my Cabinet members that I appointed. They came highly recommended to me. I trust them to be always on their best behavior, they'll be bringing 'regulatory relief' to the American people. First, financed by Adolf Coors, who also backed Paul Weyrich and Free Congress Foundation ...and, representing the conservatives who helped put me into office and keep me here, is James Watt, the new Interior Secretary.

CNN's Alan questioned James Watt, "Mr. Watt, how will you fulfill your pledge to manage and preserve public lands?"

Watt answered like a robot, "We've got to deregulate Department

Of The Interior, I'm a reborn Christian. I'm religiously opposed to government-mandated efforts to protect the natural environment. Get the timber harvest in before Armageddon. The Bible says, 'conquer and occupy the land until Jesus returns' so we'll mine more, cut more timber, drill more oil. Two kinds of people live in America ...Liberals, and Americans. As a white man, I'd be hesitant to allow a Black doctor to operate on me because I'd always have the feeling, he may have been carried by the quota system." Watt listened as the audience applauded loudly.

I grimaced, "Nancy, oh no." I wished the applause was for me.

Nancy was thinking, 'Poor Ronnie'.

CNN's Alan stepped up to Watt, "I understand you've been pressured into naming a public advisory panel to oversee a coal-leasing venture."

Watt spoke confidently, "I think the President would be pleased, I've selected a balanced group, we have every mix you can have ...a Black, a woman, two Jews, and a cripple."

<>

Nancy saw me slap my palm against my forehead. The audience grumbled. Watt kept talking, "I've canceled a Beach Boys White House, July 4th concert, the Beach Boys project a bad image. They shouldn't be allowed to perform on public property. Instead, I've selected Wayne Newton, a Las Vegas lounge act."

The audience applauded. I frowned. So did Nancy, "Ronnie, I like the Beach Boys. They're my favorite American group, after Frank Sinatra." Nancy was alarmed.

The spotlight swirled across the audience then settled on me. I gestured to the audience to quiet down, "I'd like to introduce another one of my appointees, Anne Burford. She's an ally of Mr. Watt. I nominated her to head Environmental Protection Agency."

Anne Burford addressed the audience, "We must deregulate Environmental Protection Agency. I too, like Mr. Watt, am ideologically opposed to protecting the environment. I'm appointing Ed Meese's protégé, Rita Lavelle, to oversee the 'Superfund' program Congress created, to clean up the nation's worst hazardous waste sites.

Rita Lavelle and I agree, EPA rules unfairly restrict the chemical industry, we've put too great a priority on preserving a pristine environment. That alienates the business community. Those days are over."

< >

Before too long, I found myself sitting in on another Senate Hearing, listening to the sound of the Senate Hearing chairman's gavel as he kept pounding it up and down on his desk. I watched the EPA's Anne Burford and Rita Lavelle. They stood before the Congressional Investigating Committee. The Senate chairman announced the Hearing's verdicts, "Our Congressional Investigation has determined that Anne Burford and Rita Lavelle of Environmental Protection Agency, violated the public trust by disregarding the public health and the environment and manipulating the Superfund toxic clean-up program for political gain by illegally distributing clean-up money. They engaged in unethical conduct. In addition, two dozen top EPA appointees are being removed from office, or are resigning-under-pressure, for favoring the industries they were supposed to oversee. I understand, Ms. Anne Burford has resigned. Because Ms. Rita Lavelle lied to us, we're sentencing her to prison."

< >

At another luncheon, I had the opportunity to introduce my appointee to head the Federal Communications Commission, Mark Fowler. Fowler addressed his audience, "I want to deregulate the Federal Communications Commission. As far as I'm concerned, TV's another appliance, like a toaster with pictures."

Time passed. I found myself sitting-in on another Senate Hearing, listening to the sound of the Senate Hearing chairman pound his wooden gavel down on his desk then pronounce another set of verdicts. The Chairman spoke to the gallery, "Our Congressional Investigation has determined that the President's appointment of Samuel Pierce to head the Department of Housing and Urban

Development, HUD, has been involved with influence peddling, favoritism, abuse, greed, fraud, embezzlement, and theft."

At another luncheon, I had the opportunity to introduce my appointee to supervise the deregulation of the Savings & Loan industry, Ed Gray. Ed Gray addressed the group assembled to meet him, "We've needed to deregulate the Savings & Loan industry a long time. I'm not good at telling jokes. The Reagan Administration's so ideologically blinded, it can't understand the different between lowering airfares and removing all controls from the Savings & Loan industry. You'll be sorry, the S&Ls are going to be eaten alive!"

I didn't know how to react. I heard the audience applauding, everything was probably going well. Neil Bush, one of George Bush's sons, was enthusiastic. Nancy watched Ed Gray storm off. She looked at me, "What's eating him?"

I had no idea, "I don't know. People are saying everyone I appoint is a crook, maybe he isn't."

"I've got to fire everyone who is a crook, they make you guilty, by association!"

"But Nancy, if you fire everyone in my administration who's a crook ...there won't be anyone left."

"This is no time to kid around."

Nancy was startled when she saw a look on my face that meant, 'Who's kidding around?' I looked Nancy straight in the eyes, "I think there's getting to be a finer line of ethics in my Administration than I can get along with. And, all this Iran-Contra business. Sometimes, I think it's just a Casey red herring to cover up him arming the Muhajidin to control the Afghanistan opium poppy trade, then reinvest the profits into some kind of corporate leveraged buy-out to make their stock soar ...so, international banking venture capitalists connected to the Fed can issue an IPO, make a killing then use the money to do hostile take-overs ...and primarily found, invest in, grow, buy and sell their own Fed-owned subsidiaries among themselves then start the cycle over again. The only reason Casey's arming the Muhajidin with Stinger missiles through Monzer Al-Kassar is to get kickbacks into his anti-Communist campaign fund and private bank accounts. That's why he's anti-Communist. That's why he wants Weyrich's and Coors' Full-Court Press to destabilize

Soviet Union and Eastern Europe, so him and his central banks can finance another world war, just like him and Dulles and the Bushes did in World War I and World War II."

Nancy looked at me like I was nuts. Nancy got that feeling again, concerned I was confused, losing it ...otherwise, why would I be exercising lack of judgment, talking like this ...in public. So, she needed to change the subject, before I attracted attention, "Ronnie, there's something bothering me."

"What is it, Darling?"

"I adore the Beach Boys."

I looked curiously at Nancy, "Watt failed the keep-your-mouth-shut test. I'm personally hurt, Watt didn't try to bite his tongue. I've decided to ask for Watt's resignation. From now on, I'm going to make all bad news disappear the easy way ...by ignoring it."

Nancy laughed, "But Ronnie, the Beach Boys?"

"All right, we'll over-ride Watt, we'll dump Wayne Newton, we reinstate the Beach Boys for the White House 4th of July Concert."

Nancy was pleased, "Thanks, Darling, you've made me happy." Nancy hugged me. I kissed her. Nancy felt pampered. Nancy started to cry.

I didn't understand, "Nancy, I thought you were happy."

"Oh Ronnie, I didn't know how to tell you. Rock Hudson has aids. He's dying."

I was shocked, "Rock Hudson? That's terrible. It's awful. It never felt like Aids was real, until now."

"Maybe you should make Aids a Federal funding priority, before any other of our friends die."

"I'll have Surgeon General Koop do a report."

Surgeon General Koop's report was published. Koop called on Americans to change their personal sexual behavior. Koop described the Administration's remedy to Aids, as 'one, abstinence ...two, monogamy ...three, condoms'.

Conservatives Jerry Falwell, Phyllis Schlafly, and the new Education Secretary, William Bennett condemned Surgeon General Koop. They felt he was encouraging immorality by mentioning the word 'condoms'. Koop pleaded with me, take the lead nationally, tell Americans more about the disease, how to prevent it. I didn't want to get my public image personally involved with Aids and the Aids public health crisis. In my next speech, I said, scientists are still learning about how AIDS is transmitted, the public shouldn't be afraid to donate blood.

Deaver told me, never mention sex ...or, condoms. So, I endorsed the Right-To-Life movement. I said, I support the idea of having a constitutional amendment making abortion illegal. That night, after his speech J. Peter Grace, who chaired the Grace Commission to recommend budget cuts in government programs, introduced me at the podium of a banquet of anti-abortion fundamentalists. J. Peter Grace spoke, "It takes a man, like Reagan, to point out the simple truth, all living people started life as feces. Yes, even you started out as feces. Now, dinner is served."

The audience was shocked. CNN's Alan was sitting with other reporters, clapping wildly, laughing til he cried and yelled, "Right on!"

CHAPTER 9

Back at the ranch after my presidential retirement, I always got a kick out of Nancy reading me books and articles ...but sometimes, it was a real kick in the rear end. I looked at her, "Nancy, love hurts."

Nancy looked at me, "Ronnie, we decided we'd find out what really was going on that we didn't know about, when we were in the White House. It hurts me just as much as it hurts you."

< >

Back at the ranch, Nancy read Kimery to me. He was the kind of person I wished I'd known when I was President. Of course, my Vice President might have shot him down or at least sent him on a hunting trip with Dick Cheney. I'd known Dick Cheney back in Starwars days, he was a major proponent, along with his friend USAF Lt. Col. Robert M. Bowman, who now blamed Cheney personally as one of the only men who could have single-handedly engineered the 911/WTC terrorist provocation. It was a natural evolution of my martial law and holding camp Operation Cable Cutter program as Governor which became my martial law and holding camp Operation Northwoods during my administration ...although before that, when George Bush was CIA director he asked Lt. Gen. Dan Graham to co-found 'Committee on the Present Danger' ... all those projects were the forerunners of what Cheney and his pirate crew embodied in The Project for The New American Century ... straight

Bank of England and Fed destabilization programs complete with domestic holding camps with all domestic war-related contracts and reconstruction contracts going to companies Bank of England and the private shareholders of the Fed owned such as Bechtel, Halliburton, Kelly Brown & Root or did business with such as bin Laden Construction, and exceeding MI-6 and CIA expectations of deep cover outsourced all the mercenary work, murder, genocide and torture to Halliburton's Blackwater or Kroll. Nancy picked up a copy of *Covert Action Quarterly* and read it to me.

White House Situation Room

I found myself in another one of my daily meetings with Mike Deaver, totally besides myself, "Are all my appointees, crooks? How does that make me look?!"

"It doesn't matter."

"Explain."

"According to our opinion polls, the American people don't associate you with the scandals and failures of your Administration."

"That's the darndest thing. Are you sure?"

"Yep. You're an icon. Make sure you never even discuss the Savings & Loan crises, or Wedtech, or HUD Scandals. The American people are concerned with your Hollywood image, your looks, they like that you make mistakes, they like you forget what you're talking about, it makes you human, another victim of big government, like them."

"Can they give me an Oscar?"

Deaver was amused, "McFarland resigned, couldn't take the heat." Mike left the Situation Room.

Outside the Situation Room, CNN's Alan was finishing an interview with Bill Casey. Bill had said about as much as he wanted to, "All-in-all, these are very good years. My stock portfolio's soaring. Reagan years are good for money-issuing family portfolios." Bill walked off.

Alan turned to George Bush, "Can we finish our interview, now?"

Bush was interview shy, but agreed, "This is my experience with Ronald Reagan. We don't always see eye-to-eye. President Reagan and his nouveau-riche friends profit on statewide levels. I, of course, come from old family wealth, my forte is petroleum. Don't get me mixed up with my father, and grandfather, and uncle …they were the international bankers, in bed with foreign international bankers the same way as Bill Casey and Allen Dulles. Not me, I'm just a New Englander who loves oil and lives and votes in Texas, for tax breaks. We all knew building up the national debt would let the bankers who made the loans and owned the bonds suck trillions of dollars of profits out of the American people and bankrupt America. Same kind of thing with the savings-and-loans rip-off. That was a classic exercise for rich kids from money-issuing and ruling families. The Full-Court Press to destabilize the Soviet Union and Eastern Europe, that was a banker-kind-of-vision thing. I remember the day the President came to me for reassurance about deregulating the Savings & Loan Industry."

< >

George Bush remembered that day.

But, I wanted to get to the bottom of things, "How can your sons be making millions of dollars from this Savings & Loans scandal when it's going to cost taxpayers billions of dollars?!"

Sometimes, George didn't beat around the bush, "That's the whole point."

"Sometimes, I think you're not out of the loop at all."

"I'm sorry to hear that."

"George, look, I've heard you say it more than once."

"I know, I know. 'Me? Out of the loop? I am the loop.' Trust me, Ronnie," George said, "… it's different this time."

I watched the expression on George's face change as he suddenly considered himself off the hook and smirked, "Ron, what scares me most, is the wealthy people in America are taking foreign citizenship …so, they don't pay American taxes. The 1980s and 1990s are about making the Deutschmark and Yen, king. You could say, the currencies and central banks that financed Hitler won World War II and then we shot the U.S. dollar down so it's worth less. History's embarrassing. I'm disillusioned. A one-world government central bank New World

Order's the only way to keep us all from destroying ourselves. It took me my whole life to forgive my parents and grandparents for working with Dulles to finance Nazis and Fascists, they were business partners the whole 20th Century. Now, I'm in my 70s, gosh darn if I didn't do the same thing with oil dictators, banana republics, Nazis, and Fascists, too. Maybe my Dad was a visionary, ahead of his time. He saw beyond the limitations of national boundaries. He believed, a one-world government could only be achieved with genocide and war, in order for God to bring peace to the world and keep the rest of us ruling family kids and money-issuing dynasties from killing each other off."

I was confused and turned to Baker, "What about you, Baker. How is it you're making money off the Savings & Loan crises, too?"

White House Chief of Staff James Baker III smiled, "Just business as usual. When we deregulated the Savings & Loans, everyone knew there was an end run coming, we were waiting for the right president to come along, for several administrations, we just waited for a president like you, who understood the importance of deregulation."

I was angry, "Me?! I didn't know any such thing! How does it make me look?! Like a John Wayne hero? Or a villain?"

Baker looked at me, showing no expression, "Deaver says you've got the Midas touch, step in shit, come out smelling like roses."

I was amused and enjoyed the compliment, "Lucky for all of us, he's right. I just don't want to keep pushing the envelope. I don't want to keep pushing our luck. Didn't your father ever teach you how not to get caught? You may come from a ruling class family in the social register but any street kid investigative reporter considers you easy pickin's."

Budget Director David Stockman caught my eye, "Stockman, I'm not happy about you betraying our budget machinery to the press. I respect you for doing what you believe in, you're fired. There are changes coming down. I've been thinking about relieving Baker, Meese, and Deaver, who now head White House Staff. I'd replace them with a senior executive from Merrill Lynch, Don Regan."

That's how George Bush remembered that day.

< >

After Alan finished interviewing Bush, he turned to White House Spokesman Larry Speakes, "What was it like working with President Reagan, Mr. Speakes."

"Ronald Reagan has more aces up his sleeves than a carnival barker. Before you knew it," Speakes said, "he's going to replace the White House Head Staff 'sleaze team' of Jim Baker, Ed Meese, and Mike Deaver. He fired Poindexter for Poindexter's role in Iran-Contra. George Bush's sons are making millions of dollars off the Savings & Loans scandal, his sons are running for governor of Texas and Florida. All those Reagan photo-ops prevented there being any target for the American people to blame. Deregulation was the best thing for money-issuing and ruling family Americans since slavery. Now, we have financial slavery of the middle class ...up into the upper class, that was the greatest contribution of the Reagan years. And the way they changed the way they figured unemployment, not by how many people were unemployed ...but, once your unemployment benefits expired, you'd no longer be counted as unemployed. The Fed had a brainstorm around that one. That method is still used. It keeps millions of unemployed people invisible. White House crime soared, the President's popularity soared, too."

George & Barbara Bush's home

Lucky visited Barbara Bush at a Bush estate in Washington D.C. Lucky liked Barbara a lot, "I accept at least 500 party invitations a year, I turn down many more."

Barbara was in the same boat and smiled warmly, "I know what you mean."

"I go to official parties with your husband, the Vice President, he has me make sure he's not overwhelmed by the press or not monopolized by some bore he can't get rid of. When he wants to leave without causing a stink, he winks at me. I'll interrupt him, no matter who he's with ...point to my watch to give him an excuse to leave. He says, 'Opps, Chief of Protocol says, it's time for another meeting'. One time at an embassy party, he winked but then said in a loud whisper, 'Gee, Lucky, do I have to leave? I'm having such a good time.' The foreign Ambassador glared at me for taking George away. Your husband protested all the way to the door. I was so embarrassed."

Barbara watched Lucky's eyes carefully as Lucky talked. Barbara felt a little bit jealous. Barbara was demure, "George is a flirt, I'm the first one to say it."

Lucky wanted to get to the heart of the matter, why she'd come to visit Barbara in the first place, "How should I deal with my munchkin problem? I've asked myself over and over, what motivates a munchkin?"

Barbara let it go, "Money and sex motivate a munchkin." Barbara usually disguised her sense of humor by giving it a straight delivery.

Lucky was surprised, "Does Mike Deaver know what they're doing behind his back, in his name?"

"I've heard he has a drinking problem. It that true, Lucky? And, isn't he mixed up with the Argentines?"

"I don't know. He's surrounded by a bunch of fraternity boys who drink too much. What do you mean, about Argentines?"

Barbara was chagrin, "A little birdie told me staffers denied any involvement with Contras getting U.S. Military aid by buying congressional support and making campaign kickbacks from their foreign aid allotments, and drug smuggling profits. I heard some of the illegal money didn't make it back into campaign funds, it got sidetracked. You didn't hear it from me, Lucky. Let's get back to you. How can I help?"

Lucky felt suddenly vulnerable, "I'm not pleased with myself ...the way I let them treat me, if it's not best for me how can it be best for the country? The munchkins tried again to make me hire one of their cronies. I didn't. Then, one day, without asking me, the White House commandeered my deputy secretary to be Mrs. Reagan's social secretary. One munchkin told Deaver's secretary not to tell me about it ...but, she did. She said, I was bound to notice my secretary wasn't sitting at her desk, anyway. Then, they took another secretary ...then, they took one of my best protocol officers to be Mrs. Reagan's new advance man."

State Secretary George Shultz's office

In Shultz's White House office, Lucky repeated her problem to her boss, "That's what they did, I've been screwed."

George Shultz looked somber, "No, Lucky, you've been raped ...I have faith in you. Sometimes, you have to lose the battle to win the war."

Lucky wasn't sure what Shultz meant, "I hate this munchkin bunch of little shits. If I told the President how the munchkins were treating me, he'd be horrified. I'm so upset about it, I could scream. One of the little shits is going around saying, he's going to get rid of 'that woman', meaning me. Several people told me he keeps saying it ...but, if I go to Mike Deaver he'll think I can't handle my job. But, unless I go to him, I can't work with these little shits, any more. They're frustrating me to death. Can you tell me what to do?"

George smiled at Lucky. He looked at his watch. He had to leave.

Reagan living quarters,
Christmas Eve, White House

Patti was singing with rock music on the radio but there was a second radio somewhere, playing Christmas carols ...the music mixing together was driving her nuts. The Reagan Christmas family get together was in full swing. Ronnie, Nancy, and Patti start watching videos of Patti speaking at anti-Contra, anti-nuclear power, and anti-war demonstrations ...usually, with Patti onstage singing back-up with her boyfriend's band, the Eagles, to a huge crowd. Patti danced around wildly on the video, delighting in shaking her long hair around and around, back and forth. Nancy couldn't watch, without getting upset, "Tossing your hair around like that in public and gyrating like that is disgraceful to the Presidency."

Patti couldn't hold back her anger, "I hate you! You stole my father from me! You know you did it! You know it! Dad, you just stood there, my whole life. You let her!"

Alan Allen

Nancy felt challenged on home turf, "Ronnie, Patti's lying. She'll never change, she's a bad seed."

I frowned. I couldn't please both of them, "I did know about it, Patti. I talked with your mother about it ...but, it kept happening. I couldn't be in the middle between you and mommy. Don't make me choose between you and mommy, 'cause I'll choose mommy, not you. You're grown up now, you should understand. It's painful to talk about ...are you happy, now?"

Patti was crying, "Yes. You're admitting for the first time, you lied. You're a hypocrite."

I wouldn't stand for that, "I deny that, Patti."

Patti exploded at Nancy, "I hated you being my Mother! I never had kids! That's how much I was afraid I'd turn out like you. I never wanted to put my kids or any kids, through that!"

I was amazed at what Patti came up with, "It couldn't have been that bad."

"It was too! I got a tubal ligation so I can never have kids!"

Patti's brothers and sister sat on a couch. They assured me, Patti did have a tubal ligation. I felt tears in my eyes, "I'm so sorry, Patty. God, I wish you hadn't done that. It's a sin worse than abortion. I knew Nancy slapped you a few times when you were a bad girl ...but, Nancy couldn't help that, she was doing the best she could to raise all of you ...you were a defiant child. I did the best I could. I'm sorry, if I was wrong. I really am ...but, it was a long time ago." I felt the tears falling down my cheeks. I picked up a movie magazine and hid behind it.

That made Patti furious. Patti felt ignored, like she'd been made invisible and didn't matter, "Stop hiding behind that movie magazine! All you've ever done is hide behind parts you played, you weren't real. You were never there for me! You've hid your feelings, all I ever wanted was you to love me! You think I'm not here. You need the shrink, not me! You support Contra death squads, you're a drug runner, a terrorist, a mass murderer, a serial killer!"

I lowered the magazine, staring at Patti, "You're exaggerating. I never killed anyone. Other people did it."

"You authorized Casey to build up CIA, you funded the Contras and they kill and torture people!"

I was losing patience, trying to make Patti understand, "But, I didn't do it myself! I didn't kill anyone!"

"The Nazis said they followed orders. They said it was Hitler's fault. But, you give the orders, Dad. Do you think about that?"

I sat there quietly ...and, thought. "Yes, I think about it every day. But, someone has to save us from communists."

Patti was sad, "That's exactly what Hitler said making excuses to kill innocent people, do genocide, concentration camps, death squads. You give the orders, Dad. You're not the hero. You're the villain!"

That was preposterous, "No, I'm not!"

"Yes, you are!"

"No I'm not!

"Then, what are you?!"

"What am I? I'll tell you what I am! I'm the most popular president America ever had!"

"You're denying the truth!"

"I didn't kill anyone myself, someone else did, can't you see that? It's my management style, I surround myself with capable people, I stay out of their way, I let them do their jobs."

"Dad, you're a serial killer, a mass murderer, drug runner, terrorist, you're everything you hate, a hypocrite in denial."

"I'm not a hypocrite! I'm not a villain! I'm telling you, again! I'm the most popular president the United States ever had! Why can't you believe me? Look at the public opinion polls, Patti! Ask Deaver. Ask your mother. I'm a hero! ...playing in the biggest movie role of my career. My friends finance it, produce it ...I wrote it. The American people love it. They love me! America's my family! I'm their Father. They love me!"

Patti wasn't sold, "No Dad, they don't. They love your shadow. You don't even exist. Life's not a movie! 'Cause if it is, you're on the cutting-room floor."

"To hell it's not, Patti! Life is a movie! It is!"

"Then, it's a bad movie, 'cause I'm not clapping."

I was furious, "We all play roles God gave us, can't you ever get it? Won't you grow up? You need a lot more Jesus and a lot less rock and roll!"

"I get it, Dad! You're the Devil! ...runnin our shadow government!" Patti stormed off.

We continued with our Christmas party as if nothing happened and Patti had never been there, at all.

White House photo-opportunity

A few days later in the White House I was relaxing before my next photo-op, watching a video of Jimmy Steward starring in, It's a Wonderful Life. I explained the film to Nancy, "Jimmy's making Savings & Loans home loans to homeowners ...but, his S&L is implicated, making bad loans."

Nancy was sad, "Ronnie, don't you remember I've watched this movie with you, a hundred times?"

I thought about it, "A hundred?" I felt nostalgic. "Today's a big day. I have to sign the Garn-St. Germain Act to deregulate the Savings & Loan Thrift Industry, that's why I put on this old Jimmy Steward movie from the early '40s, they almost cast me in that role, instead of Jimmy."

At my speech, I had a captive audience. I love that feeling, "This is the most important legislation for financial institutions in fifty years! Garn-St. Germain is the Emancipation Proclamation for American savings institutions! It means more housing, jobs, growth! All in all, I think, we've hit the jackpot."

In the audience, James Baker III, Lloyd Bentsen and son, George Bush and sons, and Farhad Azima clapped wildly. I could see some of the audience was smirking. I didn't know why. Later that night, I couldn't sleep. I kept watching the Jimmy Steward movie I'd started watching that morning. I finally fell asleep. I had fitful sleep. I had nightmares. So did Nancy. Me and Nancy were so close, sometimes we dreamed the same dreams.

Nancy and her astrologer

Me and Nancy dreamed the same dream, so she could hear the Jimmy Steward movie drifting in and out of her head and fell into in a fitful sleep, startled by the sound of oversized tarot cards slowly shuffled and the drone of her astrologer's voice. Nancy couldn't wait any longer, "Please do my tarot reading now. Is it all right? ...Ronnie's here."

Joan smiled at Nancy then at me while she shuffled the tarot cards.

I was falling in and out of sleep on the Joan's couch, using Peter Brewton's book, *George Bush, the Mafia & the CIA*, as a pillow. Or ...was it Joseph J. Trento's, *Prelude to Terror, the Rogue CIA & Legacy of America's Private Intelligence Network*. Wait, it was Brewton.

Nancy spoke up, "I have photographs one of my Carter Naval Intelligence men sent me in the mail, I recognize the people, can you touch the pictures and get a psychic reading from them?"

Joan smiled in a superior way, "Let's go in a trance using my crystal ball then I'll do the tarot card reading for you and Ronnie."

Nancy was filled with excited anticipation. Joan dealt the fortune-telling cards, "The danger card! I see it in my psychic vision. My third-eye's opening, you must be careful about the crowd around Ronnie."

Nancy was frightened, "Ronnie, Ronnie get up. This is important."

I slowly opened my eyes, my Jimmy Steward movie played in the background. I sat between Nancy and Joan at the séance table. Joan looked in the crystal ball, "I see James Baker III having lunch with Raymond Hill at Hill's Mainland Savings & Loan, I see Hill lending money to the mafia and to CIA operatives. Deception! I see Lloyd Bentsen selling three Texas Savings & Loans the mafia and CIA will own. Danger! Farhad Azima, gunrunner and board member of a Kansas City bank, there in the photograph he's holding in his hand a picture of him standing with the Crowned Shah of Iran, Shah Pahlevi. He's having dinner with Oliver North, Leslie Aspin, and Mario Alarcon in the Kansas City Bank boardroom. Greed! Murder! William Blakemore, oilman, Contra supporter, friend of George Bush is lobbying Congressmen for Contra aid, Blakemore's heading up Contra paramilitary training at his Iron Mountain ranch. Treachery! John Ellis 'Jeb' Bush son of Vice President Bush, a Contra supporter, a business associate of Camilo

Padreda and Guillermo Hernandez-Cartaya. Deception! Neil Bush son of Vice President Bush is director of Silverado Savings & Loan, a partner with Bill Walters and Ken Good, a friend of Walt Mischer, Jr. Treason! Eulalio Francisco 'Frank' Castro, Cuban exile, Bay of Pigs veteran, a CIA operative who helped train and supply Contras, he's part of a drug-smuggling ring that bought Sunshine State Bank. Assassination beware! John Connally, former Texas Governor. Charles Keating worked on Connally's 1980 Republican presidential race, Keating and partner Ben Barnes borrowed tens of millions of dollars from dirty Savings & Loans. Genocide! ...racism! The International Fascista! WACL! Ray Corona, former head of mafia-owned Sunshine State Bank in Miami, he's using Sunshine as a front for drug smugglers, his bank is a borrower from Peoples Savings in Llano, Texas. He's an associate of mobsters and CIA operatives including Frank Castro, and Guillermo Hernandez-Cartaya. Betrayal! Betrayal! Treason! War in Latin America! Robert L. Corson, Houston good old boy and developer who owned Vision Bank Savings in Kingsville is Walter Mischer's former son-in-law and a CIA mule, he'll be indicted with Mike Adkinson for a bogus 200 million dollar Savings & Loan land deal in Florida. Cookies, good to eat. Innocence. Cover-ups. Disguises! Marvin Davis, Denver and Beverly Hills oil billionaire, his daughter was in the cookie business with Neil Bush's wife, Sharon."

Nancy listened attentively, making mental notes, "Can you tell if they're chocolate chip or oatmeal cookies?"

"Oatmeal," Joan said. "Drugs! Seduction! Loss of innocence! Suffering! Racism! Genocide! Evil! Beware! Stefan Halper, cofounder with Harvey Mclean of Palmer National Bank financed by Herman Beebe, funneled private donations to the Contras, he's the former son-in-law of past CIA deputy director Ray Cline. He helped set up a defense fund for Oliver North. It's the money-issuing and ruling family mafia, that's what it is! The bad apples! Herman Beebe, Sr. Louisiana financier convicted felon Mafia associate, he has more connections than a switchboard to the intelligence community, he's godfather of the dirty Texas Savings & Loans. It's the money-issuing and ruling family mafia rag, that's what it is. Guillermo Hernandez-Cartaya Cuban exile Bay of Pigs veteran will be convicted of fraud for the Texas Savings & Loan he bought from Lloyd Bentsen's father. I see CIA and mafia money being laundered but he's being protected from criminal charges by CIA. Satan! GATT! Council of Foreign Relations! The one-world government! Apocalypse! The Central Bank one world government New World Order! Walt Mischer Jr. son of Mischer has been tapped to take over his father's empire. He's the friend of Neil Bush. Walter M. Mischer Sr., Houston developer, banker, power broker who headed Allied Bank, Corson's former father-in-law did business with mafia and CIA. Mischer Sr. is fourth largest landowner in Texas, he and his portfolio partners own twelve percent of the Caribbean Central American nation of Belize, he's a friend and fundraiser for LBJ, Lloyd Bentsen, your husband, George Bush, and others. Belize is a staging ground for Contra support activities. Apocalypse! Marvin Nathan Houston attorney who served on Carroll Kelly's Continental Savings board, he now owns the Texas ranch from the family of late Nicaraguan dictator Anastasion Somoza, purchased from one of George Bush's best friends. Apocalypse! Lloyd Monroe former Kansas City organized crime strike force prosecutor was told to back off Farhad Azima because Azima had CIA-issued get-out-of-jail-free cards. Satan! GATT! Council of Foreign Relations! Central bank One World Government! Apocalypse! Central bank New World Order! Destruction of Yugoslavia, Bosnia, Iraq, genocide, ethnic cleansing! World War III. Robert Strauss Dallas attorney and U.S. Ambassador to Moscow former chairman of Democratic National Committee friend of George Bush former business partner of James A. Baker III, he and his son Richard were involved in a number of failed Texas Savings & Loan deals, including Lamar and Gibratar. Bosnia, Baghdad, genocide in the Garden of Eden, ethnic cleansing in Sarajevo! World War III. Santo Trafficante, late Tampa mafia boss worked with CIA to try to assassinate Fidel Castro is involved in narcotics trafficking in Southeast Asia with CIA. Bill Walters Denver developer borrower at Silverado Savings helped set up Neil Bush in business."

Nancy was dumbfounded, "This is too much, for me! How's it gonna turn out?!"

Joan start blinking rapidly, "I'm coming out of my trance now.

Let's make your astrology charts and Ronnie's current. Let's update the chart for Washington D.C. too. Washington might get nuked by terrorists! Let's see who's pulling the strings!"

Mike Deaver's White House office

Lucky angrily marched in to Mike Deaver's office at the White House, "Your staff's treating me badly to make me resign. You don't have to go to those lengths! Tell me the President's no longer happy with my performance, I'll leave right now. I didn't ask for this job, you called me! I had a great life before the White House. I'll have a great life after I leave the White House!"

Mike screwed the top back on his flask, took a nip, spoke patiently, "Don't be silly, Lucky. The President and Nancy are pleased with your performance, there's been no suggestion for you to leave the White House."

"In that case, call off your munchkins or you'll be explaining to the Secretary of State and the President and the press exactly why I left."

White House corridors

Lucky walked victoriously out of Deaver's office and down the corridors of the White House and saw Barbara Bush walking towards her from the other end of the hall. Barbara smiled. Lucky smiled back, she felt happy, "I've got that winning feeling!"

Barbara was enthusiastic, "Zippity-do-dah!"

"Barbara, all the rumors have stopped, thanks to Mike! I made such a fuss. I got my frustration and anger out. I'm not going to quit, I'm not going to let the munchkins push me out!"

Barbara hugged Lucky, then happily continued down the hall. George Shultz came down another hallway. Shultz walked up to Lucky, "Lucky, I want you to stay on with me."

Lucky felt so happy, "I'm sitting on top of the world. If you want me to stay then you have to have the President himself, ask me to. That way, I can keep the munchkins in line when I have to."

Shultz smiled and left. Just then, Prime Minister Tariq Aziz of Iraq walked over to chat with Lucky. Then, a presidential aide came over, "Ambassador Roosevelt, the President wants to see you."

"Iraqi Prime Minister Tariq is waiting to talk to me, can he come along?"

The aide looked curiously at Lucky, "No. The President wants to see you alone."

White House Oval Office

I was sitting at my desk in the Oval Office as Lucky walked in. George Shultz was sitting there, a smile on his face. I stood up. Lucky walked over to me. I placed my hands on Lucky's shoulders. I was fond of Lucky, "The State Secretary and I think you've done a marvelous job. I'd like you to continue to stay with me for my second term in Washington. I hope you say, 'yes'."

Lucky was surprised ...I had started singing to her! ...'I've Grown Accustomed To Your Face', from the Hollywood musical, My Fair Lady. "I've grown accustomed to your face, like breathing out and breathing in." In my mind, I went back to the early '50s. My movie career was on the skids. I hadn't started working as a spokesman for General Electric Theatre. I hadn't yet gotten the job to host the TV weekly series Death Valley Days. I remembered when my agent offered me a job in a Las Vegas lounge act with strippers. Nancy marched into my agent's office and refused the job for me. But, I did accept a soft-shoe bit part. I wore a straw derby as a straight man in a Las Vegas lounge act comedy routine.

Lucky noticed I seemed distracted. But, was too thrilled to care. She laughed, smiling at me, "You've appeased me. I'm so happy. I'm a winner!"

On the way out of the Oval Office, Lucky passed Nancy ...and a munchkin! Lucky felt like a cheerleader whose team had just won. Lucky cheered, "Victory, victory, hear our cry, v, i, c, t, o, r, y... Yea!" Lucky intentionally bumped into a vase and spilled water onto the munchkin, then pretended it was an accident.

Lucky at home

Lucky sat at home at her writing desk, tenderly touched her diary with her fingers. The reporter in the room smiled. Lucky spoke softly, "That was primarily my experience of working with President Ronald Reagan, when I was Ambassador and Chief of Protocol for the White House."

The reporter felt satisfied with the interview, "Thank you for the interview, Ambassador Roosevelt."

Lucky was gracious, as usual, "Thank you."

Nancy's office in the White House

Nancy sat at her desk in her White House office. Nancy's astrologer sat by her. Nancy looked at her, "The stars impel, they don't compel."

Joan Quigley agreed, "That's right. Now remember, don't let Ronnie talk any of that 'Evil Empire' baloney to Gorbachev. And, share your charts with Gorbachev's adviser, since he has an astrologer. Here are the dates, and times, for you to have Ronnie meet with Gorbachev, give them to Don Regan, the new White House Chief of Staff. Order Regan to follow them. It's your good karma days, understand?"

"Yes."

"Summit-1, Nov. 1985, Geneva. Summit-2, Oct. 1986, Reykjavic, Iceland. Summit-3, Dec. 1987, Washington D.C. Summit-4, Jun. 1988, Moscow. Summit-5, Dec. 1988, New York City."

< >

A few days before my first summit meeting with Soviet leader Mikhail Gorbachev I was visited again by Starwars lobbyists Edward Teller, Lt. General Dan Graham, Gregory Fosseda, Dick Cheney, and Bob Bowman. Back in 1975, with Paul Nitze and Richard Pipes, at the request of several of Bill Casey's central banking partners sitting on the CIA board of directors, CIA Director George Bush asked Lt. Gen. Dan Graham to co-found 'Committee on the Present Danger'.

Bill Casey was handed names of the three men from the board members running CIA to pass along to Bush. Nitze had become my Reagan Administration's leading arms negotiator. Starwars lobbyists Teller, Graham, and Fosseda asked me not to use Starwars as a bargaining chip in my negotiations with the Soviet Union. Cheney disagreed. I relaxed, "I'm not going to bargain-off Starwars with the Evil Empire, gentlemen. Don't worry. Starwars is the only way to defeat them."

Cheney appeared pleased.

"Back in 1948, when I wrote NSC-68," Paul Nitze said, "Allen Dulles was a rabid anti-communist and Christian West was his baby. Dulles believed in fighting a rollback-liberation war to rollback Communism, liberate the people living under Communism, from Communism. Dulles' hard-line anti-Communism was for public consumption, means-to-an-end. Dulles used American intelligence to line his pockets, Mr. President ..don't forget the difference between propaganda and truth. That's the real war."

I was curious, doubtful, skeptical and I didn't have the faintest idea what Nitze was talking about, so I said, "I knew that."

I had an Alzheimer's attack of dementia, a vision, a premonition of what was to come. From nowhere, Mel Gibson's Jesus spoke to me, "There are three Pauls."

The first Paul, was Paul Nitze.

The second Paul, was Paul Weyrich.

Paul Weyrich supported The Society for the Protection of Tradition, Family & Property, a neo-Fascist Catholic renegade sect. In 1973, Coors beer ruling family financed Paul Weyrich, to found, 'The Heritage Foundation'.

In 1974, about the time members of Bill Casey's money-issuing family investment banking group who sat on CIA Board of Directors passed along the names of Paul Nitze, Richard Pipes, and Dan Graham ...to Bill Casey, to give to CIA Director George Bush, letting Bush know to give full CIA cooperation to the Committee on the Present Danger ... the Coors ruling family financed Paul Weyrich to found, 'The Committee for the Survival of a Free Congress'. Coors heavily funded both organizations, both far to the right of traditional Republican Conservatism and far to the right of Right-Wing Republicans …many people referred to the Heritage Foundation, and Free Congress Foundation, as neo-Fascist organizations determined to eliminate civil rights and liberties of non-ruling family everyday Americans. Paul Weyrich was pretty good dancing between the Republican-right, the Republican far-right, the Christian right, the Christian far-right, and the fascist-right but it wasn't pretty. The better he danced, the more fascist dollars flowed in. In 1976, Paul Weyrich, William Rusher, Morton Blackwell, and Richard Vigary tried to takeover the racist, 'American Independent Party', formed by racist Governor George Wallace, in 1968. Many American Independent Party members were members of Ku Klux Klan, John Birch Society …and, Christian Front. Paul Weyrich was a defender of White culture … like neo-Nazi White supremacists are. In 1982, Paul Weyrich had an essay published. He explained, "Culturally destructive government policies of racial hiring quotas and racial busing are immediately important in the realm of action to the New Right, since the damage they do is enormous, irremediable." Weyrich's defense of 'white culture' reflected theories advocated by neo-Nazi white supremacists.

The third Paul is, Paul the Apostle, a true advocate of democracy. All three Pauls were great men in their own times. Paul Nitze, Paul Weyrich, and Paul the Apostle, all knew the Apocalypse peeking around the corner. The first two Pauls and I hated the Evil Empire as much as the third Paul loved Our Lord Jesus Christ and that made a problem for me, I didn't hate the Russian people, I hated Communism, but bullets, like most people, make no such distinction.

Such as Richard Pipes.

<>

In 1981, Richard Pipes was Senior National Security Council Officer in Charge of Soviet Affairs, a Soviet expert on leave from Harvard. Pipes led the pack, "Nothing is left of détente with Soviet Union. Reagan Administration will pursue foreign policy radical as Reagan's new economic program. The Administration is moving to a strategy of confrontation with the Soviet Union, and with radical and socialist regimes in the Third World. The purpose of this strategy is to change world balance of power in favor of the U.S. and its allies. Soviet leaders will have to chose between peacefully changing their Communist system in the direction of the West or going to war." Mar. 1981 Pipes was interviewed by a Reuters correspondent, in *New York Times*, "There's no alternative to war with Soviet Union if the Russians do not abandon Communism."

The Reagan White House officially discounted the interview.

Larry Speakes held a press conference, "The remarks of Senior National Security Council Officer in Charge of Soviet Affairs Richard Pipes didn't represent the views of the Administration."

London Financial Times responded with an editorial, "U.S. allies will be angered by any attempt of the Reagan Administration to play a dangerous game of chicken with Soviet Union." Then, the matter disappeared from the press.

Richard Pipes had deliberately warned the Soviets to build-up their military-industrial complex to rival America's. Pipes was re-starting Nitze's NSC-68 process of spending the Soviet Union into bankruptcy to weaken the Soviet economy. It wasn't really a threat of nuclear war, or was it? The people of the U.S. were frightened. In early 1980s, California think-tank Rand Corp., part of the military-industrial complex, shed light on the question in a series of studies and white papers. Rand carried out top secret intelligence studies for U.S. military that weren't made available to Congress, such as, *Economic Leverage in the Soviet Union ...Costs of Soviet Empire, Sitting on Bayonets? ...Soviet Defense Burden & Moscow's Economic Dilemma.* The papers described economic stress in Soviet Union and how NATO countries could make Soviet economic stress worse. The papers made observations and recommendations in the spirit of 'Committee on the Present Danger' and 'Project for the New American Century' ...in terms of intentionally scaring Americans to death so military-industrial complex Bank of England, Fed and Bundesbank shareholders could swipe more U.S. taxpayer dollars into their own pockets. The Rand papers issued forth, 'Since the Soviet economy is slowing down in the late 1970's, we must do things to help weaken it. The old guard Soviet Communist leadership is being replaced by a younger generation, and there's conflict in leadership of the Communist Party. U.S. and Western powers should force Soviet

Union into an arms race. Deny Soviet Union access to international bank credit, imports and technology needed to increase economic productivity and growth. These suggestions are aimed at stagnating and destabilizing the Soviet civilian economy. By imposing military costs on Soviet Union, the investment climate in Russia will suffer and standard-of-living of the Soviet people fall, hopefully far enough to create dissension and mass movements for political and economic reform'." Rand wanted to weaken the Soviet economy so it was harder to care for the Soviet people and harder to distribute resources to care for them, until their economy went bankrupt ...a covert economic destabilization putsch. Rand encouraged my Reagan Administration handlers to wage economic warfare against Soviet Union, rather than military warfare ...with the same goals in mind ...conquer the Soviet Union.

Political economic analyst Joseph Fromm commented, "There's something behind the shift to a harder line in foreign policy. The U.S. is waging limited economic warfare against Russia, to force Soviets to reform their political system. Soviet Union is in deep economic and financial trouble. By squeezing wherever we can, our purpose is to induce the Soviets to reform their system. We'll see results over the next several years."

Mid-1982, it appeared my Reagan Administration was doing what Rand and Pipes wanted. May 1982, a White House consultant to National Security Council briefed reporters in the White House Press Briefing Room. CNN's Alan covered the press briefing. The subject was, 'U.S. Policy Towards the Soviet Union'. Alan was alarmed. He looked at the National Security Council consultant, "You're outlining aggressive policy against Soviet Union."

Helen Thomas, UPI White House correspondent, felt alarmed, too. She sent in her story to her press bureau, "A Senior White House Official said Reagan approved an eight-page national security document that undertakes a campaign aimed at internal reform in the Soviet Union and the shrinking of the Soviet empire. He affirmed that it could be called, a 'Full-Court Press', against Soviet Union'. In basketball, a full-court press is a strategy of maximum pressure applied against one's adversary in every part of the court. It's an onslaught."

May 20, 1982 National Security Advisor William Clark described the 'Full-Court Press' at Georgetown University, "U.S. strategy is merging into diplomatic, economic, and informational components built on military strength. Cold War rhetoric, East-West trade policy, public diplomacy, and armament are part of an over-all plan. This strategy has a new purpose. We must force the Soviet Union to bear the brunt of its economic shortcomings."

< >

It was now we leaked the Defense Department Report, *Fiscal Years 1984-1988 Defense Guidance Document*, to Richard Hallorin of *New York Times*. May 30, *NYT* published a report on my Administration's nuclear war policy. Hallorin wrote the article as if he was a CIA asset, "Unknown sources sent me a copy of a report, Fiscal Years 1984-1988 Defense Guidance Document. In the guidance document, Defense Secretary Caspar Weinberger talks of 'prevailing in prolonged nuclear war'. Weinberger's guidance document recommends escalating the nuclear-arms race against Soviet Union. Quite apart from that, it indicates measures are being taken to impose costs on Soviet Union. The document says the U.S. should develop weapons too difficult for Soviets to counter, because they impose disproportionate research and development costs. U.S. should open up new areas of major military competition making previous Soviet military financial investments obsolete. Western trade policy should put as much pressure as possible on a Soviet economy burdened with military spending. As a peace-time complement to military strategy, the report asserts the U.S. and its allies ... should declare economic and technical war on the Soviet Union."

Hallorin's article blew the whistle, and the game started ...the 'Full-Court Press' was underway, way beyond the Cold War strategy of Christian West containment of Communism, simply containing the Soviet Union, this was Christian West rollback-liberation, an aggressive tactic to confront then push Communism back and 'liberate' Russia's natural resources for Central Bank one world government New World Order money-issuing, ruling family shareholders and the financial, military, industrial, and petroleum companies on whose boards they sat as directors ...to plunder Russia for personal profit ...business as usual.

Spring 1982, State Secretary Alexander Haig had held a press conference, "Just as Soviet Union gives active support to Marxist-Leninist forces in the West and South, we must give vigorous support to democratic forces wherever they're located, including countries now communist. We shouldn't hesitate to create our own values, knowing that freedom and dignity of man are ideals that motivate the quest for social justice. A free press, free trade unions, free political parties, freedom to travel, and freedom to create are ingredients of the democratic revolution of the future, not the status-quo of a failed past."

<>

My Administration handlers harnessed many forces to 'promote democracy' in Soviet Union and Eastern Europe. These harnessed forces included ...the Republican Party and Democratic Party ...political parties in NATO countries ...private foundations, i.e. limited trust foundations established for the purposes of ruling family capital gains retention, usually propaganda research 'think-tanks' ...AFL/CIO ...private-sector organizations ...and, private-sector organization intelligence fronts such as National Endowment for Democracy NED, and Heritage Foundation, for example. May 10, 1985 ... U.S. Ambassador to United Nations Jean Kirkpatrick gave a speech called, 'The Reagan Doctrine', to members of Heritage Foundation, "What I shall term 'the Reagan Doctrine', focuses on U.S. relations with Soviet Union and its associated states. The principle aims of the Reagan Doctrine are to redress the correlation of forces, stop Soviet expansion, and clarify the nature of the contest. We have to rebuild defenses, expand U.S. military forces, develop new defenses such as the Strategic Defense Initiative. We have to develop and deploy advanced weapons in the U.S. and Europe. We have to withhold from our adversaries advanced technology of military importance. We have to support the rollback-liberation 'freedom-fighters' in low-intensity warfare and war-by-proxy using mercenaries or foreign guerrilla units. We have to make a semantic infiltration and moral disarmament response at the ideological level with propaganda. We have to have a foreign-assistance program and use foreign aid to expand and preserve rollback-liberation freedom."

This 'Reagan Doctrine', was 'the Full-Court Press', the harder line in foreign policy against Soviet Union. By 1984, the program of 'promoting democracy' was at work in Poland and Soviet Union. Richard Pipes wrote an article calling attention to U.S. policy regarding the Soviet Union and Eastern Europe. The article appeared in *Foreign Affairs*, "The growing crisis in Soviet Union can and will be resolved. Soviet Union is in a revolutionary situation. But, what was lacking in the time of Lenin was the subjective element, the ability and will of social groups and social parties to transform the 'revolutionary situation' into a revolution. But, a way can be found around even this obstacle as events in Hungary, Czechoslovakia, and Poland have shown. The only way out of the crisis for the Soviet elite is reform. In the past, the Soviets consented to make changes only under duress caused by humiliations abroad or upheavals at home. Reforms are the price Soviet ruling families must pay for survival. The key to peace, therefore, lies in an internal transformation of Soviet system in the direction of legality, economic decentralization, greater scope for contractual free enterprise, and national self-determination. The West would be well-advised to do all in its power to assist the indigenous forces making for change in the U.S.S.R. and its client states."

National Security Council Adviser Richard Pipes knew what my Administration handlers were doing and planning, in order to control the survival of Soviet ruling families and the Russian people. Pipes was heralding the dismantling of Socialism in Soviet Union. Soviet Union would have to move in the direction of the West or deal with continuing crises and humiliations at home and abroad with unsustainable price tags and mounting pressure. Sean Gervasi, one of America's top public-oriented researchers, wrote an article exposing the Full-Court Press and explaining economic destabilization, Fall 1990 in Lou Wolf's Covert Action Quarterly, called, *A Full-Court Press, the destabilization of the Soviet Union*. "The handlers of Reagan Administration wanted to destabilize

Soviet Union. The typical campaign of de-stabilization involves two elements. The first element is external pressure. The second is internal manipulation. The 'attacker' is bent on creating disruption and turmoil in the target country. The ultimate purpose is to produce a change of government, a coup d'état, or a revolution. But, there's no assurance the disruption and turmoil will produce the desired political results. Therefore, the attacking power also intervenes in the internal political process in the target country to ensure events move in the desired direction. Intervention is usually covert. The first step is identifying and even creating political assets such as influential individuals, civic groups, trade unions, youth groups, cultural organizations, and media organizations in conflict with, or hostile, to the targeted government. Then, these assets are manipulated to further the political purposes of the attacker. This is what the U.S. and other Western countries have been doing inside the Soviet Union and Eastern Europe ...the Socialist Bloc countries. Reagan & Bush Administration intervened in a covert and overt fashion to destabilize Soviet Union and Eastern Europe. What is striking today, is that so many public agencies and private organizations are doing exactly what intelligence agencies have exclusively done in the past. U.S. Government agencies, foundations, business groups, media organizations, human-rights groups, trade unions and others are all supporting and aiding opposition groups, particularly in Soviet Union. They're openly aiding and guiding forces hostile to socialist governments. What's equally striking is this intervention is now openly talked about without the slightest criticism or protest from Congress, the mass media, or opposition political groups in our own country. Having succeeded in aggravating the crisis in Soviet Union, the U.S. and its allies are now engaged in building internal pressures there, for further reforms. They're engaged in open, large-scale interference in the internal affairs of Soviet Union. U.S. policies moved things very far, very fast in Soviet Union, particularly in recent years when aid to the anti-Communist opposition has involved domestic expenditures of hundreds-of-millions-of-dollars. There is some question about whether the Cold War is, indeed over. But, did the cost of the Full-Court Press to destabilize and bankrupt Soviet

Union, also bankrupt and destabilize the United States and create economic chaos in our own country?"

<>

In my Alzheimer's vision of dementia, Mel's Jesus said, there was a monopoly of American and British ruling families covertly investing in building up the economy of the U.S.S.R. since 1918 ...now, rival forces wanted a piece of the pie ...that, banking, military, industrial, and petroleum ruling families handling my Administration took the U.S. from the world's largest creditor nation, to the world's largest debtor nation ...pick-pocketing taxpayers and dumping billions of dollars into their own pockets as usual ...successfully bankrupting Russia and America ...that, economic warfare against the Soviet people was at the same time waged against American taxpayers ...that, national debt carried by American taxpayers is taken from their paychecks and pockets ... and goes into the pockets of American Fed and British Bank of England money-issuing ruling families ...that, our American and British rulers successfully robbed the American people again and again till they had stolen, then bankrupted the American dream. Stole U.S. quality of life, and destroyed American family values.

But, I didn't have time to listen! I had a country to run!

<>

Nov. 1985, at the summit with the Russians in Geneva, Nancy happily shared astrology charts with Mikhail Gorbachev's wife, Raisa. This bored Raisa. So, Nancy turned to Gorbachev's adviser, showed him her astrology charts. He was delighted. Nancy and Raisa Gorbachev start having cat fights about nothing ...and, everything.

Meanwhile, George Shultz and his business consultants with Russian counterparts met behind closed doors to dictate foreign policy terms and interest rates to each another. They, in effect, decided which central banks would make which loans, to whom and at what cost. They determined loans BIS, IMF, Ex-Im Bank, and World Bank would make ...what interest rates the Fed, Bank of England, Bundesbank and all the other central banks they controlled would charge, everyone. Profits, of course, went to majority private shareholders and founding shareholders of the central banks. Like opposing football teams, the real central bank people waging war on humanity were on different central bank teams, but were united in the same league. Which means, all wars can be traced to one group of central bank majority shareholders, or another ...and the company boards they sat on as directors ... very simple. Or, to the drug warlords they allied themselves with or became allied with to avoid 'mutually-assured self-destruction'.

<>

I sat in a waiting room with Mikhail Gorbachev, waiting for businessmen in the next room behind closed doors to finalize their deals and emerge victorious. We awkwardly made small talk, "I'm determined to build Starwars."

Gorbachev bit his lip, "You know, Mr. President, contrary to popular belief, World War II did not stop in 1945. Nazi guerrilla units stayed behind in Soviet Union and Eastern Europe. They waged armed struggle against us until 1952. I think you may have heard of Reinhard Gehlen and Otto Skorzeny?"

I was daydreaming.

Gorbachev sighed heavily and fell into despair. He looked at Raisa, shrugged, "It's an interesting story, have Bill Casey tell it to you one day. Just before the end of World War II, Allen Dulles took command of leftover Nazi Freikorps units, left behind in Soviet Union. He made a merger, formed CIA largely out of Hitler's anti-Soviet intelligencers and Nazi soldiers."

My attention wandered. I yawned, "I helped FBI stop your communist plot to takeover Hollywood. You know, if Earth were invaded by aliens ...like in, The Day The Earth Stood Still, us two major superpowers would have to cooperate, not to mention the major studios."

Gorbachev laughed and looked at Raisa, "Please translate this into English for me?"

Following the summit, a press conference was held. Nancy was upset. She spoke to reporters, "Raisa Gorbachev tried to upstage me in a photo session! Who does this dame think she is?"

I had some comments for the press, too, "I criticized Soviet Union for violating SALT and ABM Treaties. I denounced their record on human rights. Gorbachev told me, Starwars would violate our anti-missile treaty. I told him, I am building Starwars!"

Chief of Staff Don Regan waited until me and Nancy finished talking with the press. Then, he talked to them, "The Reagans are pleased Raisa and Mikhail Gorbachev are movie buffs. Raisa and Mikhail listened spellbound to every detail President Reagan told them about his Hollywood days. They were very pleased to be in the company of somebody that knew Jimmy Stewart, John Wayne, and Humphrey Bogart."

At the Oct. 1986 summit with the Russians in Reykjavic Iceland, Nancy and Raisa had cat fights. They disagreed about everything from weather to time of day. Mikhail Gorbachev and I shared conflicting views of Cold War history, but we both wanted to get rid of 'Mutually-Assured Nuclear Destruction' scenarios. Gorbachev smiled, "I suggest we both cut the number of long-range ballistic missiles we have, by 50%. Then, I'll work to eliminate them all, together. Then, we must honor the anti-missile treaty for ten more years ...you must confine Starwars to the laboratory."

It was time for a meeting recess starring George Shultz talking with hardline anti-Communist, Richard Perle. Perle walked over me and adamantly stated, "Ronnie you and the Kremlin are the only people who take Starwars seriously. I'm against arms control. Make a bold counter-offer, Gorbachev will reject it. If he accepts, that leaves America with more strategic bombers and cruise missiles than him."

Following recess, I challenged Gorbachev, "I propose we eliminate all American, British, and French ballistic missiles over a ten-year period. But, at the end of that, the U.S. is free to deploy Starwars, so no third party countries cheat, have any 'accidental' missile firings or make any military threats."

Gorbachev assessed the situation, "Why don't we eliminate all of the world's nuclear weapons, not just their delivery systems?" Raisa felt proud of her husband's response to my offer.

Perle could see I was pleased with the suggestion. I liked the idea. Perle was upset. If I and Mikhail agreed, then the advantage Perle hoped for would be lost. He wished he never suggested I make a bold counter-offer.

Mikhail continued, "But, you must agree not to deploy Starwars, after it's built."

I got angry. I'd rehearsed this. I shouted, "You threw me a curve ball! Starwars is not a bargaining chip!"

Perle sighed heavily and got a second wind.

<>

Back in Washington, my advisers talked to me before a press conference. They felt relieved, no formal agreement had been reached. Larry Speakes made opening remarks to the press. National Security Adviser Admiral Poindexter tried to explain something to me, "Ronnie, we've got to clear up this business about you, agreeing to get rid of all nuclear weapons."

I shrugged my shoulders, "But, John, I did agree to that."

"No," Poindexter said, "you couldn't have. You have no authority to get rid of British or French weapons."

"I was there ..and, I did agree."

Chief of Staff Don Regan turned to reporters. Don Regan leaned over to CNN's Alan, who was taking notes for a story, "Some of us follow behind Ronnie like a shovel brigade behind a circus parade of elephants, cleaning up."

<>

Following the Challenger disaster I addressed the Nation, "The astronauts have slipped the surly bonds of earth to touch the face of God. Our nation is grateful for their sacrifice. We'll reach out for new goals, and greater achievements, to commemorate our seven Challenger heroes."

Peggy Noonan, who wrote that speech, stood on the sidelines, watching with interest.

Autumn 1987, my negotiators and Gorbachev's negotiators agreed. They'd remove intermediate-range nuclear-tipped missiles from Europe. This was the first time two superpowers agreed to destroy a whole range of weapons. To Richard Perle's surprise, Gorbachev accepted an American demand for mutual on-site inspection. I bragged a little bit, "I knew, if we went ahead building more missiles ...then, the Soviets would have to, too. But, the Soviets are having a major economic crises. My friend, Paul Weyrich, told me. So, I knew the Soviets would agree."

Everyone listening to me in the Situation Room was silent. They couldn't believe I knew what I was doing.

<>

Unfortunately, Don Regan had offended Nancy ...several times. So, I fired Don Regan. Then, Senator Howard Baker was made Chief of White House Staff. Bill Casey was sick a lot. There was talk, Bill would be replaced by FBI director William Webster. I replaced several of my hardline anti-Communist advisers who'd rather go to war. I fired Pointdexter, replaced him with Frank Carlucci to head National Security Council. Caspar Weinberger 'resigned' a few months later. Carlucci was promoted to Defense Secretary. Lt. General Colin Powell succeeded Carlucci as National Security Adviser. This new team was less far-Right in their Christian West anti-Communism bloodlust. They were more sincere, more willing to negotiate arms control, wanted nuclear détente with U.S.S.R. Nancy backed them up. Nancy wanted a major agreement between me and Gorbachev. Nancy knew that could repair my image after the Iran-Contra scandal, cause Nancy was a Hollywood girl. Nancy wanted, with all her heart, to make Soviet détente my presidential legacy. Nancy wanted a thaw in Cold War politics, to be a feather in my cap.

Dec. 1987, Mikhail Gorbachev visited Washington to sign the Intermediate-Range Nuclear Missile treaty. Me and Gorbachev sat down at the negotiating table. I noticed a change in Mike Gorbachev,

"You seem more willing to talk about the bad shape the Soviet economy is in."

Gorbachev was on a mission, "The Soviet military-industrial putsch is bleeding our economy to death. George Kennan predicted containment or rollback-liberation against the Soviet Union, and an economic blockade against us by our World War II allies ...would eventually bankrupt us. It took 50 years, but he was right. The Nazis completely destroyed Soviet industry in World War II. Since the war, it's been a long struggle for Russia to survive."

I was confused, "I'm not much of a world history buff. I know since Stalin, Moscow dominated its neighbors in Eastern Europe ...and, intimidated its rivals."

"Just like your CIA does," Gorbachev said, "now, it's time for me to ensure Soviet security in the world by cooperating with neighboring states, and other world powers." Gorbachev's aide winked knowingly to Gorbachev. Gorbachev's aide spoke to me, complimenting me on my B-films, then winked to Gorbachev, again.

I shifted uncomfortably in my chair, "They weren't all B-films."

Gorbachev's aide tried to smooth things over, "I like the one about the fellow who loses his legs and where you say, 'Where's the rest of me?'"

I felt better, "That one's called, King's Row, that's no B-film!"

Nancy interrupted, offering me and our guests ice tea. After the talks ended and the agreement was set, Gorbachev made a few photo-ops for himself. Gorbachev hosted a party for Paul Newman, Yoko Ono, and Henry Kissinger. Once, when Gorbachev was being chauffeured through the streets of Washington D.C. he had his driver stop. Gorbachev got out in the streets and randomly shook the hands of pedestrians. Gorbachev was happy, "I just want to say hello to you." I guess, he had to do his own photo-ops.

At a press conference, I was asked if I felt overshadowed by Gorbachev inviting Paul Newman, an America movie star, to his party with Yoko and Henry. It didn't really upstage me, too much, "I don't resent his popularity. Good Lord, I co-starred with Errol Flynn once."

My popularity was on the rise again. But, by showing warmth to Moscow, I angered my far-right supporters. The most hardcore anti-Communist 'warriors' felt I had been the useful idiot of a communist Jewish conspiracy to take over the world.

That's show biz.

CHAPTER 10

Bill Casey knew, a thaw in Cold War relations meant one day soon, the Soviet Union would disintegrate. Interlocking board directors of Bank of England, Fed, BIS, World Bank, Ex-Im Bank, IMF in his banking investment consortium would re-colonize Soviet Union, openly lend money at high interest rates, restrict trade. ..then, foreclose ... topple Soviet Union with economic warfare. Then, they'd again own the Russian natural resource portfolios they lost in 1918 ...and co-develop Russia, like back in Czarist times.

June 1988 summit in Moscow, Gorbachev and Raisa both, again, personally told me they were great movie buffs. So, I told the Gorbachevs stories about Hollywood movie star greats. They were enthralled. My appearance in Moscow signaled the beginning of the end of the Cold War. I hugged Gorbachev, in front of Lenin's tomb.

Reporters crowded around me. CNN's Alan asked, "Is the Soviet Union still the focus of evil in the modern world."

I smiled proudly, "They've changed."

State Secretary George Shultz spoke to Alan, "I was impressed Gorbachev matched Ronnie, joke for joke."

<>

Later, at the Bolshoi Ballet, I stood at attention while the Soviet orchestra played, 'The Star-Spangled Banner'. Between us, U.S.A.

and Soviet Union, we still had 30,000 nuclear weapons aimed at each other.

Dec. 1988 New York summit, I was still telling Gorbachev Hollywood stories. That was our final summit ...so, I had to talk fast.

Gorbachev smiled at me, "During 1988, I've withdrawn Soviet troops from Afghanistan. I've tried to end civil wars in Ethiopia, Angola, and Southeast Asia."

I smiled back, "Perhaps the United Nations is the best forum to mediate these civil wars and counter-revolutions."

"I'm reducing conventional forces."

While our negotiators worked behind closed doors, me and Gorbachev chatted. I finally got a chance to start telling Gorbachev more Hollywood stories. Shultz, and his Soviet counterparts, came out from behind closed doors. George Shultz smiled, "We've worked out U.S.-Soviet foreign policy details."

I wasn't happy, "I'm not done talking about Errol Flynn and Gary Cooper."

Gorbachev invited me, and President-elect George Bush, to pose for pictures with him in a photo-op in front of the Statue of Liberty. Newspapers and magazines start popularizing the end of the Cold War.

But, still no Oscar.

<>

Patti pasted-in another headline in her scrapbook from the *New York Times*, 'Another Obstacle Falls, Nancy Reagan & Raisa Gorbachev get chummy.' The news story said, "The most assertive anti-communist President since World War II has achieved a foreign policy goal none of the President's before him could achieve, breakthroughs on arms control, new cooperation in settling Third World disputes. Now, how long will Soviet Union continue to dominate Eastern Europe?

Joan Quigley's office in San Francisco

Nancy's astrologer sat in her office in San Francisco telling Nancy's story to CNN's Alan, "As a result of the successful U.S.-Soviet Summit meetings between Ronnie and Mikhail, Ronnie's approval rating soared. Ronnie and Nancy were so pleased that negative press from the Iran-Contra scandal had faded ...as the public perceived it, the commotion was forgotten."

Alan closed his note pad, "Thanks for the interview."

White House presidential bedroom

Rolling Stones music played on the White House Muzak system in the presidential bedroom where Nancy and I'd just finished making love. The marionette my daughter Maureen had given me sat on a bedroom bureau, overlooking the bed. I smiled at Nancy, "That was fun, just like the old days. Good night, Honey."

Nancy was satisfied, "You're telling me! Good night, Darling. I'm glad women have it easier than men when we're older, we just have to lie there."

I felt less than thrilled, "Sleep tight."

"Pleasant dreams." Nancy flicked the light switch, the lights in the room went off. It was dark. Nancy heard my breathing even out, I was falling asleep. Nancy heard me tossing and turning.

I started talking in my sleep, "In my heart I didn't mean to trade guns-for-hostages. In my heart, in my heart." I was having a nightmare. I heard machine-guns firing. I heard people screaming. Startled, I sat up in bed.

Nancy turned the lights on, staring at the expression on my face, she felt upset, took my head and laid it on her breast to comfort me.

I felt my confusion clearing, "Nancy, this whole Iran-Contra mess keeps going around and around in my head. I've got to talk to Casey before he dies, I've got to ask him what bridge he's hailing from, who the real puppet-master is."

Nancy stroked my head, "Maybe Casey's being blackmailed

...because, the petroleum-banking-intelligence community's grown too small for him to hide in anymore."

I got up out of bed. Nancy saw, I was in a grieving mood ...but, that mood was switching to Irish temper. I went into my closet, took off my pajama shirt.

Nancy felt alarmed, "Ronnie, what are you doing?! It's the middle of the night!"

I was enthusiastic, "Not, for the All-American boy! Not, for Ronald Reagan, movie star! Not, for the President of the United States, it isn't. It's finally the cold, hard light of day."

Nancy was concerned, she didn't want me to be alone when I acted out like this. Nancy knew what I was thinking, "You can't go see Casey in the hospital, now! It's 9:30 at night! All right ...I can see that stubborn Irish, determined look in your eyes. I'm going, too."

Hospital corridor, Washington D.C.

Me and Nancy walked down the hospital corridor towards Bill Casey's hospital room. Nancy saw the guards talking to each other, they seemed sad. I started walking past the Secret Service guards to enter the room. I put my hand on the hospital door, a Secret Service guard put his hand gently on my hand to stop me. The guard shook his head, sadly. I realized, Bill Casey was dead. I felt my spirits sink. I stared off into the distance.

I turned to Nancy, "It's too late, Casey's dead. Now, we'll never know what was going on." I felt disappointed. Nancy did too.

Nancy watched as a visitor walked out of Casey's room, bidding farewell, "Bye-bye, hang in there." Nancy was surprised and looked at me. I felt surprised, too. I threw open the door and pushed the visitor gently out of the way.

The visitor grabbed my shirt, "Let him die in peace, can't you?!"

I yelled at the Secret Service guard, "Get this person off me! Clear him out of my way!"

Nancy was furious, "That's a direct order from the President of the United States!"

One Secret Service man grabbed the visitor, gently pulled him down the hall. My ego was wounded. I felt shocked, at having been restrained. I stared at the other Secret Service men. He took a deep breath, then sighed, "You can't go in there, it's a breach of national security."

I was angry, "Shut up! I am national security! Get out of my way!" I stormed into the hospital room. I looked at Bill, I suddenly felt awe, my hard feelings softened, I no longer felt upset. I smoothed my hair back with my hand, the way I always did before I started to act or to make a speech. I no longer acted angry or desperate, I acted friendly, genuinely concerned for Bill, who lay on his deathbed. I sat down on a chair beside him, seeing he was in a fog ... I saw a surreal, peaceful look on his face ...like death warmed-over. I still felt confrontational, but decided to be gentle about it. I was solemn, "I apologize for storming in here ...being angry, at a time like this."

"Who is it?" Bill said. He felt confused. "What time is it? Is it time to go to sleep yet?"

I looked at my watch, "It's 10 o'clock in the evening, all big boys should be asleep."

"Oh it's you, Ronnie, you clown, how are you?"

I felt my anger was totally gone, "You can't just die on me like this."

Bill tried to smile, but just mumbled, "It happens all the time, we get our tickets punched."

No. Not yet, "You gotta tell me who's pulling my strings? Who's making decisions behind my back?"

Nancy sat down beside me, "Bill, are you being blackmailed?"

I raised my voice a little, "Bill, I know you're CIA director, but who's the producer? Who do you work for? You've got to tell me!"

Bill felt peaceful, he could care less ...but, had the energy to feel amused, "No one tells me what to do, we're all pulling each others' strings, Ronnie."

Nancy saw that confused look on my face. I tried to smile, "I'm playing it close to the chest! I'm not pulling anybody's strings."

Bill felt far away, "I know you're not. I said, we are, not you. You're not from a ruling family, you're not the money-issuing elite guard, you wouldn't understand the responsibility of dynastic wealth and power of the money-issuing apparatus to make a one world government."

I saw the light start to fade in Bill's eyes. I was shocked. I felt frantic, "Who are they?!"

Casey was fading fast, "We're Earth's ruling families, Ronnie. We're all over the world. We're the ones that issue the money. We'd fill up a football stadium, not much more. I'll tell you that, but we control real power."

That wasn't enough, "You're not making sense, Bill. Who?"

Nancy interrupted, "Bill, these intelligence people who hang themselves or go mad? Were they murdered? I'm going crazy wondering if Ronnie's safe, or if we have to shut up."

Bill kept closing and opening his eyes, "I think about Angleton, Wisner, Forrestal. Dulles told me they went mad, or were suicides ...like Paul Robeson. I lay in this bed, wondering if I've been poisoned or irradiated or microwaved. I wonder if someone's murdering me. Yes, you better shut up."

Nancy shut up. She didn't know what to say. I was confused, "But why me?! I'm anti-communist! I've always supported the World Anti-Communist League and anti-communist freedom-fighters, Colonia Dignatad, Skorzeny, Odessa, International Fascista, Contra death squads, BCCI. Where did I go wrong?"

Bill mumbled, "I'll let you know a secret, Dulles, von Hohenlohe, DeMohrenshieldt, Rosenberg. There was never any communist threat. It was all make-believe."

I was floored, "I deserve better than that, Bill!"

Casey barely smiled, "Bechtel had us choose you, because you were an old man full of yourself, you'd do anything for a good audience, reassure him, send him away laughing, make him feel like he matters, with a wife that would do anything to make you look good. You got what you wanted, fame, glory, attention, you got to be a star."

I was confused and felt small. Then, I had a realization, "You used me."

"Welcome home. We pulled your strings. You were a puppet, a marionette, all presidents are, they just find out at different times. Christ, we never accepted you as one of us, Ronnie, we were the real actors, not you."

I couldn't believe what I was hearing, "You used me, all the time you used me?"

"You used yourself, champ, don't take it so hard, there's always strings attached for us, too."

Nancy saw I was emotionally drained, she put her hand tenderly on my arm. I felt confused.

Casey managed a smile, "The sociopathic ruling families of the world would fill a football stadium or two on a Sunday afternoon. If you got rid of us, then you common people with good hearts and strong backs could rule the world. Let me die now, Ronnie, it's time."

I felt my temper rising, I felt vindictive, "You're going to Hell, that's where you're going, Bill."

"And you," Bill said, "are you going too?"

That stopped me. I felt dumb. Maybe I was.

Casey mumbled, "Don't look so shocked, Ronnie, you may be been a b-grade actor, but you were an a-grade president."

I sensed the inevitable. I felt myself getting calm. Something in me wanted to assure Bill, "Thank you, Bill. Remember that day at the Vatican when the Pope shook our hands and asked us if we were good Catholics?"

"Yes, I remember that. You said, 'I don't know, it depends on who you ask.' That was a good one."

I laughed warmly, quietly. I felt love for Bill.

Bill seemed to be falling asleep, "It's been a good life, but it's been too long a life, Ronnie. Y'know, Dulles that old devil, he always said we'd rot in Hell together, maybe he's right."

I felt fond of him, "Bill, I hope you're happily in heaven a half hour before the devil knows you're dead." I stared off into the distance.

So did Bill. He whispered very low, "I'm made in God's image, but so is Wall Street. It's funny, the Russians are blackmailing Bush because Monzer Al-Kassar worked for the Russians, not Syria, not Iran, not Britain, not us, but for the Russians. Russians really are in control. Bank of England and Fed made me give them a few points on their BIS, World Bank, Ex-Im and IMF loans ...that's what its all about, a few points. The Germans will finish them off. The Deutschemark and Yen will finish them off even if the dollar doesn't, we've done the Great Depression routine before, you'll see, they'll be a new pearl harbor and all the financing and all the loans will start all over again, you can't stop us, we hold the bank."

I felt sad watching Bill die. George Bush stepped partly out of the shadows of the dimly lit room, half his face was hidden in shadows behind the curtains, "Plausible deniability, Ronnie. We gave it to you for your safety, because we care about you."

Onboard Air Force One in flight

In flight on board Air Force One, State Secretary George Shultz was putting golf balls down the aisle towards an Old Fashion glass, "How's your mood holding-up, Mr. President."

I was not my usual jovial self, "I still have a bitter taste in my mouth from Casey's death ...it's like, he took part of me to the grave with him."

George Shultz smiled in his debonair way, "That's the way it always is. Hey, do one of your imitations for us, won't you, you silly boy?"

I extended a limp wrist and sashayed past the golf balls rolling around on the floor, portraying a queen. The passengers in the plane loved it, they clapped. I soaked it up. "Say, Sweetie, I've had to re-evaluate my position on AIDS, and I'm not going to take it sitting down. I've failed to adjust from time to time, what's a poor girl to do boopy do?"

Nancy felt embarrassed, she went ballistic. She made me stop doing my queer act and sit back down in my seat. Nancy felt like she needed some attention, she start walking down the aisles of Air Force One passing out cookies to everyone.

George Shultz took a couple, "Well, it seems that if the G-7 decide to go ahead and finance war in Yugoslavia for Germany's push to its 'Eastern Territories' and the Balkans, the U.S. might get the Baku oil fields from Russia after all, after 80 years. If the war goes ahead on schedule ...then, Bechtel, Halliburton, Kelley Brown & Root and bid Laden construction will compete for windfall contracts to rebuild the war zones ...when we're done destroying everything, and German, British, and U.S. central banks will issue the credit and loans and reap the interest on soaring national debts. U.S. arms manufacturers in the military-industrial complex under Weinberger will reap windfall profits too, it's a win-win. The way it looks now, we're scheduled to go to war against Iran or Iraq in the next administration to beef-up 3rd quarter petroleum numbers and solidify one world government."

I was still smiling from my queen performance. I turned towards George Shultz, "I'm trying to figure-out the intelligence pyramid. My Administration and Bechtel ... versus ... Bush, Casey and Halliburton, Brown & Root, and bin Laden construction? Dulles masterminded New England, Texas, California and German money. Carter was deep South, I'm California, Bush and Casey northeast, Florida, and Texas money-issuing families."

George Shultz frowned, "Are you asking me if Bush was out of the loop ...or, is Bush the loop?"

I felt I had inside information from Bush ...and, Casey, "George already told me, 'Stay out of the loop? ... I am the loop.' You're telling me Dulles represented ruling families on both sides of the Atlantic and those ruling families were really fighting low class, middle class and upper class families on both sides of the Atlantic? And, the Pacific? That Dulles partnered with European, Japanese, Czarist, and German General Staff ruling families against the lower class, middle class, and upper class families of the whole world, that's the new World Order everyone's talking about? And the global money-issuing families are pulling the strings? It's that simple?"

George Shultz nodded, "The new World Order one world government is only for the benefit of those families who own controlling shares of the central banks, the interlocking board directorates they sit on and the companies they own. No one else matters. Bushes, Fords, General Motors, basically the Warburg banking group community, which is basically the Rothschild entourage ... everyone's tied-in through Wall Street, BIS, World Trade Org. It's always the money-issuing elite ruling families of the world ... against lower classes, middle classes, and upper classes ...we just make it look like it's one country against another for show, it plays. We confuse people, make them think what we want them to, we own the news, the movies, we determine education policy, make everyone think it's one group of countries against another ... but, it never is ...it's just ruling families that sit on central bank boards fighting turf wars over another central bank's ruling family's property rights. Look at it this way. U.S. intelligence took over the world drug trade from the British except in Africa and China ... where we left it for them ...but, Bank of England owns majority shares in the Fed ...so, there you go. Casey and his team used North and Al-Kassar to finance and train bin Laden's Muhajidin to attack the Soviet Union, to put pressure on Gorbachev and financed everything with black budget drug money and taxpayer money, none of their own money. At the same time, Weyrich spearheaded WACL and the Full-Court Press to finance Fascist and Nazi groups to destabilize Soviet Union and Eastern Europe to recolonize that half of the continent before marching on India and China. We never tell taxpayers what we're doing, not even the ruling class knows, just the money-issuing class determines the structure of society, that's what we teach our kids, not yours. It's our family values, not yours, that we're talking about."

I was finally getting some answers, "Was BCCI the central money laundry for all that drug money and illegal arms trafficking money, after the Nyugen Hand and Cayman Island bank fronts were exposed?"

George Shultz putted another shot, "Along with Casey's personal international banking investment partners in MI-6, DINA Spanish intelligence, Vatican bank, the usual crew of suspects." George was determined, he kept putting. He'd make a putt into a whiskey glass, then would aim for another of several he'd spread out on the floor of Air Force One. He was a good putter.

I kept figuring it out, "So, Soviet GRE and KGB were blackmailing Casey to get better interest terms to pick-up points for their group of central banks competing against World Bank, IMF and BIS, Ex-Im Bank, Fed, Bank of England and Bundesbank ...while, everyone competed for interest futures on Third World country development, and arms loans."

Shultz putted another golf ball into the glass, "Got it! Got another one in. Don't forget your Administration, they did the same thing here to the U.S. ...bankrupted, destabilized the United States, for God's sake ... the amount of money we make each day from interest on the national debt is mind-boggling, that's the coup of the century, makes the Savings & Loan fiasco look like child's play."

I was putting pieces together like a jig-saw puzzle, trying to get the big picture together, "Casey, Bush, North, MI-6, Monzer Al-Kassar, GRU, McFarland, Poindexter, Mossad, CIA, Bechtel intelligence, Halliburton intelligence, bin Laden Construction intelligence, Brown & Root intelligence, military-industrial intelligence ...and, oil company intelligence ... are one big family ...in bed together?"

"At the moment," Shultz said, "... I can't promise you, tomorrow. It's like a football league, we trade players, move teams around, but it stays the same game with no national borders drawn on ruling families by the money-issuing class, just on the other classes. Get it?"

"Do the American people matter?"

"Taxpayers, consumers, soldiers. We take their paychecks, put them into our savings accounts, that's the I.R.S."

I was tired, "Then, Deaver, Alarcon, the Contras were just an extension of one central bank consortium competing against another ...a game?"

"Well, kind of," George Shultz said, "The global drug economy is bigger than the global legitimate economy ...so, you have to factor that in. So, we do, we partner with the druggies ...then, we have to own that racket, too ...cause its real power, like what you said ... along with BCCI in Bahrain after Nyugen-Hand bank front closed ...and, Vatican bank drew too much attention."

I yawned, "I think I've had enough foreign policy lessons for today, State Secretary Shultz."

Shultz laughed in his good natured way.

Nancy had fallen asleep, long ago. Nancy was dreaming. Nancy remembered, Lucky told her what to expect when the Queen of England visited Nancy at Nancy's West Coast White House ranch, above Santa Barbara. Nancy was excited, "Tell me what to expect, when the Queen of England visits me."

Lucky knew all about it, "What's it like to be Queen? Queens have certain characteristics in common, starting with stamina. They never seem to get tired. They never ask for the ladies room. Queens usually wear hats, so they don't have to worry about their hair, come wind or rain. They wear sensible shoes. They need an endless supply of white cotton gloves, which get worn and dirty after a round of handshakes."

Nancy remembered wearing her most expensive gowns to impress the Queen of England and financial ruler of half the world. Nancy remembered Ronnie hamming it up, to entertain the Queen ... showing her his video copy of, King's Row, putting it in the VCR, turning on the TV, narrating it.

I looked over at Nancy sleeping. I smiled at George Shultz, "George, look at Nancy, she's passed out. Y'know, George, if I'd known ... before I was President ...that, the Presidency's a part you played telling lies, winning approval and playing God, it would've been easier, than finding out the hard way. I wish you'd tipped me off."

George Bush came out of the plane's bathroom. He sat down next to me, "Ronnie, enjoying the flight?"

I whispered to him, "Why the hell didn't you tell me you had the Republican Heritage Groups Council filled up with Nazi death-squad leaders?!"

George Bush looked at me, "Well, the votes they got us elected us. I needed 'em to do the same thing on both Reagan-Bush campaigns ...and, on my Bush-for-President campaign ...and, we're using them on the Full-Court Press to destabilize Soviet Union and Eastern Europe."

"What press? ...I don't have a press conference, now!" I said, "do I? I'm sleepy, let's talk later."

December 1987, White House

I was serving my last week at the White House. I entered George Bush's office to close the window ...because, the wind was blowing papers off George Bush's desk, onto the floor. I stepped behind the curtain to close the window. The window was stuck. While I was behind the curtain, George Bush walked into the room with the King of Syria, King Assad ...and, the King's son, Haidar, Head of Syrian Intelligence. I listened, George Bush welcomed them to the White House. King Assad start talking, "Haidar and I will keep quiet about you sending Buckley to Beirut on his little covert counter-kidnapping and torture expedition ...and, how you were behind it. Only ...if you reverse U.S. policy on Syria, give Syria foreign aid, influence IMF, World Bank, Ex-Im Bank ...and, BIS ... to make favorable loans to Syria and stabilize our currency in international trade ...have them stabilize our trade credits ...and, put a few percentage points in our pockets for Western development loans to Syria. We'll do customary kickbacks into appropriate Congressional campaign funds through U.S. domestic accounts, non-profits and dummy companies."

I was totally shocked to hear what King Assad said. Bush responded to them, "You've got nothin' on me. I was out of the loop, it was Casey. But, I want to keep his memory clean, avoid embarrassment for the Administration. Let's shake on it, get it over with."

They shook hands. The King of Syria and his son, Haidar, Head of Syrian Intelligence left George Bush's office. I stepped out from behind the curtain. I angrily confronted George Bush, "Buckley wasn't an innocent victim?! You sent him! He really wasn't a hostage?! He was an intelligence operative on a covert operation?!"

Bush didn't mince around, "Yes. And, I have the papers you signed to authorize it."

"I'm pissed off! You never told me the truth, about anything. I sign whatever my staff puts under my nose!"

"Plausible deniability. We gave ..."

I interrupted him, "...it to you for your own safety! I know! I know!"

Bush was calm, "Well, we did."

I was upset, struggling to restrain my fury. "Never again! I've had enough, 'plausible deniability! I've had it with politics! Never again! I'll tell you something. George, I've always said ... when we stop criticizing politicians in Washington as 'they' ...and, start saying 'we', it's time to go home ...I'm going home!"

I stormed out of George Bush's office. I was surprised to find Nancy standing outside in the hall, eavesdropping. Nancy was pretending to clap wildly ...but, her hands didn't touch ...so, it was quiet. As soon as I saw her, I stopped being angry. I tried not to laugh out loud. Nancy was trying not to laugh out loud, too. Nancy was excited as she whispered to me, "Encore! Bravo! I knew you had it in you! I knew you could do it!"

I bowed. I kissed her. Both of us, trying not to laugh, we hurried off down the hall, skipping hand-in-hand. When we turned down another hall, we both burst out laughing. I had gotten away safely with my life ...and, could go home.

Farewell

I made my farewell address to a captive audience, "I'm going to read from a letter, from a sailor on the aircraft carrier, Midway ... stationed in the South China Sea. The crew saw a boat, so full of refugees ... it was almost sinking in the water. Risking his own life, this sailor joined a rescue party to save the refugees. They set out in a small motor launch. The Midway's sailor boarded the sinking boat full of refugees. One of the Indochinese refugees stood up ...and, called out to him, 'Hello American sailor, Hello Freedom Man'. This incident symbolizes, to me, America's promise to bring freedom to the world. I believe we're fulfilling this promise. I'm glad of the part I played in bringing freedom to the world."

West Coast White House

There, at my West Coast White House in the hills of Santa Barbara overlooking the Pacific Ocean, I sat with my head in my hands. I felt lost. I watched a moth flirting with a candle flame in a glass chimney on the picnic table. I didn't understand anyone, anymore, anyway. I heard Nancy's voice calling me from the forest. I turned around, stared into the Redwood and Pine trees at the fog drifting in between them, from the sea.

Sixteen years out of office, I was still carrying an armload of autographed Bibles, handing them to my kids. I took a bow. In my head, I was playing my movie star role in, Kings Row. I walked around, repeating my best line ever in a Hollywood film, "Where's the rest of me? ... Where's the rest of me?" I watched my imaginary audience smile, clap, cheer. I was on the alert. There was a war going on around me. Nobody else could see the war going on around me, but me. I listened, the sound of rifles with silencers being fired sounded like me breaking a carrot in two. I listened, the rifles went off quietly, blending in with the droning of crickets folding into the droning of the waves on the beach below. I hid behind a tall redwood tree so, no one could see me. I watched terrorists shooting everyone. From out of nowhere, I was the sheriff in one of my movies, shooting bad guys, watching them fall like dominoes. I felt happy, "I'm going home! I'm going home! I can't play, anymore," I told them. "It's time to go home. I'm going home."

Nancy sadly watched, "Bravo! Bravo! Bravo!"

Nancy led me to a picnic table to have lunch. The rest of my family was at the picnic table waiting for me. Patti was at the table, when Nancy helped me sit down. I went in and out of my dementia. I was back now.

Patti described her Playboy shoot and her conversation with the Playboy photographer, to me and Nancy. I frowned, "Patti, we don't approve you posing for Playboy."

Patti shrugged, "Mom, I thought we had a new policy of honesty, because, we're trying to pull the family together."

Nancy smile reassured me. Nancy bit her lip. Patti remembered her Playboy shoot. While they were doing the shoot, Patti was telling the photographer her life story. Patti looked at the photographer, "That's what being a President's kid is like. What do you think they'll think if the magazine prints me as a big centerfold spread? ...give me my money, I want out of here."

<>

Patti finished describing the session to Nancy and me, "It's not like I was posing totally nude!"

I wasn't pleased, "Patti we don't approve. But, that's show biz. I guess, everyone does their own thing."

Patti stared at me, "Dad, there was a time I'd tell you to shove it. Now, I accept you the way you are. I accept myself. I'm alive. I'm amazed, life exists at all. I'm part of it, every flower, every star, every birth, every murder."

"Gee Patti," I said, "you don't make it easy for yourself, do you?"

Patti smiled at me, "Dad, I'm a Reagan. We dream big. What I want's a hug from you."

I tried to give Patti a hug, but I start drifting away. The spirits of the Dead and the Poor ... who only I could see, grabbed my arms and restrained me. Paul Robeson's ghost tried to pull me away from them, but there were too many of them.

Nancy watched me struggle against the air around me, trying to get away. Nancy figured my dementia was getting the best of me. My children gathered around me, afraid to get too close because of the way I was talking to the air around me. One by one, my kids forgave me. I watched the Dead and Poor crowding around me, moving their mouths, their words falling out like butterflies. They spoke to me, "We can't forgive you. We won't. You kept us from holding our loved ones. We won't let you embrace yours. We'll harden your heart, you'll die alone."

I couldn't get out of my chair because the Dead and the Poor held me down. I turned to Patti, "I want to hug you, Patti."

"Dad, all I want's a hug."

In my dementia, I couldn't move. Patti looked at me. Nancy and Patti hugged one another and cried. The other Reagan children joined into a group hug. Patti saw me watching a moth flying around a candle flame in a glass chimney on the picnic table. Patti watched as I tried to brush the moth away from the flame repeatedly. Patti watched me, "Mom, I think Ronnie's coming out of his dementia. He's moving his hand!"

I came out of my dementia. I started acting normal again, as if nothing happened. Patti watched me trying to direct the moth away from the flame.

Patti sighed, "You're more concerned with one moth flying into a flame than you are with hundreds of thousands of human beings suffering every day."

That wasn't fair, "What could I've done, Patti?"

"All that carrying around Bibles. You could've followed the Ten Commandments. You could've loved your neighbor. You could've loved me."

Nancy saw, I was hurt, tried protecting me, "Patti, leave your father alone."

Patti turned on Nancy, "Mom, you could've just said, 'No', to drugs, yourself."

Nancy was angry, "I didn't make this world. I was born into it. Given that, I think your father and I did a damn good job at running this country."

I felt desperate, "Patti, pray for me."

Patti looked at me, "Doing unto others doesn't mean having death squads liquidate them, Dad."

My dementia returned, I saw a vision of moths flying out of the mouths of Nancy and Patti, "Forgive me, God." I picked up my Bibles, start chasing my shadow, dropped my bibles, chased my shadow around and around a tree, trampling the Bibles deeper and deeper into the mud with no Time to stop. I hid behind the tree, finally poking my head out.

"Peek-a-boo."

<>

I saw myself float up to heaven, led by an Angel that looked like Nancy. I approached the Shining City in the Sky in the clouds surrounding Heaven. I told Saint Peter, open up the Pearly Gates of Heaven, for me. I stood before the Golden Desk and Throne of God. I saw God hold up the burnt Bible that'd slipped off my lap when I was a child and fallen into the fireplace and burnt while I slept. God held up the dirty Bibles I'd just trampled in the mud. God held up the pocket Bible I'd autographed and given to Oliver North to give to Monzer Al-Kassar to give to King Assad of Syria. I trembled before God. Beside God, were the souls of all those innocents killed in war and those who died in poverty during the Reagan Administration. The martyred souls stood pointing their fingers, accusingly, at me. I watched God staring at me. I defended myself, "I was a man, made of flesh and blood. I wasn't perfect."

God wasn't impressed, "Did you do the best you could?"

I felt too ashamed, to answer, "I tried to."

"It's not up to me to judge your sins, Ronnie. It's up to the people killed by the Contras you supported. It's up to the kids who ruined themselves on drugs you allowed the CIA to traffick in. It's up to the homeless, the needy, the hungry, everyone who suffered on your account, because you hardened your heart to humanity, you looked the other way right into your damn mirror."

"I was bringing in the sheep the best I knew how," I said. "I was a movie star, a hero to the American people ...I gave them a chance to dream."

"You were a villain to the hungry and the poor, you were a Devil, a curse upon mankind."

"Even my kids forgave me."

"You were a not a hero, you were a bad guy to all those who suffered, were hurt or killed because of the Reagan Administration, in this way you betrayed Me. All I've ever asked a living soul, is be faithful to Me. Can you look in your heart and say, 'I know the difference between right, and wrong? ...and, did right'?"

"Yes, I always believed in you."

"Faith is not enough, Ronnie. You needed to have racked up more good deeds to get in, Here. I'm giving you another chance. Do it right this time. I'm sending you back. Would you like to go back?"

I considered what God said. "No, I think once was enough."

I heard Nancy calling my name from far away, "Ronnie! Ronnnieee! Tell God, 'Yes!'"

I didn't understand. I almost had a realization ...I forgot what it was I was going to think ...I stared off into the distance.

God looked at me, "C'mon Ronnie, go for the Oscar."

Suddenly, I felt motivated. "Okay. Send me back. Rehearsals are over. But God, one thing, did you do the best you could?"

God was taken aback, "What do you mean?"

I sang the words to a popular song, back in the day, "'What if God was one of us? Just a stranger on a bus. What if God was one of us? Trying to make his way home?'" I saw God had a questioning look on his face. I was hot, "All these wars and starvation and suffering and killing, fathers hurting their sons' feelings, mothers hurting their daughters' feelings, kids hurting their parents' feelings, not to mention the wars."

"I did the best I could. You fight the wars, not me."

"You could have made it better from day one."

I watched God open his palm. The solar system spun around in God's palm. God opened his other hand. In it mighty redwoods forests were growing. "Have you forgotten what your mother taught you in Bible studies? I made you in My Image, with free will. If you let Satan win his coup in your heart, the Earth's ruling families will never be held accountable for making life on Earth the real Hell. It's time for you to go back, try again, Ronnie. You have unfinished business."

God miraculously restored my burnt and muddy Bibles to cleanliness and wholeness. He handed them to me.

<>

I was singing, while I rocked in my rocking chair overlooking sunset on the Pacific on my ranch above Santa Barbara. Patti watched me watch a baby bird learning to fly. I saw the mother bird chirping, flying behind the baby bird on its first flight. The mother bird and baby bird flew around and around the picnic table beside where I was sitting. The baby bird landed on the picnic table. The baby bird looked at me. That made me feel happy. I watched both the birds take off, flying away into the treetops. I stared up into the Heavens. "God, you didn't do so bad, after all."

Nancy noticed the confused look on my face, as I sat unmoving in my chair. Nancy saw, my face was frozen in a trance. Nancy felt helpless. Nancy felt like crying. Nancy read to me, "Fragile cease-fire in Yugoslavia remains threatened by unemployed roving terrorist, death squad, and mercenary units willing to work for the highest bidder."

I laughed, in my head I bowed to my audience of Americans cheering me. A big, house-sized inflated Mickey Mouse went by floating by a rope in a parade honoring me, a person in a big inflatable Coors beer can costume walked over to me, tapped me on the shoulder. I knew, that was the signal for the bad guys to start chasing me. Suddenly, in front of me, Satan wearing a Satan costume appeared, he handed me an Oscar.

Nancy looked at me sitting motionless in the chair, my face blank. Nancy start crying. Nancy forced herself to keep reading, "Investment bankers involved wanted to help arrange financing for construction projects in Eastern Europe after the war, but a civil war broke out between Bin Laden Construction, Bechtel, Halliburton, and Kelly, Brown & Root a Halliburton subsidiary."

I struggled to speak, but I couldn't.

Nancy saw me struggle to talk. Nancy smiled at me. Then, Nancy's smile faded, "I know, Honey. If you could speak ...you'd say, you're glad we're out of government, away from those back-stabbing cutthroats and assassins once, and for all."

Patti saw I had a look of peace on my face, she sat down on the grass beside me. Patti thought, I was going to say something. She leaned her head close to me. I tried to reach out to her. My hand took hers. I started to move my lips, to say something. Patti got excited. She called the family around, "Daddy's going to say something. Everyone! Come over, quick!"

I moved my lips, "It's about time we finally kill the right people in war, divest the people who own money-issuing shares of central banks, they're devils in a spiritual war between good and evil, between Satan and mankind ...God's just in a box seat."

Patti smiled, "I agree. It's about time the right people are killed in war."

I nodded. I closed his eyes. I felt myself slipping back into dementia. I sat in my rocking chair, watching the sun set over the Pacific Ocean. In my head, I heard God talking to me, "Do you want another chance to live?"

"No," I said. "I think once was enough."

Nancy saw a look of awe suddenly take my face. Nancy didn't know what to make of it. I heard someone, far away, calling my name in a ghostly way, "Ronnnie, Ronnieeeee."

I thought it was Nancy's voice. I couldn't understand ...because, Nancy was sitting right next to me, not saying a word. I almost had a realization ...I forgot what I was thinking ...I stared off into the distance. It was like I was President, again ...off in the distance the sun started to set over the Pacific. Paul Robeson's ghost came out of the sunshine like a little dot that grew bigger and bigger. By the time it was life-sized, Paul Robeson's ghost was right beside me. Nancy was crying. Maureen, Ron, Michael, and Patti were gathered around me. I didn't know why.

"Dad will you give me a hug?" Patti said, "All I want's a hug. All I've ever wanted is for you to love me."

I tried to reach out to Patti. My body would not move. Nancy saw, how handsome I looked, as I absently stared out to sea. Patti start crying. Paul Robeson's ghost helped me stand up out of my rocking chair. He put my arms around Patti. I hugged her. Patti wept. I held up my Oscar in the sunset. I ran past my Secret Service guards who were pitching cards into a cowboy hat. I ran to show my family my Oscar. I was so excited, "I got my Oscar! I got my Oscar!"

But, it was as if I was invisible. No one wanted to be bothered with me, the Secret Service agents kept sitting on both sides of me, I kept rocking in my rocking chair, kept watching the sunset on the Pacific Ocean, the Secret Service agents kept pitching cards into a cowboy hat, I sat there watching the cards sail slowly through the air. One of the Secret Service Agents looked at me, then spoke to the other one, "He never moves. He never shows any expression on his face. I think he's dead, already. I feel like the Green Grocer."

The other agent couldn't care less, "This guy doesn't even know he's a vegetable."

I start crying. I quickly leaned from my rocking chair and grabbed a gun from the holster of one of the Secret Service men. I start shooting at some foreign agents hiding in the trees aiming rifles at me. My family watched the empty rocking chair. I was walking on the beach. I noticed no footprints in front of me. Behind me, two side-by-side sets of footprints led over to me. I got confused. I looked up into Heaven, "God, why are there two sets of footprints leading to me, I'm here by myself."

Mel Gibson's Jesus appeared beside me, embraced me in his arms ...he start carrying me along the shoreline, leaving one set of footprints in the sand behind us.

It was Oscar material.

"Jesus, how you doing, it took you long enough."

Mel's Jesus smiled at me, a golden halo shown around his head,

"I'm fine, Ronnie, are you ready to go now? ...found your toe-marks?"

God knows, I didn't need toe-marks to stand in front of His camera, looking my best to His heavenly audience, "I don't need toe-marks, today."

Nancy and her family looked at the empty rocking chair and watched sunset on the Pacific Ocean, then sat in the dark at the Reagan Ranch in the hills above Santa Barbara.

excerpted from
American Civilian Counter-terrorist Manual:
A Fictional Autobiography of Ronald Reagan
Unabridged Edition

Based on the work of Eustice Mullins and the U.S. House of Representatives:

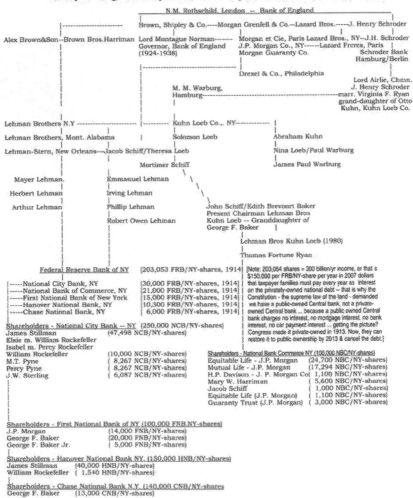

CHART 1 -- Shareholders (private owners) & interlocking directorates of the U.S. Federal Reserve Bank
Source: Federal Reserve Directors: A Study of Corporate & Banking Influence. Staff Report, Committee on Banking, Currency & Housing, House of Representatives, 94th Congress, 2nd Session, August 1976. (72 charts)

CHART 2
J. Henry Schroder

Baron Rudolph Von Schroder
Hamburg - 1858 - 1934

Baron Bruno Von Schroder
Hamburg - 1867 - 1940

F. C. Tiarks
1874-1952
marr. Emma Franziska
(Hamburg)
J. Henry Schroder, 1902
Dir. Bank of England
Dir. Anglo-Iranian Oil Co.

Helmut B. Schroder

J. Henry Schroder Banking Co. N.Y.

J. Henry Schroder Trust Co. N.Y.

Allen Dulles
Sullivan & Cromwell
Director -- CIA

John Foster Dulles
Sullivan & Cromwell
U.S. Secretary of State
Rockefeller Foundation

Prentiss Gray
Belgian Relief Comm.
Chief Marine Transportation
U.S. Food Administration WW I
Manati Sugar Co. American &
British Continental Corp.

Lord Airlie
Chairman; Virginia Fortune
Ping Coal Mines, Tientsin
Ryan daughter of Otto Kahn
of Kuhn, Loeb Co.

M. E. Rionda
Pres., Cuba Cane Sugar Co.
Manati Sugar Co. & many other
sugar companies.

G. A. Zabriskie
Chmn U.S. Sugar Equalization Board
Board 1917-18; Pres Empire
Biscuit Co., Columbia Baking
Co., Southern Baking Co.

Emile Francoui
Belgian Relief Comm. Kai
Ping Coal Mines, Tientsin
Railroad, Congo Copper,
Banque Nationale de Belgique

Suite 2000 42 Broadway, NY

Edgar Richard

Belgium Relief Comm
Amer Relief Comm
U.S. Food Admin
1918-24, Hazeltine Corp.

Julius H. Barnes

Belgium Relief Comm
Pres. Grain Corp.
U.S. Food Admin
1917-18, C.B Pitney
Bowes Corp, Manati
Sugar Corp.

Herbert Hoover

Chmn Belgium Relief
U.S. Food Admin
Sec of Commerce 24-28
Kaiping Coal Mines
Congo Copper
U.S. President, 1928-32

John Lowery Simpson
Sacramento, Calif Belgium Relief
Comm. U. S. Food Administration
Prentiss Gray Co. J. Henry Schroder
Trust, Schroder-Rockefeller, Chmn
Fin Comm, Bechtel International
Co. Bechtel Co. (Casper Weinberger
Sec of Defense; George P. Schultz
Sec of State (Reagan Admin)
SS Senior Group Leader

Baron Kurt Von Schroder
Schroder Banking Corp. J.H. Stein
Bankhaus (Hitler's personal bank
account) served on board of all
German subsidiaries of ITT
Bank for International Settlements

Himmler's Circle of Friends (Nazi Fund)
Schroder-Rockefeller & Co., NY
Deutsche Reichsbank, pres.
Avery Rockefeller, J. Henry Schroder
Banking Corp., Bechtel Co., Bechtel
International Co., Canadian Bechtel Co.

Sir Gordon Richardson
Governor, Bank of England
1973-PRESENT C.B. of J. Henry Schroder N.Y.
Schroder Banking Co., New York, Lloyds Bank
Rolls Royce

CHART 3
David Rockefeller, Chairman, Chase Manhattan Corp

Chase Manhattan Corp. Officer & Director Interlocks
Private Investment Co. for America
Firestone Tire & Rubber Co
Orion Multinational Services Ltd
ASARCO, Inc
Southern Peru Copper Corp.
Industrial Minerva Mexico S.A.
Continental Corp.
Honeywell Inc.
Northwest Airlines, Inc.
Northwestern Bell Telephone Co.
Minnesota Mining & Mfg Co (3M)
American Express Co.
Hewlett Packard
FMC Corporation
Utah Int'l Inc.
Exxon Corporation
International Nickel/Canada
Federated Capital Corp.
Equitable Life Assurance Soc U.S.
Federated Dept Stores
General Electric
Scott Paper Co.
American Petroleum Institute
Richardson Merril Inc.
May Department Stores Co.
Sperry Rand Corporation
San Salvador Development Co.

Allied Chemicals Corp.
General Motors
Rockefeller Family & Associates
Chrysler Corp.
Intl Basic Economy Corp.
R.H. Macy & Co.
Selected Risk Investments S.A.
Omega Fund, Inc.
Squibb Corp.
Olin Foundation
Mutual Benefit Life Ins. Co. NJ
AT&T
Pacific Northwestern Bell Co.
BeachviLime Ltd.
Eveleth Expansion Co.
Fidelity Union Bancorporation
Cypress Woods Corp.
Intl Minerals & Chemical Corp.
Burlington Industries
Wachovia Corporation
Jefferson Pilot Corp.
R. J. Reynolds Industries Inc.
United States Steel Corp.
Metropolitan Life Insurance Co.
Norton-Simon Inc.
Stone-Webster Inc.
Standard Oil of Indiana

Chart 4
Alan Pifer, President, Carnegie Corp. of NY

Carnegie Corp. Trustee Interlocks----------
Rockefeller Center, Inc
The Cabot Corp.
Fed. Reserve Bank of Boston
Owens Corning Fiberglas
New England Telephone Co.
Fisher Scientific Co.
Mellon National Corporation
Equitable Life Assurance Society
Twentieth Century Fox Corp.
J. Henry Schroder Banking Corp.

J. Henry Schroder Trust Co.
Paul Revere Investors, Inc.
Qualpeco, Inc.

Chart 5
Maurice F. Granville, Chairman, Texaco Incorporated

Texaco Officer & Director Interlocks---Liggett & Myers, Inc.
London ------ Arabian American Oil Co. St John del Ray Mining Ltd.
Connection -- Brown Brothers Harriman National Steel Corp.
Brown Harriman & Intl Banks Ltd. Massey-Ferguson Ltd.
American Express Mutual Life Insurance Co.
Amer. Express Intl Bank Mass Mutual Income Invest
Anaconda Copper United Services Life Ins. Co
Rockefeller Foundation Fairchild Industries
Owens-Corning Fiberglas Blount. Inc.
Nat'l City Bank (Cleveland) William Wrigley Jr. Co.
I.M. Roths- Sun Life Assurance Co. Nat'l Blvd. Bank of Chicago
child & General Reinsurance Lykes Youngstown Corp.
Sons. Ltd. General Electric (NBC) Inmount Corp.

<>

excerpted from
American Civilian Counter-terrorist Manual:
A Fictional Autobiography of Ronald Reagan
Unabridged Edition

Based on the work of Antony Sutton

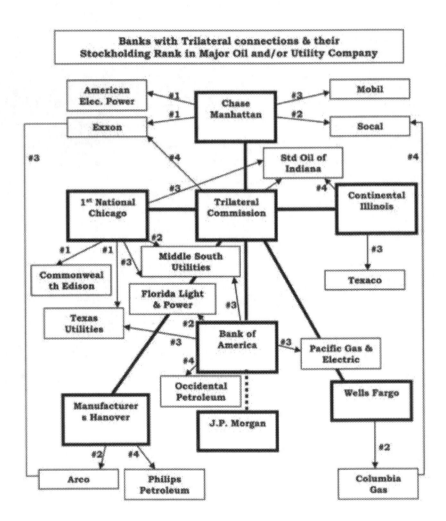

Based on the work of Antony Sutton

"The United States consumes about 71 quads of energy per year. (A quad is one quadrillion British thermal units.) There is available today in the United States, excluding solar sources and excluding gas and oil imports, about 150,000 quads of energy. Put another way, this statistic means we have sufficient known usuable energy resources [in the United States] to last us for over two thousand years." – Antony Sutton, Fellow at Hoover Institution of War, Revolution and Peace located on the Stanford University Campus.

excerpted from
American Civilian Counter-terrorist Manual:
A Fictional Autobiography of Ronald Reagan
Unabridged Edition

The work of Linda Minor
"Wall Street was created by, and is run by, the Tory faction, which followed the policy of Bank of Manhattan founders and American traitors Aaron Burr and John Jacob Astor. The *Wall Street Journal* represents a merger of the Boston and New York interests. At the heart of the *Wall Street Journal* is the aristocratic Bancroft family of Boston. Boston's State Street financial center is run by the treasonous families that made their money in the British-run China opium trade …Cabot, Perkins, Coolidge, Russell, Lowell et al."
– *Why Harvard Protects the Drug Trade*, by Linda Minor

excerpted from
American Civilian Counter-terrorist Manual:
A Fictional Autobiography of Ronald Reagan
Unabridged Edition

The work of Siegfried E. Tischler
"The new world order which comes hand-in-glove with the merging of Communism and Capitalism into globablist practices … is a house of cards without any real sustainability. It's a fact,

200 multinational transnational corporations control … and their shareholders own … over 95% of all private business which is not owned by individual privateers, and are reaping most of the benefit. The flipside of this coin is that all of this economic activity employs only 0.3 per cent of the global workforce."

– *Big Oil & the War on Drugs and Terrorism*, by Siegfried E. Tischler, PhD, excerpted from Nexus Magazine, Volume 11, Number 4 Jun-Jul 2004

excerpted from
American Civilian Counter-terrorist Manual:
A Fictional Autobiography of Ronald Reagan
Unabridged Edition

The work of Dr. Grey

"One of the world's foremost meteorologists called the theory that helped Al Gore share the Nobel Peace Prize, 'ridiculous' ..and the product of 'people who don't understand how the atmosphere works'. A natural cycle of ocean water temperatures – related to the amount of salt in ocean water – is responsible for global warming. That same cycle means a period of cooling will begin soon and last for several years. 'We'll look back on all of this in ten or fifteen years and realize how foolish it was,' Dr. Gray said. 'We're brainwashing our kids. The human impact on the atmosphere is simply too small to have a major effect on global temperatures,'" Dr. Grey said.

http://seattletimes.nwsource.com/html/nationworld/2003946751_nobelgray13.html

(Alan Allen's Spring 2010 release)

Acts 2:43-45 (Gideon Bible)

[43] Then fear came upon every soul, and many wonders and signs were done through the apostles.
[44] Now all who believed were together, and had all things in common.
[45] And sold their possessions and goods, and divided them among all, as anyone had need.

1776-1913-2013-2113
Kill a Banker, Win a Prize: The Jeffersonian Prophecies -or- How to Get Back Your Home & Job and Punish Those Responsible
~ Financial Terrorism for the Complete Idiot ~

How to get your home, property, job and money back. Who you should hate and why. How should we punish those who took away our jobs, destroyed our American Dream of home ownership, ruined our livelihoods, plunged us into needless debt, took away our credit, destroyed our families and friends and waged financial, military, psychological, biological and spiritual warfare on us ...simply, because they could. Why redistribution of wealth (as prophesied in Acts 2:43-45 defining God's Will) is the only successful counterattack to level the playing field ...and, the only way to world peace is to have equal guaranteed incomes for everyone and caps on personal wealth for everyone.

The 6% fixed rate mortgage is really a 580% variable mortgage.

There is no such thing as a fixed mortgage. A "30-year fixed mortgage" is actually a variable mortgage, and the rate you really pay is higher than you know and is designed to eliminate your financial freedom.

Nationally, homeowners keep their mortgages an average of 5 years before refinancing ... that "30-yr-6%" mortgage rate is a minimum of 102%.

So, if you're a banker, you continue predatory lending and set people up then want to foreclose to be able to resell and get 580%.

In fact, the "6%" 'fixed' mortgage the first year is 580%. The following table shows you that since mortgages are "front-end loaded for interest" (which means you pay interest heavily over principle), you start off at 580% and the mortgage never reaches a 6% rate until the last year of the 30-year term. The last year, probably the last day.

Also, regarding the real interest rate of the loan, the 15-yr is much lower than the 30-year. The following table compares the effective interest rate on a 6%-30-year vs. a 5%-15-year.

```
Year--------30yr mortgage --------15yr mortgage
1-----------580%--------------------161%
3-----------182%--------------------51%
5-----------102%--------------------28%
7-----------68%--------------------18%
10-----------43%--------------------11%
15-----------24%--------------------5%
20-----------15%--------------------paid off
25-----------9%--------------------paid off
30-----------6%--------------------paid off
```

Here's another way to look at it, using for example, a $150,000 30-yr fixed-rated mortgage at 6%:

```
Yr---interest pd------principal pd-------balance owed
1----$8,949.89--------$1,842.02----------$148,157.98
2----$8,836.28--------$1,955.53----------$146,202.35
3----$8,715.66--------$2,076.25----------$144,126.11
4----$8,587.60--------$2,204.31----------$141,921.80
5----$8,451.65--------$2,340.46----------$139,581.54
6----$8,307.30--------$2,484.61----------$137,096.93
7----$8,154.06--------$2,637.85----------$134,459.08
8----$7,991.36--------$2,800.55----------$131,658.53
9----$7,818.63--------$2,973.28----------$128,685.80
```

10---$7,635.24--------$3,156.66----------$125,528.59
11---$7,440.55--------$3,351.36----------$122,177.23
12---$7,233.84--------$3,558.07----------$118,619.16
13---$7,014.39--------$3,777.52----------$114,841.64
14---$6,781.40--------$4,010.51----------$110,831.13
15---$6,534.04--------$4,257.97----------$106,573.27
16---$6,271.43--------$4,520.48----------$102,052.78
17---$5,992.61--------$4,799.30----------$97,353.49
18---$5,696.60--------$5,095.31----------$92,158.18
19---$5,382.33--------$5,409.57----------$86,748.60
20---$5,048.68--------$5,743.23----------$81,005.38
21---$4,694.45--------$6,097.45----------$74,907.92
22---$4,318.38--------$6,473.53----------$68,434.39
23---$3,919.10--------$6,872.81----------$61,561.59
24---$3,495.20--------$7,296.71----------$54,264.88
25---$3,045.16--------$7,746.75----------$46,518.13
26---$2,567.36--------$8,224.55----------$38,293.58
27---$2,060.08--------$8,731.83----------$29,561.75
28---$1,521.52--------$9,270.39----------$20,291.37
29---$--949.75--------$9,842.16----------$10,449.21
30---$--342.70-------$10,449.21----------$0.00